Complete Traditional Recipe Book

Complete Traditional Recipe Book

Sarah Edington

THE NATIONAL TRUST

For John

First published in the United Kingdom in 2006
by National Trust Books
10 Southcombe Street
London W14 0RA

An imprint of Anova Books Company Ltd

ISBN-10 190540042 X
ISBN-13 9781905400423

A CIP catalogue record for this book is available from the British Library.

15 14 13 12 11 10 09 08 07
10 9 8 7 6 5 4 3

Printed and bound by Craft Print International Ltd, Singapore
Reproduction by Anorax Imaging Ltd, Leeds

Design by Lee-May Lim
Home economist: Jane Suthering
Stylist: Penny Markham

This book can be ordered direct from the publisher at the website: www.anovabooks.com,
or try your local bookshop.
Also available at National Trust shops.

Contents

Introduction

Welcome to the *National Trust Complete Traditional Recipe Book*. This book is a celebration of British cooking, complete in the sense that it contains recipes across the whole spectrum of traditional British food – from soups to drinks, via fish, meat, and vegetable dishes, together with sweet and savoury sauces. Those high spots of British cooking, puddings and teatime recipes, are also well represented, with more than 50 recipes for hot and cold puddings, and more than another 50 recipes for breads, tea breads, cakes, scones and biscuits. We have not forgotten recipes for preserves, drinks and even confectionery, and there is also advice on roasting the excellent meat and poultry raised in the British Isles. The recipes are mostly modern versions of traditional recipes from all over England, plus some recipes from other parts of the United Kingdom. They reflect two strands of cooking – the 'posh', and the more homely. Recipes from the more prosperous kitchens were those most likely to be written down, but we also know the basic ingredients for pottage, the ancestor of soup – vegetables for the less well-off, fish or meat for the rich – and there are modern recipes for pottage, and for soup, here. Much baking, especially on a griddle, was done in the poorest homes with only a simple hearth, as well as in the well-equipped kitchens of the grander households. So you will find griddle recipes for Welsh Cakes, Drop Scones and the delightfully named 'Singin' Hinnies'. Some recipes are elaborate and take time, but some are very simple. A number of these recipes have hardly changed in hundreds of years, while others are modern versions of the original. At the top of each recipe I have provided a short explanation of why I have chosen it, its name or its history.

The original sources for this book are four books of recipes that I collected between 1986 and 1992, from cooks in restaurants attached to National Trust properties all over England, Northern Ireland and Wales. I was inspired by what I found on that journey: across the length and breadth of the United Kingdom, cooks were preserving culinary traditions. Not only that, but they were using the excellent ingredients that we take for granted in this country, they were cooking classic recipes and they were making them their own. Not every recipe given to me was suitable for this book. Some recipes, like lasagne for instance, are traditional to other cultures and have been adopted by ours. Some recipes were repetitious: I had no less than seven recipes for Apple Cake, and had to choose just two. Some recipes, particularly those for special-occasion food with expensive ingredients, were not in my original books, because the cooks I had spoken to had needed to keep to a strict budget. These recipes, and others that deserved inclusion, have been gleaned from a rich variety of sources. I have delved, fruitfully, into other cookbooks published by the National Trust, and I have myself cooked professionally for twenty years for other peoples' weddings, birthdays and special events. Other cooks gave me their recipes and I have devoured – it seems an appropriate word – a huge number of cookbooks, published over the last 200 years or so. Inspiration has come from all quarters. Some omissions are, I admit, subjective. I remember, with something approaching horror, the brawn I was forced to eat as a child; the smell of the pig's head cooking, and the result – gristly pieces of pig, some still with bristles on it, suspended in opaque jelly. So there is no recipe for brawn in this book, nor is there much for offal. Lovers of milk puddings can pick holes in this book, too, because there is no sago, no semolina and no tapioca. The preserve recipes here make up a small shelf only, and there are many more puddings and teatime recipes than I could include. I collected most of the recipes here over a period of 18 years. I did not ask their authors whether they invented them, or whether they wrote down recipes their grandmothers, mothers or friends had given them to them. I was simply interested in whether they tasted good. I found – to paraphrase Mark Twain's telegram after reading his own obituary in *The Times* – that 'reports of the death of British Cooking are greatly exaggerated – it is alive and well.'

Soups

'Soup of the evening – beautiful soup' sang the Mock Turtle, in Lewis Carroll's *Alice in Wonderland*. And soup is fine for every other time of day, as well. Since man or, more probably, woman discovered that food cooked in water tasted good, everyone has eaten soup.

But it wasn't always called soup here. In Britain, in the Middle Ages, soup was called pottage, and was a staple part of everyone's diet. Made from meat or fish (or just vegetables, for the poor), cooked in water or broth that was thickened with oatmeal or bread, it was both filling and nutritious – the food of life. Then, as now, it was difficult to tell where pottages stopped and stews began, and the three recipes described as pottage in this book were certainly intended as main courses.

There are soups in this chapter that are direct descendants of pottage. Scotch Broth is one – a complete meal of meat, vegetables, barley and parsley. Sometimes the broth contained potatoes or dumplings as well, to fill up the hungry. Other close descendants are Vegetable Barley Broth and Cock-a-Leekie Soup, while Chicken Noodle Soup is a more modern descendant. Cook any of these recipes and you need look no further for your nutritional needs. Some vegetable pottages can be found in the chapter on Vegetables and Side Dishes.

The description 'soup' came into use in the 16th century, at about the same time as the dish began to change, becoming thinner and less homely. At the same time, the pottages that were now called stews or ragoos became more solid, more elaborate, and joined the main courses. A soup was now considered as an appetiser, or opening course, for a large meal. It was the 'removed course' – the empty bowls being taken away before the main eating began, as they are today. Golden Cider Soup and Asparagus Soup are these kinds of soups – both use ingredients local to their origin, and are elegant enough for the grandest table.

Soups are often made to use up a glut of ingredients. Derbyshire Carrot Soup results from the arrival, at certain times of year, of quantities of fine-flavoured, locally grown carrots. I make Game Soup when I am lucky enough to have been given some game, and after we have eaten it roasted or casseroled and still have some leftover meat. Other soups in this chapter also use up leftovers, though not in the gloomy, 'better use them up' sense. Pea and Ham Soup and Butterbean and Ham Soup both require chopped ham. Elsewhere in this book you will find a recipe for Gammon Poached in Cider with Clove and Mustard Glaze (see page 80), and a gammon is nearly always too big for one meal. Cold ham is all part of the pleasure, but save some to make these soups, using the wonderful cider-flavoured stock that you have left after cooking the ham. Stilton and Onion Soup is perfect for early January, when the Stilton cheese bought for Christmas is still fine, but everyone has seen it too often.

Some medieval soups were thickened and flavoured with almonds. The almond soups here are Celery and Almond, where almond is the predominant flavour, and Cauliflower and Almond, where it is used more as a thickener. The use of herbs in soups also stretches back across the centuries. Dame Alice Soup is based on a very old recipe. It is named after Dame Alice Whitgreave, who sheltered the young Charles II while he was on the run after the Royalist defeat at Worcester in 1651. Celery seeds are an essential ingredient of this soup, and the recipe also uses bay leaves, fresh thyme and parsley. Green peas team up naturally with mint in Green Pea and Mint Soup, while aromatic rosemary is in both Rosemary Soup and Tomato and Rosemary Soup, where it perfectly complements the flavour of tomato.

Mulligatawny Soup is a tasty curiosity, with Indian roots. There is no tradition of a 'soup course' in Indian cookery, and Indian meals are taken as ours were before the 19th century, with all the dishes placed on the table at once, so that guests may pick and choose what they want. Mulligatawny is a derivation of the Tamil words *milagu-tannir*, meaning 'pepper water', a soup that developed into a more hearty dish, to please the British palate. It is slightly Indian and slightly British, like that other stalwart of Anglo-Indian cuisine, Kedgeree (see page 49). I love the idea of wild food, and collecting and eating my own food is one of my greatest pleasures. The cliffs near my Devon home have crops of delicious mushrooms which we have collected over many years. When we tire of mushrooms on toast, or with bacon, we make the Mushroom Soup recipe in this book. Mushrooms are at their best in the early autumn, but the beautiful green Nettle and Watercress Soup must be made in the spring when the nettle tops are young. Nettle tops can't be bought, but asparagus can – even so, the Asparagus Soup is still best made in May when the English season, so tantalisingly short, is in full swing. I think the taste of home-grown asparagus can't be improved on – and, of course, the price is more reasonable.

There are two recipes for stock in this chapter. Home-made chicken stock is an essential for Chicken Noodle Soup. Many other soup recipes specify vegetable stock as an ingredient. Of course you can use instant stock but there may be occasions where you want to control, for example, exactly how much salt is in your stock – and the recipes here let you do that.

Soup is a dish that is easy to prepare, almost impossible to spoil, and often uses inexpensive ingredients – and it brings the cook compliments out of all proportion to the effort and cost involved.

Nettle and Watercress Soup

Make this soup in the spring or early summer and use only the young new shoots of the nettles, which incidentally have the fiercest sting. Use rubber gloves to collect them. Once cooked, the sting disappears. If you have a stream that grows watercress nearby as well, you nearly have food for free in this green soup, high in iron and vitamins A and C.

175g (6oz) nettle tops
25g (1oz) butter
1 medium onion, finely chopped
1 litre (1¾ pints) vegetable stock
1 bunch of watercress
300ml (½ pint) creamy milk
Pinch of chilli pepper
Salt and pepper to taste

FOR GARNISH
Single cream
Paprika

Serves 4

Pick only young, tender nettle tops and wash well. Cook over a low heat just in the water they hold on their leaves until they are tender. Drain in a colander. Melt the butter in a large pan over a low heat. Add the onion and cook gently until it is soft but not brown. Pour in the vegetable stock. Add the cooked nettle tops and stir so they are well mixed in. Roughly chop the watercress and add to the pan. Bring to the boil and simmer for 5 minutes. Liquidise the soup, which should be a rich, dark green purée. Season with the chilli, salt and pepper and add the milk. Serve with a swirl of cream and a dusting of paprika.

Vegetable Stock

Vegetable stock is an essential ingredient of many recipes. The perfectly acceptable short cut is to use instant vegetable stock, in either liquid, cube or granule form, but there may be occasions when a home-made vegetable stock is preferred, for instance when preparing fresh food for babies or when cooking for someone with a food intolerance, or just when you want to use the real thing.

2 large leeks
2 large carrots
2 large onions
1 celery head
2.5 litres (4 pints) water
1 teaspoon salt
8 peppercorns

Peel as necessary and chop all the vegetables. Put in a pan, add water, salt and peppercorns. Bring to the boil and simmer uncovered for 20 minutes. Allow to stand until cool, then strain and use as necessary.

This stock will keep well in the fridge for at least two weeks. You can also freeze it.

Vegetable Barley Broth

Barley is the oldest cultivated cereal in Europe and the Near East. It was supplanted by wheat, which makes better bread, but has retained its importance in soups, stews and barley water (see page 306). This is a main-course soup from Northumberland – traditional fare to keep out the cold winds from the North Sea. Northumbrians say, 'You should be able to stand your spoon up in it.'

1.2 litres (2 pints) strong vegetable stock
25g (1oz) pearl barley
25g (1oz) red lentils
1 carrot, peeled and grated
1 onion, peeled and finely chopped
1 leek, finely chopped
½ medium turnip, peeled and grated
1 celery stick, finely chopped
½ red pepper, finely chopped
Salt and pepper to taste

FOR GARNISH
Chopped parsley
Grated hard cheese

Serves 6

Put everything in a large pan, bring the mixture to the boil, then cover the pan and simmer for at least an hour. Season to taste. Everything should be well cooked and the flavour of the mixed vegetables brought out. Serve piping hot, sprinkled with chopped parsley and grated cheese, allowing a large bowl per person.

Rosemary Soup

Rosemary soup is breathtakingly simple but gives a subtle, sophisticated, creamy soup fit for any dinner party. Make it with the young rosemary leaves of early summer, which are especially fragrant. You can vary the amount of rosemary according to taste. I love rosemary and use four sprigs for a strong flavour. I am in good company. In the 16th century, Sir Thomas More wrote, 'I lett it runne all over my garden walls, not onelie because my bees love it but because it is the herb sacred to remembrance and therefore friendship.'

600ml (1 pint) milk
7.5cm (3in) rosemary sprig
25g (1oz) butter, chopped
25g (1oz) Cheddar cheese, chopped
A little extra rosemary for garnish

FOR THE VEGETABLE PURÉE
1 medium onion, finely chopped
1 tablespoon sunflower oil
450g (1lb) potatoes, peeled and chopped
600ml (1 pint) vegetable stock

Serves 6

In a pan bring the milk up to the boil with the rosemary. Turn off the heat, cover the pan and allow the milk to stand for at least an hour to be infused. While the milk is infusing, make the vegetable purée as follows. Sauté the onion gently in the oil in a large pan until it is soft but not coloured. Add the potatoes and the vegetable stock. Bring the mixture to the boil, reduce the heat and simmer until the potato is cooked. Purée the mixture.

After an hour, discard the rosemary and add the milk to the vegetable purée (see above). Reheat gently to just below boiling. Mix in the butter and cheese and serve immediately with a little chopped rosemary in each soup bowl.

Cauliflower and Almond Soup

The almonds in this soup not only add to the subtle blend of flavours, they also help to give the soup its creamy texture. Ground almonds or hazelnuts were often used in medieval cookery to thicken sauces and soups, so this recipe may have a long history.

75g (3oz) butter
1 medium onion, peeled and chopped
1 medium cauliflower, divided into florets
110g (4oz) flaked almonds
¼ teaspoon nutmeg
¼ teaspoon turmeric
850ml (1½ pints) vegetable stock
Salt and pepper to taste

Serves 4–6

Melt the butter in a large pan. Sauté the onion until soft but not coloured, then add the cauliflower, almonds (retain a few almonds to garnish when serving), nutmeg and turmeric. Stir well so that all the ingredients are thoroughly combined and cook gently for 5 minutes. Add the vegetable stock, bring to the boil, cover the pan, reduce the heat and simmer until the cauliflower is cooked. Blend the soup until it is smooth, then season with salt and pepper to taste. Reheat if necessary and serve with a scatter of toasted almonds on the top.

Right: Cauliflower and Almond Soup

Dame Alice Soup

This is based on a very old recipe and is named after Dame Alice Whitgreave. She was the mother of Thomas Whitgreave, known as 'the preserver', who sheltered the future Charles II in Moseley Old Hall, Staffordshire, in 1651. The young prince was on the run with a price on his head after his disastrous defeat at the Battle of Worcester. Did she cook him a soup like this? We shall never know. We do know that Charles escaped to France disguised as a serving man to Jane Lane, a neighbour, and you can still read his letter of thanks at Moseley Old Hall.

1 small onion, peeled and chopped
2 small carrots, peeled and chopped
50g (2oz) butter
1 bay leaf
1 teaspoon celery seeds (these are essential)
1 teaspoon fresh thyme
1 teaspoon fresh parsley
6 peppercorns
50g (2oz) plain flour
600ml (1 pint) vegetable stock
250ml (9fl oz) full cream milk
1 teaspoon Marmite
salt and pepper to taste

Serves 4–6

Fry the chopped onion and carrots in the butter in a large pan for a minute or two. Add the bay leaf, celery seeds, thyme, parsley and peppercorns, and continue to cook to bring out the flavours of the herbs. Stir in the flour, add the stock and bring to the boil, stirring frequently. Cover the pan and simmer gently for 15 minutes. Pour in the milk, season with salt and pepper and stir in the Marmite. Bring almost to the boil and serve.

Left: Dame Alice Soup

Leek Soup with Cream

The delicate flavour and texture of leeks makes for particularly good soup. There's no waste here either – you can use the whole of the leek, including the green tops. Competitions are held in Northumbria to see who can grow the largest leek. However, you are better off with younger, slender leeks for this soup.

1 large onion, peeled and chopped

700g (1½lb) leeks, peeled and chopped

50g (2oz) butter

25g (1oz) plain flour

425ml (¾ pint) chicken or vegetarian stock

425g (¾ pint) milk

Salt and pepper to taste

FOR GARNISH

1 tablespoon cream per serving

Chopped parsley

Serves 4

Wash any grit off the leeks and sauté with the onion gently in the butter until soft but not coloured. Add the flour and stir well, then add the stock and milk, cover the pan and simmer until the vegetables are cooked. Taste and season with salt and pepper. This soup can either be liquidised at this point or served as it is. Either way it is nicest with a spoonful of cream added at the last minute and a scattering of chopped parsley.

Stilton and Onion Soup

Stilton is a protected cheese, its manufacture limited to an area on the borders of Leicestershire, Rutland and Derbyshire. Its creamy yet salty flavour combines perfectly with the sweet flavour of the onion. It is also extremely good chilled, and makes an excellent starter for a summer party.

2 large onions, peeled and finely chopped
50g (2oz) butter
1 level tablespoon cornflour
600ml (1 pint) milk
850ml (1½ pints) chicken stock
225g (8oz) crumbled Stilton cheese
Salt and pepper to taste

Serves 4–6

Soften the onions in the butter over a gentle heat. Add the cornflour and stir for a minute or two. Gradually pour in the milk, stirring all the time, and bring to the boil. Add the stock and simmer for 5 minutes. Remove the pan from the heat and immediately add the cheese, allowing it to melt without boiling. Liquidise the soup until it is smooth. Season to taste and serve hot with crusty bread.

Green Pea and Mint Soup

This soup, with its beautiful colour and lovely delicate flavour, is unbelievably simple to make.

600g (1¼lb) frozen peas
1 tablespoon fresh mint
850ml (1½ pints) chicken stock
1 medium onion, chopped
50g (2oz) butter

FOR GARNISH
Double cream
A few fresh mint leaves

Serves 4

Place the peas, mint, chicken stock and onion in a large pan. Bring to the boil, cover the pan and simmer gently for 20 minutes. Liquidise in a blender or food processor with the butter. Serve either hot or cold with a swirl of cream and a few fresh mint leaves.

Derbyshire Carrot Soup

The name of this soup refers to the excellent carrots grown in Derbyshire rather than a particular regional soup.

25g (1oz) butter
450g (1lb) carrots, grated
1 onion, peeled and chopped
1 celery stick, finely chopped
750 ml (1¼ pints) vegetable stock
2 tablespoons double cream
½ teaspoon sugar
Salt and pepper to taste
Chopped parsley, for garnish

Serves 4

Melt the butter in a large pan and stir in the carrots, onion and celery. Cook for 15 minutes, stirring frequently, over a low heat without allowing the vegetables to colour. Pour in the vegetable stock. Bring to the boil, cover the pan and simmer for a further 15 minutes. Add the cream and sugar and season to taste with salt and pepper. Serve with a sprinkling of chopped parsley.

Country Vegetable Soup

This is a modern version of an old idea. The variety and amounts of vegetables are not set in stone — they have been chosen here for their colour as well as their flavour. If you do not like peppers or sweetcorn, just substitute something else. You need to end up with 700g (just over 1lb) of vegetables, not including the potatoes, which are there to thicken the broth.

25g (1oz) butter
2 red peppers, chopped
110g (4oz) peas (fresh or frozen)
110g (4oz) carrots, peeled and diced
110g (4oz) swede, peeled and diced
110g (4oz) sweetcorn (fresh or frozen)
450g (1lb) potatoes
Milk (optional)
Salt and pepper to taste

FOR GARNISH
Freshly chopped parsley
A few spring onion tops, chopped

Serves 4

Melt the butter and sauté all the vegetables gently, except the potatoes, until cooked. Peel the potatoes and barely cover them with water. Cover the pan and boil until soft. Drain, reserving the cooking liquid, and mash until creamy. Stir the mashed potato and the potato cooking liquid into the pan containing the cooked vegetables and stir together. If you think the soup is too thick, add milk until you get the right texture. Season with salt and pepper, reheat and serve piping hot, sprinkled with parsley and a few chopped spring onion tops.

Golden Cider Soup

This recipe was given to me by the cook at Montacute, Somerset, a glorious, golden house set in lush countryside of orchards and green fields, so use Somerset cider for preference. The cider gives this simple recipe a wonderful luxurious flavour. I have served this soup hot and cold – it is equally delicious either way. I think it is best very smooth – I know pushing a soup through a sieve is tedious, but in this recipe the result is rewarding.

50g (2oz) butter
225g (8oz) carrots, diced
225g (8oz) potatoes, diced
2 garlic cloves, crushed
400g tin chopped tomatoes
450ml (¾ pint) medium or sweet cider
450ml (¾ pint) vegetable stock

FOR GARNISH
Salt and freshly ground black pepper to taste
Crème fraîche
Basil leaves

Serves 6

Melt the butter in a large saucepan and sweat the diced carrots and potatoes for 5 minutes. Add the crushed garlic, tin of tomatoes, cider and vegetable stock and bring to the boil. Cover and simmer until the vegetables are tender. Season with salt and pepper. Pour into a food processor and blend until very smooth. Then press the mixture through a sieve before returning it to the pan and reheating before serving. Garnish each bowl with a spoonful of crème fraîche and a couple of basil leaves.

Celery and Almond Soup

A rich soup with a delicate flavour.

1 large onion, chopped
50g (2oz) butter
1 small celery head
1 large potato
2 vegetable stock cubes dissolved in 125ml (4fl oz) boiling water
1.2 litres (2 pints) milk
110g (4oz) ground almonds
Few drops of almond essence
Salt and pepper to taste
Handful of chopped parsley and chives for garnish

Serves 6

In a pan large enough to hold all the ingredients, cook the chopped onion gently in butter until soft but not coloured. Chop the celery into chunks and cube the potato and add to the onion. Pour in the dissolved vegetable stock and milk, cover the pan and simmer until the vegetables are soft (20–25 minutes). Remove from the heat and liquidise in a blender or food processor; add the ground almonds and a few drops of almond essence and blend for a further few seconds to make a smooth soup. Season to taste with salt and pepper. Return to the heat and serve piping hot with chopped parsley and chives stirred through the soup so that it is a pretty green and white colour.

Asparagus Soup

Although asparagus is available all the year round now, English asparagus is a luxury food. For a few blissful weeks in April and May, we can buy home-grown spears and the price comes down. If you are lucky enough to be out and about in the countryside, look out for the sign 'Fresh Asparagus for Sale', and stop and buy some. If you tire of fresh steamed green spears with vinaigrette or melted butter, this soup has a beautiful colour and the authentic individual taste.

1 bundle fresh asparagus (about 450g/1lb)
110g (4oz) butter
1 small onion, peeled and chopped
425ml (¾ pint) vegetable stock
25g (1oz) plain flour
425ml (¾ pint) extra strong vegetable stock (double strength)
300ml (½ pint) double cream
Salt and freshly ground black pepper to taste

Serves 4

Remove the asparagus tips and reserve for garnishing. Cut off the tough ends, scrape the stems clean and cut these into 2–5cm (1–2in) pieces. Melt the butter, add the asparagus pieces and chopped onion and cook until barely tender, stirring regularly. Add the ordinary vegetable stock, cover the pan and simmer until the stalks are cooked and soft. Whisk in the flour. When it is smoothly blended, add the double-strength stock and continue stirring until the soup comes to the boil. Pour into a food processor and blend until smooth.

Steam or simmer very gently in water until the asparagus tips are cooked but still crunchy.

Return the soup to the pan and just before serving reheat. Pour into individual bowls, swirl in some double cream to give a marbled effect and scatter the asparagus tips on top.

Carrot, Coriander and Orange Soup

Coriander and orange have an affinity with each other, and just sharpen the taste of the carrots without drowning it. We have been growing carrots in Britain since the Dutch set up market gardens here in the reign of Elizabeth I. The first carrots were pale yellow or purple – the orange carrot we now take for granted was cultivated later.

450g (1lb) carrots
1 large onion
50g (2oz) butter
1.5 litres (2¼ pints) vegetable stock
½ teaspoon crushed coriander
2 tablespoons ground rice
Zest and juice of 2 oranges
Salt and pepper to taste

Serves 6

Slice the carrots and onions thinly and sweat with the butter in a large pan with the lid on until soft. Pour in the stock and crushed coriander, bring to the boil, cover the pan and simmer for 15 minutes. Add the ground rice and orange juice and zest and continue to simmer for a further 30 minutes. Liquidise in a blender or food processor, return to the pan and season to taste.

Parsnip, Paprika and Mustard Soup

Parsnips are one of the few vegetables native to Britain. In the Middle Ages, before sugar was regularly available, they were often used in sweet dishes. During the Tudor period, they were a substitute food for the poor when the grain harvests failed. Now their subtly sweet flavour is again appreciated in fine cooking. This soup has both a fine colour and a smoky, interesting flavour.

450g (1lb) parsnips
1 medium leek
1 tablespoon oil
25g (1oz) butter
1 heaped teaspoon paprika – use smoked paprika if possible
1.25 litres (2 pints) vegetable stock
1 tablespoon Dijon mustard
1 teaspoon sugar
Salt and pepper to taste

Serves 6

Peel and dice the parsnips, wash and dice the leek. Heat the oil and butter together in a pan large enough to take all the ingredients. Sauté the diced leek and parsnips for 5 minutes. Add the paprika, stir well to coat the vegetables and cook for a couple of minutes more. Add the vegetable stock. Bring to the boil, cover the pan and simmer until the vegetables are soft. This takes approximately 20 minutes. Liquidise the mixture; return to the pan and stir in the mustard and sugar. Adjust seasoning, reheat until very hot and serve immediately with warm buttered bread rolls.

Game Soup

The Romans created the first game reserves in Britain, enclosing land to form parks for the hunting of deer and boar. The pastime remained popular with many British monarchs: Henry VIII gave Anne Boleyn, his second queen, a haunch of venison as a love token when they were courting.

For this recipe I am assuming that you have some leftover game. Perhaps you have roasted a couple of pheasants and are left with the carcasses, which still have quite a lot of meat on them, or you may have already made a recipe that required saddle of rabbit and have the rest of the beast on your hands. In these situations, I have never regretted making the leftovers into a rich, nourishing soup.

FOR THE STOCK
1kg (2¼lb) game carcasses or bones (pheasant, rabbit, grouse or hare)
1 small onion
1 celery stick
1 small carrot
1 bay leaf
1 black peppercorn
1.8 litres (3 pints) water
Salt to taste

FOR THE SOUP

25g (1oz) butter

1 tablespoon olive oil

1 small onion, peeled and chopped

1 carrot, peeled and finely diced

1 celery stick, peeled and finely diced

850 ml (1½ pints) stock, made as above

225 g (8oz) game of any kind (pheasant, grouse, hare or guinea fowl) diced into small pieces

1 small glass sherry

1 teaspoon redcurrant jelly

Grated zest and juice of ½ lemon

Serves 4–6

To make the stock, put all the ingredients in a pan and cover them with the water. Bring to the boil, then turn the heat down, cover the pan and simmer for at least 1½ hours. Season with salt and strain.

For the soup, melt the butter and oil in a large pan and sauté the onion, carrot and celery until softened and beginning to brown. Add the stock and the chopped game. Bring to the boil, cover the pan, turn the heat down and simmer for 10 minutes. (If you want a thicker soup, this is the moment to take half of the liquid out, purée it and return it to the pan.) Add the sherry, redcurrant jelly and the lemon zest and juice. Heat the soup until just below boiling and serve.

Mushroom Soup

Any kind of mushroom is fine for this soup but the best, of course, are ones you have picked yourself. There is something intensely satisfying about eating food for free, even if the soup it makes does look like a muddy puddle. Please take care when picking mushrooms.

50g (2oz) butter
1 tablespoon olive oil
1 large onion, peeled and chopped
3 garlic cloves, peeled and chopped
1 potato, peeled and diced
600g (1¼lb) mushrooms, chopped
1 litre (1¾ pints) vegetable stock
1 small glass medium or cream sherry
Grated zest and juice of 1 lemon
Salt to taste
Crème fraîche, to serve

Serves 4

Melt the butter with the oil in a large pan. Put in the onion, garlic and potato, and fry gently for 5 minutes. Stir in the mushrooms and then add the stock and sherry. Season with salt to taste. Bring to the boil, then cover the pan and simmer until everything is cooked. This will probably take about 20 minutes. Purée the mixture. Don't worry if it isn't very smooth; a little texture is good. Add the lemon zest and juice and reheat until piping hot. Serve with a bowl of crème fraîche for people to stir in as desired.

Chicken Noodle Soup

Chicken Noodle Soup has a bad reputation thanks to the pale imitations you can buy in supermarkets. Made properly, it is sustaining, soothing and tasty in equal proportions. If you haven't got time to make your own stock, use chicken stock cubes made up according to the packet instructions.

2 tablespoons olive oil
1 large onion, peeled and chopped
2 garlic cloves, peeled and chopped
1 leek, peeled, sliced and washed
1 large carrot, peeled and finely chopped
2 litres (3½ pints) chicken stock
450g (1lb) cooked chicken pieces
1 nest of egg noodles
A handful of chopped parsley, for garnish

Serves 4

Heat the olive oil in a large pan and add the onion, garlic, leek and carrot. Fry for about 5 minutes. Add the stock and simmer the mixture for about 20 minutes, until the vegetables are cooked. Add the chicken and the noodles, and simmer for a further 5 minutes. Just before you serve the soup, stir in the parsley. Serve piping hot.

Tomato and Rosemary Soup

This soup is simple and economical, and is good made with tinned tomatoes. Make it with fresh tomatoes and it is very special.

225g (8oz) chopped onions
3 teaspoons chopped fresh rosemary
3 397g tins of tomatoes (if you have fresh tomatoes use the equivalent
   in weight)
2 teaspoons tomato purée
25g (1oz) sugar
900ml (1½ pints) chicken stock
1 level tablespoon cornflour
300ml (½ pint) single cream
Salt and pepper to taste
Chopped parsley, for garnish

Serves 6

Place the chopped onions, rosemary, tomatoes, tomato purée, sugar and stock in a large pan. Reserve a little of the stock to cream the cornflour. Add the blended cornflour to the pan, cover it and simmer all the ingredients for approximately 20 minutes. Remove from the heat and liquidise. Adjust the seasoning. Reheat and stir in the cream just before serving. Serve very hot with a garnish of chopped parsley.

Right: Tomato and Rosemary Soup

Butter Bean and Ham Soup

This is the perfect soup to make after you have poached the gammon on page 80. If you haven't got the full two litres of ham stock, extend it with vegetable stock to the right amount. You need to begin this recipe the day before you want to serve it.

225g (8oz) butter beans
25g (1oz) butter
1 onion, peeled and sliced
1 carrot, peeled and chopped
2 litres (3½ pints) ham stock

FOR GARNISH
50g (2oz) diced ham
1 tablespoon chopped parsley

Serves 6

Soak the butter beans overnight. In a pan large enough to take all the ingredients, melt the butter, gently fry the onion and carrot for 5 minutes. Add the butter beans and the stock. Bring to the boil, cover the pan, then simmer until the butter beans are cooked, which will take up to an hour. Take off the heat, liquidise the mixture and adjust the seasoning if you wish. Add the diced ham and the parsley and serve piping hot.

Left: Tomato and Rosemary Soup

Mulligatawny Soup

Mulligatawny Soup originated in Kerala, southern India, during the rule of the Raj. The name is an anglicised version of the Tamil word milagutannir, *meaning 'pepper-water'. It was very popular in Queen Victoria's reign, different recipes being introduced by British families returning from the sub-continent. If you make your own curry paste, the result will be even more interesting.*

50g (2oz) butter

1 large onion, peeled and chopped

2 carrots, peeled and chopped

1 cooking apple, peeled and chopped

1 tablespoon sultanas

1 tablespoon sweetish pickle – mango is particularly good

Pinch of cayenne

1 teaspoon curry paste (mild or hot according to taste)

1 teaspoon sugar

850ml (1½ pints) vegetable stock

Salt and pepper to taste

Serves 6

Melt the butter in a largish pan and sauté the onion and carrots. Add the apple, sultanas and pickle. Cook gently with the lid on until the carrots are tender. Put the mixture in a food processor and process briefly – the mixture should be chunky, not a smooth purée. Return to the pan. Stir in the cayenne, curry paste, sugar and stock and reheat, stirring all the time. Season the soup. Serve very hot.

Pea and Ham Soup

This soup is made in the same way as the Rosemary Soup on page 15. It requires vegetable purée made in the same way. This soup should be very thick, but if you prefer it less so, thin it down with more stock. It is a winter soup, perfect on Boxing Day after a cold, invigorating walk, made with the stock from the Christmas ham. Note: you need to start this recipe a day in advance.

110g (4oz) dried split peas
600ml (1 pint) chicken or ham stock
Vegetable purée (see Rosemary Soup recipe, page 15)

FOR GARNISH
50g (2oz) smoked ham, diced
Chopped parsley

Serves 2–3

Soak the peas overnight. Drain and cook in the chicken or ham stock. Liquidise and combine with the purée base (see above). The soup should be very thick but if you prefer a slightly thinner soup, dilute with a little more stock. Bring to the boil. Add the diced ham and a little chopped parsley. Serve very hot.

Cock-a-Leekie Soup

A famous old Scottish recipe, this is the alternative to Scotch Broth on Burns Night or St Andrew's Day. Kettners Book of the Table *describes this as the modern version of Malachi, a 14th-century recipe that featured a 'Ma', the old name for a fowl or chicken. Modern cookery writers have questioned the addition of prunes, but I think they give the dish a distinctive flavour.*

Leg and wing joints of 1 chicken, plus the carcass
700g (1½lb) leeks, chopped and washed
3 bacon rashers, chopped
1 mixed bunch of parsley and thyme
1 bay leaf
1.2 litres (2 pints) water
110g (4oz) stoned prunes
Salt and pepper to taste

Serves 4

Put the chicken leg and wing joints, and the carcass, in a large pan, together with all but two of the leeks, the bacon and the herbs. Cover with the water. Bring to the boil, turn down the heat, cover the pan and simmer for at least 1 hour, until the chicken is tender. Season to taste, then strain off the liquid, picking out the chicken meat and cutting it into pieces to serve. Put the broth and the chicken pieces back in the pan together with the stoned prunes and the remaining leeks. Simmer very gently for 15 minutes and serve piping hot.

Scotch Broth

'At dinner, Dr Johnson ate several plates of Scotch Broth, with barley and peas in it and seemed very fond of the dish. I said, "You never ate it before?" Johnson replied, "No, sir, but I don't care how soon I eat it again." '

James Boswell, Diaries, *1786*

This soup can be a meal in itself. Originally mutton would have been used but lamb shanks are more readily available today.

2 lamb shanks, chopped
1.5 litres (2½ pints) water
25g (1oz) pearl barley (usually available at health-food shops)
1 large onion, peeled and finely chopped
2 small turnips, peeled and finely chopped
3 carrots, peeled and finely chopped
2 leeks, trimmed, chopped and washed
Grated zest and juice of ½ lemon
At least 2 tablespoons finely chopped parsley
1 teaspoon salt
Black pepper to taste

Serves 4

Ask your butcher to chop the lamb shanks into chunks for you. Put the meat in a large pan and cover with the water. Bring to the boil, add the pearl barley and simmer for 20–30 minutes.

Add all the vegetables to the pan with the salt and black pepper to taste. Cover and simmer for 1½ hours. Lift out the meat, extract the bones and stir the meat back into the soup. Check the seasoning, stir in the lemon and parsley and serve very hot.

Fish Dishes

Fish tastes good, and is good for you – we are even exhorted to eat at least two portions of oily fish a week. And Britain is a maritime nation, where it is geographically impossible to be more than a hundred miles from the sea. So, why is this chapter so short, compared to those for meat dishes or vegetables?

There are several reasons, one being the good reason that you don't need a complicated recipe to cook very fresh fish. By and large, those people who lived by the sea and had access to fish that was 'straight from the boat' did not bother to write down their recipes.

The best place to obtain very fresh fish is as near to the sea as possible. Buy it from stalls by the harbour, in fishing ports like Whitby, Brixham or Aberdeen. Buy it, as I have done, from a fisherman with a box of plaice or lemon sole, standing by his boat on the beach at Dungeness in Kent, or from a boatman selling cod on a quay in Ireland. Fish this fresh needs only covering in seasoned flour, brushing with butter, and then grilling, frying or roasting in a hot oven until it is cooked – 15 minutes for steaks, fillets or small flat fish, or 30–40 minutes for a larger fish. The test for 'doneness' is when the flesh falls away from the bone, and is white or cream-coloured rather than opaque. For similar reasons I have no recipes here for shellfish – except Potted Shrimps and Crab. We eat oysters uncooked. We eat whelks, cockles, winkles, queens and mussels boiled, and eaten plain or with vinegar. Lobsters and crabs are best simply boiled, as soon as they come out of the sea – serve them with Mayonnaise or Green Sauce (see page 119).

In the Middle Ages, England was still part of the Roman Catholic church and Fridays and saints' days were nominated 'fast days', when meat could not be eaten. People ate far more fish than we do today – huge shoals of herring were caught and, in winter, fresh sea fish was transported inland. 'Stockfish' (dried cod), and pickled or salted herrings were also important staples. Meanwhile, both the aristocracy and the monasteries caught carp and pike from their own 'stew ponds', and there are accounts of fish traps and weirs on many rivers.

At the beginning of the 19th century, poor people in the cities survived mainly on a bland diet of bread and potatoes. But the advent of the railways brought with it a wider distribution of food – the availability of fresh fish, often fried in beef dripping (and later with its inseparable companion, deep-fried potato chips) was greeted with understandable enthusiasm. In fact the one fish dish that probably every British person has eaten at one time or another is battered cod, or haddock, with chips.

Today, most of us buy our fish from a supermarket, partly because we are lucky if we have a fishmonger within easy reach. We probably have no idea when our fish was actually caught – how fresh it is – although we are at least told these days if it has been deep-frozen. Fish is also expensive in comparison to other foods. And, finally, we get so many mixed messages from the media – about over-fishing, pollution, sustainability, farmed or wild fish – that we can find ourselves confused. My advice is to buy from a fishmonger if you have one locally, because he or she knows their stock, and what fish is freshest and best, and cheapest, on any particular day. Sometimes, for instance, mackerel and herring are cheap. On those days, use the recipes here for potting and pickling fish. If you have to buy fish at a supermarket, choose fish from the counter rather than the pre-packed fish in the cabinet. Not only can you choose exactly how much you want – and the thickness and shape – but it is likely to be fresher.

Fish is wonderfully simple to cook with. Look at the recipe for Poached Salmon – it is absolutely foolproof. A cooked salmon can be central to several meals, rather in the way you would treat a joint of meat. Eat it warm first – a poached salmon, huge and impressive on a platter, makes any meal into a celebration. Then eat it cold the next day, and afterwards make fishcakes out of what is left. When you count up the meals one salmon has provided, you will find it is not that expensive at all.

The Salmon Pie is another dish that is perfect for a special occasion – it looks spectacular and tastes even better. Kedgeree, an Indian dish that was brought here in the days of the British Empire, was a favourite breakfast dish for the Victorians. In our modern lifestyle, with no time for huge breakfasts, it makes an excellent supper dish. Cullen Skink is officially a smoked haddock soup, but as one of those soups that is a meal in itself, it fits well in this chapter.

Some recipes reflect the regionality of fish. Stargazey Pie uses Cornwall's most famous fish, the pilchard. Not only a staple of the Cornish diet, huge quantities of pilchard were caught with seine nets 'between harvest and all hallowtide' and exported – at first salted and smoked, later canned. Incidentally, the complaint that all our prime fish ends up elsewhere is a continuing one.

So keep eating fish. Not only will you keep the fishmongers in business, but you ensure that fishermen have an income. And what could be better than eating fish? You can enjoy eating it with family and friends, and it is good for everyone's health. Perhaps fish is best summed up by Andrew Boorde, physician and writer, in his *Compendyous Regyment or Dyetary of Health*, of 1542: 'Of all nacyons and countres, England is bests served of Fysshe, not onely of al maner of see-fysshe, but also of fresshe-water fysshe, and al maner of sortes of salte-fysshe.'

Potted Crab

'Potting' – preserving cooked fish or meat in fat – is a very old process. Even cheese can be potted. This recipe comes from south Devon where crabs abound – the taste is superb.

2 tablespoons dry or medium sherry
Juice and zest of 1 orange (reserve 1 teaspoon of the zest to use in the
   clarified butter)
150g (5oz) softened butter
225g (8oz) dressed crab (white and dark meat)
¼ teaspoon ground ginger
Salt and pepper to taste
50g (2oz) butter
2 tablespoons water

Serves 4

Bring the sherry, orange zest and juice to the boil and boil hard until reduced to 1 tablespoon of liquid. Remove from the heat, cool and beat with the softened butter until creamy. Combine with the crab meat and ginger. Add salt and pepper to taste. Mix well and spoon into ramekins. Seal with orange clarified butter made as follows.

Bring the reserved orange zest, the butter and water slowly to the boil. Remove from heat, allow to cool slightly and gently spoon over the ramekins.

Chill in the fridge for at least a couple of hours. Serve with hot toast or melba toast. Potted crab keeps well for two or three days in the fridge.

Cullen Skink

Cullen is a village in north-east Scotland. Skink *means 'essence' in Gaelic. All the villages on the north-eastern coast had their own particular stews and soups, but this one seems to be the most famous – perhaps it's the intriguing name. I have put this in the fish dishes rather than the soups as it's a meal in itself. Crusty bread is all the accompaniment it needs.*

450g (1lb) smoked haddock or cod
1 medium onion, peeled and finely chopped
600ml (1 pint) full cream milk
600ml (1 pint) fish stock
225g (8oz) cooked potato, cubed
1 small tin sweetcorn, approximately 225g (8oz)
Salt and pepper to taste

FOR GARNISH
Paprika
Chopped parsley

Serves 6

Steam or poach the fish for 5 minutes. Remove from the water with a slotted spoon. Discard the skin and any bones. Divide the fish into chunks with a fork. Use the water to make up the fish stock.

Peel and finely chop the onion and place in a large pan with the milk and stock. Simmer until tender (about 10–15 minutes), then add the potatoes and sweetcorn. Reheat until just below boiling, add the fish and season to taste. Serve immediately, garnishing the soup bowls with a dusting of paprika and a little chopped parsley.

Salmon Fishcakes

This is an excellent way to use up leftover fish if you have poached a whole salmon (see page 50).
The contrast between the crisp outside and the pink, cream and green inside of the cake is
particularly appetising.

225g (8oz) salmon fillet
450g (1lb) potatoes cooked, mashed and cooled
2 tablespoons onion or spring onion, finely chopped
2 tablespoons parsley, finely chopped
Grated zest and juice of ½ lemon
1 egg, well beaten
2 tablespoons plain flour
25g (1oz) butter
2 tablespoons olive or sunflower oil
Salt and pepper to taste
Lemon wedges

Serves 4

Steam the salmon until cooked (approximately 10 minutes). Put in a mixing bowl and flake,
removing any bones. Allow to cool. Then add the mashed potato, onion, parsley and lemon. Use
the rest of the lemon for the lemon-wedge garnish. Stir in the beaten egg and season to taste. The
mixture is quite soft, but if you wet your hands before forming the cakes it will not stick quite so
much. Spread the flour on a plate and as you make each cake (the mixture will provide eight, two
per person), roll it in flour mixed with a little extra seasoning. Heat the butter and oil in a large
frying pan and fry the cakes on each side until crisp and golden. Serve immediately with a wedge
of lemon. The fishcakes are delicious with either Green Sauce or Tartare Sauce (see page 119).

Pickled Salmon (Gravadlax)

Pickling in salt was one method used not only for fish but also for meat to keep it through the lean winter months. This recipe is practical but also delicious, particularly if you use fresh dill. The salty, aromatic fish makes a perfect appetiser. Very good for entertaining, too – the work, such as it is, has been done days before it is needed.

450g (1lb) fresh salmon fillet, skinned
Coarse-grain mustard
1 packet fresh dill, finely chopped (dried dill can be used)
Rock salt
Freshly ground pepper to taste
Lemon wedges

Serves 4

Ask the fishmonger for a cut from the thick end of the fillet, and allow approximately 50g (2oz) of salmon per serving. Start this dish at least three days before you wish to serve it.

Cut a piece of clingfilm large enough to wrap the salmon in. Scatter a thick layer of rock salt on the clingfilm. Spread both sides of the salmon first with coarse-grain mustard, then with the dill, to cover the fish completely. Wrap the salmon in the clingfilm, then wrap the parcel in foil and chill for at least 3 days, turning from time to time. You can leave it to pickle for 7 days. It is not necessary to unwrap the fish.

To serve, remove the foil and clingfilm, slice the salmon thinly, garnish with lemon wedges and serve with brown bread and butter, a little green frisée and some Dill Mayonnaise (see page 119).

Pickled Herring

For centuries, huge shoals of herring have been caught around our shores, particularly on the east coast of Britain. In 1902–3, 500 million fish were caught by Yarmouth boats alone. Preserving this bounty by salting, smoking and pickling has occupied us for generations. Of course you can buy pickled herring in jars in delicatessens and supermarkets, but there is a certain pleasure in preserving your own fish – particularly if you have bought them on the quayside, as you can in the autumn in ports such as Whitby, Great Yarmouth or King's Lynn.

6 herring fillets
600ml (1 pint) water
50g (2oz) salt
50g (2oz) caster sugar

FOR THE MARINADE
300ml white wine or cider vinegar
3 bay leaves
1 tablespoon pickling spices, including chilli
¼ teaspoon black peppercorns
1 tablespoon sugar
3 gherkins
1 mild sweet onion (Spanish or red), very thinly sliced

Serves 6

If the herring fillets are large, cut them in half lengthwise. Bring the water to the boil, take it off the heat and mix in the salt and sugar. Stir until they have dissolved. Let the mixture stand until it is cool. Roll up the herring fillets and lay them in a shallow dish, just large enough to take them. Pour over the brine and leave the fish for 3–4 hours.

Meanwhile, make the marinade. Bring the vinegar, bay leaves, pickling spices, peppercorns and sugar to the boil. Remove from the heat and leave to cool. Drain the brine from the fish. Dry the fillets with kitchen paper and re-roll each one round a piece of gherkin and a slice of onion. Arrange them back in the dish, tuck slices of gherkin and onion round the fish and pour over the marinade with the spices. Cover and leave for at least 4 days before eating. Serve with brown bread and butter.

Soused Mackerel

Brought up by the sea, I was taught that a mackerel went straight from the sea into the frying pan. The catch was unpredictable and often we caught more than we could eat immediately. The extras were soused as below and were a great treat for tea the next day. (A friend of mine had another good idea, though, and disposed of his share in return for lifts as he hitchhiked back to London after a fishing weekend.)

6 mackerel fillets
1 mild sweet onion (Spanish or red) or 2–3 shallots, peeled and sliced
3 bay leaves
1 marjoram sprig
1 parsley sprig
½ teaspoon black peppercorns
4 whole cloves
200ml (7fl oz) cider
200ml (7fl oz) cider vinegar
Water, to cover
Salt and pepper to taste

Serves 4

Preheat oven to 140°C, 275°F, gas mark 1. Cut each mackerel fillet in half lengthwise. Roll each piece up from the tail and lay the rolls in an ovenproof dish just large enough to take the fish. Make sure they are all facing the same way, so that the colours match. Scatter the onion slices over the fish and tuck the bay leaves and sprigs of marjoram and parsley around it. Scatter the peppercorns and cloves over the dish and season with salt and pepper. Pour over the cider and cider vinegar, and add sufficient water to cover the fish. Cover the dish with foil and cook for 1 hour in the oven. Leave the dish to cool before serving with brown bread and butter.

Potted Shrimps

As a child I shrimped off the South Devon coast with a large sweep net that was almost as big as me. We caught netfuls of shrimps that we boiled in sea water over a driftwood fire on the beach, and peeled and ate as soon as they were cool enough to handle.

Shrimps have a delicate flavour and are best eaten as soon as possible after they are caught. Potting enables us to enjoy them for a day or two longer. If you can't find brown shrimps, you can use this method to pot crab, prawns or flaked cooked salmon. The flavour of the seafood is very important; the fish really needs to be fresh, not frozen then defrosted.

200g (8oz) butter
350g (12oz) brown shrimps, peeled
¼ teaspoon or one stick mace
¼ teaspoon freshly grated nutmeg
¼ teaspoon cayenne pepper
1 lemon, cut into 6 wedges, for garnish

Serves 6

First clarify 100g (4oz) of the butter. Cut it into small pieces and melt it gently over a low heat. Skim off any scum from the surface and pour off the clarified butter into a bowl. Leave behind the milky solids at the bottom of the pan. The clarified butter is now ready to use.

Heat the remaining 100g (4oz) butter in a pan (large enough to hold the shrimps) until it has melted. Add the peeled shrimps, spices and cayenne pepper and heat through, stirring gently all the time. Do not let the mixture boil. Take out the mace and divide the mixture between six small ramekins. Spoon clarified butter over each one. Chill until ready to serve.

To serve, unmould each pot onto a plate, garnish with a wedge of lemon and eat with hot, thin brown toast.

Right: Potted Shrimps

Florence Nightingale's Kedgeree

British-Indian cuisine was very chic in Victorian Britain, as was naming dishes after well-known people. Charles Francatelli, chef to Queen Victoria, named his version of this then-new dish Kedgeree (the English version of the Indian Khichiri*) after Florence Nightingale, heroine of the Crimean War. This dish would have been served at breakfast in the 19th century. Today, it is a good supper or party dish. I have kept pretty well to Signor Francatelli's original recipe (as interpreted by Sara Paston-Williams) but when I cook this for buffet parties, I add cooked prawns, salmon chunks and peas, and colour the rice with turmeric.*

450g (1lb) smoked haddock, cooked
4 eggs, hard-boiled
1 tablespoon Parmesan cheese, grated
110g (4oz) butter
175g (6oz) long-grain rice, cooked
Salt and freshly ground black pepper to taste
Freshly grated nutmeg
2 tablespoons chopped chives
2 tablespoons fresh parsley, chopped

FOR GARNISH
Small triangles of fried bread (optional)
Lemon wedges

Serves 4–6

Remove the skin and bones from the fish and flake coarsely. Chop the whites of the hard-boiled eggs and add to the fish. Press the yolks through a sieve and mix with the cheese. Melt the butter in a saucepan and toss the rice in it over a gentle heat until well coated and heated through. Mix in the fish and egg whites and gently continue to toss until the whole mixture is hot. Season with salt, pepper and nutmeg, chopped chives and 1 tablespoon of the parsley, then pile onto an ovenproof plate. Scatter the egg yolk and cheese mixture on top and place under a gentle grill for a few minutes until the cheese begins to colour. Arrange the triangles of fried bread around the rice and sprinkle with the remaining parsley. Serve immediately, with a lemon wedge per serving.

Left: Florence Nightingale's Kedgeree

Poached Salmon

Salmon, poached in a court-bouillon, is a traditional British favourite. For centuries, salmon, caught by net at the river mouth or by line farther up river, was expensive. It was a celebration food served at christenings, weddings, birthdays – the milestones in peoples' lives. Cooking professionally for parties for twenty years, I lost count of how many salmon I poached. Farmed salmon is not expensive today. Before buying, it is worth establishing that the salmon has been farmed ethically. The flavour will be better and it will have less fat.

Salmon is sold as steaks and fillets, but if you want to cook a whole salmon by far the best and easiest way is to poach it in a court-bouillon. If you are going to serve the salmon cold, you can twist the fish into an S-bend and cook it in, for instance, a preserving pan. Alternatively, if you buy your salmon from a fishmonger, they may allow you to borrow or hire a salmon kettle. Follow the instructions below for a foolproof method for poaching a salmon to be served either cool, at room temperature or chilled.

1 whole salmon, approximately 4kg (8½lb)
Water, to cover

FOR THE COURT-BOUILLON
½ teaspoon black peppercorns
2 lemons, chopped into chunks
1 tablespoon salt
3 shallots, peeled and cut into quarters
1 carrot, roughly chopped
1 celery stick, sliced
300ml (10fl oz) white wine vinegar
300ml (10fl oz) white wine
A few sprigs of thyme, parsley and fennel or dill
A few parsley sprigs, for garnish

Serves at least 10

If you are using a salmon kettle, lay the fish on its side on the perforated tray. If you haven't got a salmon kettle, grease or oil a large pan, then twist the fish into an S-bend and jam it upright in the pan, mouth on one side, tail on the other. Don't worry if it is right up against the edge of the pan: this will hold it in place while it cooks. Add all the ingredients for the court-bouillon to the kettle or pan. Then add water until the fish is just covered. Cover and bring the bouillon up to the boil. As soon as you are sure that it is boiling, turn off the heat and leave the fish to cool completely. This may take a couple of hours. Carefully lift the fish out of the pan onto a large plate. By this time it should be set in its S-bend, if you are cooking it in a pan.

Poached salmon needs the minimum of garnish – carefully remove the skin and fill the mouth and the eye sockets with parsley. Serve with lemon wedges for squeezing, mayonnaise (see page 119) and warm new potatoes. Celebration food indeed!

Pickled Herring and Fruit Pie

This unusual Norfolk recipe was researched and written up by Sara Paston-Williams. The mixture of fish and fruit may seem odd to our modern taste, but it is a great favourite at the Elizabethan banquets held from time to time at Oxburgh Hall in Norfolk.

FOR THE PASTRY

350g (12oz) plain flour

Salt and black pepper to taste

75g (3oz) butter

75g (3oz) lard

Cold water to mix

FOR THE FILLING

450g (1lb) pickled herring or roll mops

1 large cooking pear, peeled, cored and sliced

25g (1oz) raisins

25g (1oz) currants

50g (2oz) dates, pitted and minced

¼ teaspoon ground cinnamon

2 tablespoons dry white wine

25g (1oz) butter, cut into small pieces

Beaten egg, or milk, to glaze

1 teaspoon sugar

Pinch of salt

Serves 6

Preheat oven to 220°C, 425°F, gas mark 7. To make the pastry, sieve the flour and salt together into a bowl. Add a sprinkling of pepper, then rub in the butter and lard until the mixture resembles fine breadcrumbs. Mix with enough cold water to make a firm dough. Knead lightly until smooth. Divide into two portions, about two-thirds and one-third. Roll out the two portions and then chill them for about 10 minutes.

Grease a deep 20cm (8in) flan tin and line it with the larger portion of pastry. Bake blind for 10 minutes. Leave to cool. Reduce the temperature of the oven to 190°C, 375°F, gas mark 5. Meanwhile, prepare the filling. Unroll the herring if necessary. Remove any onions and reserve. Rinse the herring in cold water and drain. Plunge them into 1.8 litres (3 pints) boiling water in a pan, cook for 1 minute, remove and drain well. Cut into chunks.

Mix the pear, dried fruit, salt, cinnamon and wine together in a bowl and add the herring. Transfer the filling into the pastry-lined flan tin, using a slotted spoon to drain off any excess liquid. Dot the mixture with the butter and cover with the remaining pastry. Decorate the top with any pastry trimmings, then brush with the egg or milk. Make a slit in the top to allow the steam to escape and sprinkle with the sugar. Bake for 1 hour, or until golden brown.

Stargazey Pie

Stargazey Pie is Cornwall's most famous dish, but you don't see it on many menus today. Made traditionally, it is all about visual effect: the heads of the fish are outside the pastry. The Oxford Companion to Food *says that this is to prevent the rich oil in the (inedible) fish heads from being lost - it drips back into the pie. If you are squeamish about the heads, get your fishmonger to remove them, and make the pie without. (This is how I ate the dish as a child on picnics, just cooled from the oven, and it tasted wonderful).*

FOR THE SHORTCRUST PASTRY
250g (8oz) plain flour
1 teaspoon salt
75g (3oz) butter
75g (3oz) vegetable shortening or lard
Approximately 4 tablespoons cold water

FOR THE FILLING
110g (4oz) white breadcrumbs
50ml (2fl oz) milk
1 tablespoon chopped parsley
1 onion, peeled and finely chopped
Juice and grated zest of 1 lemon
8 pilchards or 8 small herring or 8 large sardines (ask your fishmonger to clean and bone the fish, but leave the heads in place)
2 hard-boiled eggs, chopped
50g (2oz) bacon, chopped
150ml (¼ pint) cider
1 beaten egg, to seal and glaze
Salt and pepper to taste

Serves 4–6

With pastry, it is important to keep everything as cold as possible and to handle the dough as little as possible. Sift the flour with the salt into a bowl. Add the butter and shortening and cut with a knife until it is all small pieces. Then rub with your fingertips until the mixture forms fine crumbs. You can do this part of the recipe with a food processor.

Make a well in the centre of the mixture and add water. Mix with a knife to form crumbs. Then work together to form a ball. Wrap it tightly in clingfilm and chill in the fridge for about 30 minutes. Knead the dough after it has chilled. Flour the work surface and work the dough with your hands until it is smooth. This should only take a minute or two. It is now ready to be rolled out.

Preheat oven to 220°C, 425°F, gas mark 7. First, grease the pie dish. (You will need a shallow, round pie dish, large enough to fit the fish tail-to-tail in the centre, with their heads resting on the rim.) Divide the pastry into two pieces. Roll out the first piece to line the dish, and prick the base. Leave it to rest while you make the stuffing.

Soak the breadcrumbs in the milk for about 5 minutes. Squeeze them out and mix with the parsley, chopped onion and juice and zest of the lemon. Stuff the fish with some of this mixture – you should have about a third left over. Lay the stuffed fish in the dish, heads on the rim, tails at the centre. Mix the remainder of the stuffing with the chopped egg and bacon, and use this mixture to fill in the gaps round the fish. Pour over the cider, season with pepper and a little salt (beware of adding too much as the bacon will taste salty).

Roll out the second piece of pastry to cover the pie. Brush the rim with beaten egg to give a good seal, but leave each head sticking out. Make a hole in the centre to let out the steam and brush the top with beaten egg. Bake for 10 minutes in the oven, then reduce the heat to 180°C, 350°F, gas mark 4 and bake for a further 40 minutes. Stargazey Pie is best served at room temperature.

Haddock and Prawn Cobbler

My recipe for Haddock and Prawn Cobbler came from the National Trust York Tea Room. York abounds with tea rooms, but this is one of the best, butting up against the Minster and serving hot dishes throughout the day as well as scones, teacakes, cakes and biscuits. I assumed cobbler *was an old Yorkshire word meaning 'dish with a scone topping'. Imagine my surprise when the* Oxford Companion to Food *told me it is from New England! However, I'm not going to leave it out, since it is a variation on the British pie and is too tasty to miss.*

700g (1½lb) haddock fillet, skinned and cut into 5cm (2in) chunks
50g (2oz) butter
50g (2oz) plain flour
2 teaspoons mustard powder
600ml (1 pint) milk
4 teaspoons wine vinegar
2 hard-boiled eggs, peeled and chopped
50g (2oz) prawns

FOR THE TOPPING
175g (6oz) wholemeal flour
1 tablespoon baking powder
Pinch of thyme
40g (1½oz) butter
1 egg, beaten
2 tablespoons milk

Serves 6

Preheat oven to 180°C, 350°F, gas mark 4. Cook the haddock in boiling water. This will take approximately 10 minutes. Allow to cool. Make a white sauce with the butter, flour and mustard powder, using the milk and wine vinegar as liquid. Don't worry if the sauce curdles; just give it a quick whisk. Lay the cooked haddock in a 20 x 23cm (8 x 9in) china gratin dish, approximately 6.5cm (2½in) deep. Sprinkle over the prawns and chopped hard-boiled eggs and cover with the white sauce. Put aside while you make the topping.

Sift together flour, baking powder and thyme into a large bowl. Rub in the butter, then make up into a dough using the egg and milk. Roll out into a sheet approximately 2.5cm (1in) thick and cut into 5cm (2in) rounds. Arrange on the top of the fish mixture. Brush with milk and bake for approximately 20 minutes, until well risen and brown. Serve with green vegetables or a green salad.

Fish and Cider Casserole

I am very happy with this casserole since it uses coley, and at the time of writing, stocks of this fish round the British coast are at a sustainable level. Coley makes a good substitute for cod and haddock, which are both under threat of over-fishing. I was given this recipe by the cooks at Fountains Abbey, North Yorkshire, the spectacular ruins of a great Cistercian monastery where the choir monks led lives of rigorous simplicity, with seven services of prayers every day and only the sick ate 'the meat of quadrupeds'. Fish must have been a welcome treat when it appeared on the frugal daily menu.

700g (1½lb) coley fillets
300ml (½ pint) vegetable stock
1 onion, peeled and sliced
50g (2oz) butter
50g (2oz) plain flour
300ml (½ pint) cider
2 teaspoons anchovy essence
1 tablespoon lemon juice
Salt and pepper to taste

FOR THE TOPPING
225g (8oz) cooked potatoes, peeled and sliced
225g (8oz) apples, peeled and sliced
25g (1oz) butter

Serves 6

Preheat oven to 150°C, 300°F, gas mark 2. Poach the coley in the stock until cooked, approximately 10 minutes. Set aside while you make the sauce. Sauté the onion in the butter until cooked but not coloured. Stir in the flour and cook gently for a further 5 minutes. Stir in the cider, anchovy essence and lemon juice. Then use as much of the stock as you wish to make the sauce thick, but not too thick. Divide the coley fillets into six portions and place in a gratin dish. Pour over the cider sauce, coating the fish evenly. Cover with foil and place it in the oven to keep warm while you prepare the topping.

At this point, preheat the grill. Melt the extra 25g (1oz) of butter in a frying pan and gently fry the cooked potato and the apple slices for a few minutes. Arrange them on the top of the dish to cover the fish mixture completely. Then pop the dish under the grill for 5 minutes to brown the top before serving.

Sedgemoor Eel Stew

This recipe comes from Jane Grigson's Fish Book. *Sedgemoor is a wetland that was created in the Middle Ages by monks from nearby abbeys, such as Glastonbury. It is a perfect habitat for eels. The recipe below is very similar to the traditional pie-and-mash shops' recipe for eel. It is just slightly richer, using local Somerset cider instead of water, and with the addition of butter from the famous local dairy herds. Allow 225g (8oz) eel per person, and ask your fishmonger to prepare it for you.*

900g (2lb) eel, heads removed, skinned and cut into chunks
700ml (1¼ pints) cider
2 tablespoons softened butter
2 tablespoons plain flour
At least 2 tablespoons chopped parsley
Salt and pepper to taste

Serves 4

Arrange the eel pieces in a single layer in a shallow pan. Pour over the cider. Cover the pan and simmer until the eel is tender. (This will take about 15 minutes.) Remove the pieces of eel and keep them warm on a serving dish. Season them with salt and pepper, and season the cooking liquid. Mash together the butter and flour and add the mixture, a little at a time, to the simmering liquid until it thickens slightly. Add the parsley – the sauce should be very green – and pour it over the eel. For authenticity, serve with mash.

Trout with Almonds

Michael Smith attributes this dish to Oxford University, but doesn't say which college. He fries the trout in oil; I prefer to reduce the fat content a little by oven-baking the trout. The result is rich and delicate at the same time. Boiled new potatoes served with the fish, and a green salad afterwards are all it needs.

4 trout, heads removed and cleaned
2 tablespoons plain flour, seasoned with salt and pepper
1 tablespoon olive oil
50g (2oz) butter
50g (2oz) flaked almonds
Grated zest and juice of 1 lemon
Salt and pepper to taste

Serves 4

Preheat oven to 200°C, 400°F, gas mark 6. Coat the trout with flour seasoned with pepper and salt to taste. Place them in a large roasting tin lined with baking paper. (This prevents the trout from sticking to the tin, making it much easier to clean.) Bake for 15 minutes, then turn off the oven and leave the trout to rest while you make the sauce. Put four serving plates in the oven to warm up.

To make the sauce, melt the olive oil and butter in a small frying pan. Shake in the almonds and sauté them until they are brown. Watch and stir the pan constantly as they can go from golden to burnt very quickly. Take the pan off the heat and stir in the lemon zest and juice. To serve, place each trout on a warmed plate and pour over the almonds and sauce.

Fish and Chips

Ask a visitor to Britain which British dish they intend to sample while they are here and the chances are that top of the list will be Fish and Chips. Traditionally, Fish and Chips is 'take out' food. Every town, however small, has a 'chippie'. Its popularity dates back to the Industrial Revolution – which meant more families trying to feed themselves in cramped circumstances – and the advent of the railways, which meant fish could be transported inland quickly. Nourishing and filling, fish and chips really hit the spot.

Home-made fish and chips, made with best-quality ingredients cooked with care, are special indeed. If you come from the north you will want vinegar and mushy peas with your fish and chips. Green peas and tartare sauce (see page 117) taste good too. Either way, a wedge of lemon to squeeze over the fish is essential.

FOR THE FISH
4 thick cod or haddock fillets, skinned
Flour
Salt and pepper to taste
Best-quality beef dripping or lard or sunflower oil for frying

FOR THE BATTER
110g (4oz) plain flour
½ teaspoon salt
1 tablespoon olive oil
1 egg, separated
About 150ml (¼ pint) beer or water

FOR THE CHIPS
900g (2lb) potatoes, preferably Maris Piper, cut into even-sized chips
Lard or oil for deep-frying
Salt and pepper to taste

Serves 4

Note: all the ingredients should be at room temperature. Sieve the flour for the batter with the salt into a bowl, make a well in the centre and gradually beat in the olive oil, egg yolk and beer or water to make a smooth batter that will coat the back of a wooden spoon. Let it rest at room temperature for about 30 minutes.

Heat the fat in a deep-fat fryer with a basket to 180°C, 350°F. Test the lard or oil with a square of bread. It should cook crisp and golden immediately.

Dust the fish fillets with seasoned flour. Whip the egg white until stiff and fold it gently into the batter. Dip the flour-covered fillets in the batter and fry immediately until crisp and golden. Drain on kitchen paper. Don't overload the pan. Better to do the frying in batches and keep the drained cooked fillets warm in the oven while you finish the rest.

Dry the chips well on kitchen paper. Fry them in batches for about 10 minutes until soft, making sure not to overload the fryer. Drain on kitchen paper.

Increase the heat to 190°C, 375°F. Salt the chips and return in batches to the fryer for a few minutes until crisp and golden. Keep an eye on them as it's very easy to overcook them at this point. Drain on kitchen paper again and add salt and pepper. They are now ready to serve with the fish.

Hobbler's Seafood Pie

This recipe was given to me by the Sail Loft restaurant at St Michael's Mount, a magical island off the coast of Cornwall. It is unusual in that it uses raw fish, which seems to intensify the flavour. At the Sail Loft, this pie is made with any fish the boats land on the Mount, so generally there are leftovers after filleting for the stock. However, if you buy fish from the supermarket it will probably be easier to use a vegetable stock cube.

350g (12oz) white fish (the Sail Loft uses ling for preference, but coley, cod or
    haddock may be easier to find)
110g (4oz) peeled prawns
1 tablespoon chopped parsley
50g (2oz) butter
50g (2oz) flour
300ml (½ pint) creamy milk
300ml (½ pint) fish stock
450g (1lb) mashed potato

Serves 4

Preheat oven to 180°C, 350°F, gas mark 4. Cut the fish into large chunks and lay it on the bottom of a pie dish. Scatter over the prawns and the parsley. Make up a thick white sauce using the butter, flour, milk and fish stock and pour over the fish. Cover the fish and sauce with mashed potato, fluffing the top with a fork. Bake uncovered in the oven for approximately 30 minutes, until the top is crisp and brown.

Right: Hobbler's Seafood Pie
Next page: Salmon Fish Cakes

Herring Fried in Oatmeal

Herring or trout fried in oatmeal have always been popular for breakfast, high tea or supper, especially in Scotland. If possible, use a food processor to produce a mixture of coarse, medium and finely blended oatmeal for use in this recipe. Plain boiled new potatoes or granary bread are the best accompaniments.

4 large herring, heads, tails and backbones removed, scaled and cleaned
3–4 tablespoons milk
110g (4oz) oatmeal
110g (4oz) unsalted butter
Salt and pepper to taste
2 lemons, cut into wedges, to serve

Serves 4

Ask your fishmonger to prepare the herring. Sprinkle salt and pepper over the inside of the fish. Return them to their original shape. Dip the herring in the milk. Put the oatmeal in a shallow dish, season with salt and pepper and press the fish firmly into it so that they are coated evenly.

Heat the butter until it is bubbling in a large, heavy-based frying pan. Fry the herring for 5 minutes or so on each side. Lift the fish onto plates, pour over any butter from the pan and serve with lemon wedges to squeeze over them.

Left and previous page: Herring Fried in Oatmeal

Meat, Poultry and Game Dishes

Aberdeen Angus, Galloways, Devons, Lincoln Reds, Sussex Old Herefords and Welsh Blacks – our beef breeds have been the envy of the world. British lamb, fed on sweet green pasture, is equally prized, with Cheviot, Herdwick, Romney, Southdown and any amount of crossbreeds. We raise splendid pork, and both chickens and ducks thrive in the mild climate. There are rabbits in the countryside, and a thriving market in game. You could say that Britain is a paradise for meat eaters.

In the 18th century the British were known throughout Europe, and particularly by the French, as 'Rosbifs' – a rather scathing tribute to what was, then, our national dish. Indeed, some would say it still is. Throughout the centuries, as today, roasting has been the preferred method for cooking the choicest cuts of meat. But, of course, we have other great traditional dishes and it is these that are celebrated in this chapter, although there is information on roasting in the Appendices (see page 315).

British cooking traditions have been built round the good quality of the meat, where there was never any need to disguise the taste. Spicing, herbs, ale, cider or wine are all there to enhance the goodness and flavour of the meat itself, and even casseroles are for the cuts of meat that need longer cooking to become tender, rather than to taste better. None of these recipes are complicated; Boiled Beef and Carrots may need to simmer for several hours, but it makes no demands upon the cook – and neither do Irish Stew, Stewed Oxtail or Steak and Kidney Pudding.

I have tried to provide at least one recipe for every beast or fowl (the old words seem appropriate) that the British not only eat today, but have eaten over the last six hundred years. That includes turkey, which had a fixed price in the London markets by the 1550s, when it was already talked of as a Christmas food – although it wasn't until the 20th century that it supplanted goose as the traditional bird. Some of the dishes are modern adaptations that stick as closely as possible to the old recipes – as in the versions of Chicken in Hocchee and Venison Casseroled with Apricots.

'Take chykens and scald them, take parsel and sawge ... take garlic and grapes, and stoppe the chikens ful, and seeth them in good broth.' This old recipe for Chicken in Hocchee, a medieval or Tudor recipe for chicken breasts stuffed with grapes, garlic, fresh parsley and sage, and then poached in stock and wine, is still very much to modern tastes. Many of the old recipes are for game or poultry. Game parks, enclosed areas where game was hunted for sport by the aristocracy, had actually been part of the English countryside since the time of the Romans. These are recipes from the rich man's table, written down as a reminder to the household cooks. Medieval and Tudor cooks did not have hard and fast rules about the use of fruit in savoury recipes, and it is interesting to notice how often the game and poultry recipes include fruit, sometimes instead of vegetables.

Certain recipes have regional roots. Recipes for lamb dishes, such as Irish Stew, come from upland areas, where sheep were the main beasts raised for market. Lancashire Hot Pot – lamb or mutton cooked in a deep pot with a layer of potatoes on the top – has a long tradition, but not just in Lancashire. There are 'hot pots' right across northern England, with slightly different names, and slightly different ingredients and side dishes. 'Tatie Pot' is made in Cumbria, from lamb, black pudding and vegetables, but with the addition of beef as well. 'Tater 'Ash' is the Cheshire name for a similar dish, where it is eaten with Piccalilli rather than the usual Red Cabbage. Interestingly, I was given a recipe for Hodge Podge, the ancestor of today's Hot Pot, in Northumberland.

There are no less than ten pies in this chapter. Pies have always been a great favourite with the British, eaten hot, like Steak and Kidney Pie, or Chicken Thyme Pie, or cold, like Pork Pie or Bacon and Egg Pie. There are two squab pies here. In old recipes 'squab' meant a young pigeon, but in Cornwall and Devon it often refers to mutton or lamb. Both of the recipes here have local apples as one ingredient. But Lanhydrock Squab Pie, from Cornwall, uses lamb as a filling and the other pie, from the rich pastureland at the other end of Devon – more suitable for raising pigs – uses pork. Medieval Britain loved joke pies – you only have to think of the old nursery rhyme, 'Sing a song of sixpence, a pocket full of rye, Four and twenty blackbirds baked in a pie'. Huge celebratory pies were cooked on special occasions; Denby Dale, a small village in Yorkshire's West Riding, still cooks a huge pie for special festivals, each pie bigger than the last. In 1988, the pie cooked to mark the double centenary of the first Denby Dale pie weighed over 9 tons (over 9,000 kg). Our pies are more manageable, with pies suitable for every meal, for picnics, and even portable pies – since pasties are a meal-for-one in a pie, originally made for the tin miners in Cornwall to take to work.

Until the agricultural Enclosure Acts, at the end of the 18th century, every cottage had its patch of land, and people could keep a pig without a licence. A pig would eat anything, and could be fed on scraps, so most people could afford one, and pork was readily available. When a pig was killed, generally in the autumn, those parts of the animal that were not immediately eaten were preserved for the leaner months ahead. Sausages and sausage meat were made, hams and bacon were smoked, tripe was soaked in brine and trotters were salted. There are recipes here for sausage dishes, for bacon and gammon and for Haslet and Faggots. If you don't want to tackle the last two yourself, find a good butcher and, with any luck, you'll find them ready-made.

British meat cooking has always relied on the good quality of its ingredients. If you have the time, hunt out a good meat supplier. Apart from the butcher, who will be only too happy to provide you with advice, there is now a network of farmers' markets across the country, where you will find specialist butchers and game dealers. Some National Trust farmers sell direct to the customer – you can find a list of those who do on pages 320–321. If the supermarket is all that is available to you, take time to choose, and look for organic or free-range meat and poultry. It may cost more but it will taste much better.

Chicken Thyme Pie

Certain herbs have particular affinities. Thyme and chicken makes a good partnership. It rescues this chicken pie from lack of flavour while still leaving it the kind of easy, non-complicated recipe that conservative eaters like.

450g (1lb) shortcrust pastry (see page 54)
1 tablespoon oil
25g (1oz) butter
1 large onion, peeled and sliced
6 large celery sticks, chopped
4 chicken breasts (1 per person), cut into thick slices
Fresh or dried thyme
Salt and pepper to taste
300ml (½ pint) chicken stock (make it with a stock cube if you
    have none fresh)
300ml (½ pint) thick white sauce made with 50g (2oz) butter, 50g (2oz) flour
    and 300ml (½ pint) milk (see page 118)

Serves 4

Preheat oven to 180°C, 350°F, gas mark 4. Melt the oil and butter and sauté the onion and celery until soft. Take out the vegetables and lay them in a pie dish. Sauté the sliced chicken in the same pan (add a little more oil if you need it) until nice and brown. Add it to the dish. Make the thick white sauce (see page 118 for method) and then stir it in to make a good thick mixture with the chicken. Cover the pie dish with the pastry and decorate with any oddments. Make a hole in the centre to let out the steam and glaze with milk. Put it in the oven and cook for about 30–40 minutes until golden brown.

Chicken in Hocchee

This is a modern adaptation of a medieval or Tudor recipe: 'Take chykens and scald them, take parsel and sawge, without any other erbes, take garlec and grapes, and stoppe the chikens ful, and seeth them in good broth, so that they may esly be boyled thereine. Messe them and cast thereto powdor-douce [a mixture of mild spices].'

4 chicken breasts
110g (4oz) green grapes
2 tablespoons mixed chopped fresh parsley and sage
1 garlic clove
250ml (½ pint) chicken stock
1 small glass white wine
½ teaspoon caster sugar
½ teaspoon ground cinnamon

FOR GARNISH
Chopped parsley
A few grapes

Serves 4

Slice the chicken breasts in half so you can stuff them. Pip the grapes if necessary, reserving a few for garnishing. Mix the rest with the garlic and the herbs and stuff the chicken breasts with the mixture. Pin each breast into a neat parcel with a cocktail stick and place in a dish that just holds them. Add the stock and wine and cover the dish with foil. Simmer until tender (about 45 minutes). Remove the breasts and place on a warm serving dish. Sprinkle with the sugar and cinnamon mixed together, the chopped parsley and the grapes. Serve with the cooking juices as a gravy.

Chicken and Ham Pie

This is a good recipe to make during periods when you are catering for a crowd, such as Christmas, when there may be a gammon to cut into and some cold chicken (or turkey) in the fridge. The addition of the forcemeat balls is an old idea – the cheaper stuffing extends the expensive chicken and ham.

225g (8oz) cooked chicken meat

225g (8oz) cooked ham

175g (6oz) fresh breadcrumbs

¼ small onion, peeled and finely chopped

1 celery stick, finely chopped

1 teaspoon mixed herbs

Zest of 1 lemon

1 egg

Salt and pepper to taste

FOR THE SAUCE

50g (2oz) butter

50g (2oz) plain flour

300ml (½ pint) chicken, ham or vegetable stock

300ml (½ pint) creamy milk

1 tablespoon chopped parsley

FOR THE SHORTCRUST PASTRY

225g (8oz) plain flour

110g (4oz) margarine or lard

Egg and milk glaze

50g (2oz) sesame seeds

Serves 6

Preheat oven to 190°C, 375°F, gas mark 5. Cut the chicken and ham into chunks. Mix together the breadcrumbs, chopped onion and celery, herbs, lemon zest and salt and pepper to taste. Use the egg to bind into a dryish stuffing. Form the stuffing into balls the size of a large marble. Fill a deep pie dish with the chicken, ham and stuffing balls.

Make a white sauce with the butter, flour, stock and milk and stir in the parsley. Season with salt and pepper and pour over the pie filling.

Roll out the pastry and cover the dish, using any trimmings as decoration. Make a hole in the centre to let out the steam. Brush with egg and milk glaze and cover with a layer of sesame seeds. Bake for 30–40 minutes, until golden brown.

Roast Duck with Sage and Onion Stuffing and Apple Sauce

Duck is a prized food worldwide and recipes abound – from Chinese Peking Duck to exotic dishes such as French Caneton à la Rouennaise, *where the dish is numbered every time it is cooked. Roast Duck with Sage and Onion Stuffing and Apple Sauce is the classic British treatment. It can be cooked all year round, but it is at its best in late spring, when you can eat fresh garden peas with it – the perfect vegetable accompaniment.*

1 duck, approximately 2kg (4½lb), with giblets

2 bay leaves

2 apples

1 onion, peeled

3 garlic cloves, peeled

2 teaspoons salt

FOR THE STUFFING

50g (2oz) butter

1 small onion, finely chopped

2 celery sticks, chopped

25g (1oz) flaked almonds

1 duck's liver, finely chopped

Grated zest and juice of 1 large orange

1 apple (Cox's Orange Pippin or Braeburn), chopped

150g (5oz) fresh white breadcrumbs

5 sage leaves, finely shredded

A large handful of fresh parsley, chopped

1 large egg, well beaten

Salt and pepper to taste

FOR THE GRAVY

425ml (¾ pint) duck stock

2 tablespoons tawny port

Serves 4

Preheat oven to 200°C, 400°F, gas mark 6. If necessary, remove the giblets from the duck and separate out the liver to use in the stuffing. Put the giblets in a small pan with a couple of bay leaves, cover them with water, put the lid on and leave them to simmer while the duck is cooking.

Roughly chop the apples, onion and garlic cloves. There is no need to peel or core the apples. Mix the apples, onion and garlic together and use to stuff the carcass. Prick the skin of the duck all over. Rub it with the salt and place it, breast down, on a trivet in a large roasting tin. Roast in the oven for 30 minutes, then reduce the heat to 180°C, 350°F, Gas Mark 4 and turn the duck the right way up for the rest of the roasting time. (It should take approximately 1½ hours.)

Make the stuffing as follows. Melt the butter in a medium-sized pan. Fry the onion and celery for about 5 minutes or until slightly softened but not coloured. Add the almonds and the liver for the last minute or so, watch them carefully and give them a good stir. Take the pan off the heat and stir in the orange zest and juice, chopped apple, breadcrumbs, sage leaves and parsley. Mix well, season with salt and pepper to taste and bind together with the beaten egg. Either press the mixture into a buttered ovenproof dish or make it into patties the size of a golf ball. Put these on a baking tray lined with baking parchment. Put the dish or the patties in the oven for the last 30 minutes of the duck's cooking time. The top of the mixture or the patties should be golden brown.

When the duck is cooked, turn the oven off. Put the duck on a serving dish, cover it with foil and put it back in the oven to rest for 10–15 minutes before carving it. Make a thin gravy to serve with the duck by pouring off the excess fat from the roasting pan, leaving about 2 tablespoons behind. Drain off the stock from the giblets. Give a good scrape to the bottom of the roasting pan and add the stock from the giblets along with the tawny port. Boil vigorously for a minute or two and season with salt and pepper.

Serve the duck with the stuffing, the gravy and Apple Sauce (see page 123). Potatoes roasted with the bird, braised red cabbage and crisp, steamed green vegetables are good accompaniments.

Devilled Fowl

'It is the fault of all devilry that it knows no bounds. A moderate devil is almost a contradiction in terms; and yet it is quite certain that if a devil is not moderate, he destroys the palate … the business of which is to tickle not to annihilate the sense of taste.'

Kettners' Book of the Table

There are wet devils (sauces) and dry devils (marinades). I have chosen a recipe for a dry devil because this is traditional in our family. My mother always bought a huge turkey at Christmas time. We only ever had turkey during the festive season: hot on Christmas Day; cold on Boxing Day; the various joints, legs and thighs devilled with whatever chutney came to hand, the day after. She fricasseed the last small cuts from the bird the next day, and finally the carcass was made into soup.

You can 'devil' any meat. The idea is to liven up something that is either rather bland or has perhaps lost a little flavour in the keeping. I have called this recipe Devilled Fowl as I think poultry responds best to this treatment. Nigel Slater suggested this marinade in Real Fast Food. *I have just added the option of including chilli if you haven't got tabasco sauce in your cupboard. This recipe is also good cooked on the barbecue.*

2 cold chicken or turkey joints

FOR THE MARINADE
1 tablespoon Dijon mustard
2 garlic cloves, finely chopped
2 tablespoons fruity chutney (apple, mango, plum – whatever is in the cupboard)
1 tablespoon Worcester sauce
1 teaspoon minced chilli or a good shake of tabasco sauce (according to taste)

Serves 2

Preheat the grill to high. Mix the ingredients for the marinade into a paste. Slash the skin and flesh of the chicken or turkey with a sharp knife and spread the spicy mixture over the flesh and into the slashes. You can leave the meat to rest and soak up the marinade for a couple of hours, but this is optional. Grill, turning once, at about 10cm (4in) from the element, till sizzling and hot throughout. This should take approximately 10 minutes. Serve with a green salad.

Casseroled Pigeon with Herbs and Spices

This recipe was researched by Sara Paston-Williams, who found a recipe for 'Peiouns ystewed' in the Forme of Cury, *our oldest English cookery book. It is a series of 'receipts' which were used at the coronation of Richard II and was written in about 1390. Pigeons were then raised for the pot, but only by the lord of the manor – he didn't want other people's pigeons eating his corn so only he had a licence.*

4 oven-ready pigeons
12 large garlic cloves
4 teaspoons chopped fresh thyme
2 tablespoons chopped fresh parsley
Dripping or lard for frying
300ml (½ pint) chicken stock
Juice of ½ lemon
Large pinch of ground ginger
Pinch of saffron strands
¼ teaspoon ground cinnamon
Salt and freshly ground black pepper to taste
4 slices wholemeal toast
Fresh herbs for garnish

Serves 4

Preheat oven to 180°C, 350°F, gas mark 4. Stuff each pigeon with 3 garlic cloves, 1 teaspoon chopped fresh thyme and ½ tablespoon chopped fresh parsley. Season with a little salt and freshly milled black pepper, then brown the pigeons all over in a little dripping or lard in a heavy flame-proof casserole which is just big enough to take them. Pour over the stock, then add the lemon juice, ginger, saffron and cinnamon. Cover with a lid, place in the preheated oven and cook for 1–1½ hours or until very tender. Taste the gravy and adjust the seasoning as necessary. Serve each person with a pigeon arranged on a slice of wholemeal toast with a little gravy poured over. Garnish with fresh herbs.

Lanhydrock Squab Pie

Squabs were pigeons, but as these were scarce and generally eaten by the rich (see recipe on page 77), lamb has been substituted in this poor man's version. The apples and onions were used to make up for the lack of meat. In latter years the cream etc. has been added to make the dish more special.

700g (1½lb) stewing lamb or cooked diced lamb
450g (1lb) onions, sliced
450g (1lb) cooking apples, peeled and sliced
Mixed herbs
125ml (4fl oz) vegetable stock (using a stock cube)
350g (12oz) shortcrust or puff pastry
300ml (½ pint) double cream or clotted cream
Salt and pepper to taste

Serves 6 plus

Preheat oven to 200°C, 400°F, gas mark 6. Arrange the meat, onions and apples in alternate layers in a pie dish. Sprinkle with mixed herbs (or just rosemary) and pour the stock over everything. Cover with the pastry and cook in the oven until the pastry is done – approximately 30 minutes. Turn the oven temperature down to 160°C, 325°F, gas mark 3, and cook for a further hour. If the pastry starts to brown too much, cover it with foil. If the meat is pre-cooked, you may need a little less time. Remove from the oven and gently lift off the pastry top. Stir in the cream and adjust the seasoning. Replace the pastry lid and reheat for a further few minutes before serving.

Haslet

Haslet is a meatloaf that can be eaten hot or cold. Local bakers in Derbyshire serve Haslet cold as a sandwich filling. Recipes for haslet can be found in several English counties: I have come across a similar recipe from Hampshire. The name comes from the Old French Hastelet, *which means 'entrails' or 'innards', but here it seems to refer to the finely chopped mixture.*

450g (1lb) minced shoulder of pork – not sausage meat

150g (5oz) brown or white breadcrumbs

2 teaspoons finely chopped fresh sage

1 teaspoon mace

110g (4oz) onion, finely chopped

Salt and pepper to taste

Serves 4

Preheat oven to 180°C, 350°F, gas mark 4. Either line a 450g (1lb) loaf tin with baking paper or grease it well. Soak the breadcrumbs in a little water, then add to the rest of the ingredients in a mixing bowl and mix well together. Season to taste and pack into the tin. Bake uncovered for 1 hour. Serve hot or cold.

Gammon Poached in Cider with Clove and Mustard Glaze

'With a roly-poly gammon and spinach, "hey-ho" says Anthony Rowley', in the song 'A Frog He Would a'Wooing Go'. This combined method of beginning by poaching and finishing with a blast in a hot oven seems to work perfectly with large or small joints of gammon or bacon. Use the wonderful stock the ham produces to help with the parsley sauce. You should still have enough left over for a generous pan of soup. I have suggested a rather large joint as it is also extremely good served cold.

1.8kg (4lb) piece of gammon
450ml (15fl oz) cider
Small quantity of onion, carrot and celery for stock
Peppercorns or freshly ground pepper

FOR THE GLAZE
2 tablespoons Dijon mustard
2 tablespoons soft brown sugar
A few whole cloves

Serves 6

Place the gammon joint in a pan. Pour in the cider and add sufficient water to cover. Add the onion, carrot and celery plus a few whole peppercorns. Cover the pan and bring the liquid slowly to the boil, reduce the heat and simmer, very gently, for approximately 1 hour 40 minutes.

Strain off and reserve the stock. Turn the oven onto full heat. Line a roasting tin with baking paper and place the joint in it. Slice off the skin, leaving a layer of fat on the joint. Smear the fat with the mustard and sugar and score with a sharp knife as if you were laying out a noughts-and-crosses game. Stud the pattern with cloves. Pour in a little of the ham stock to stop the joint sticking and return it to the fully heated oven. Roast for 30 minutes, then turn off the oven and leave the joint to rest for at least 10 minutes. Serve the ham sliced thickly with Parsley Sauce (see page 118).

Right: Gammon Poached in Cider with Clove and Mustard Glaze
Next page: Chicken in Hocchee

Toad in the Hole

How did this dish get its name and when was it invented? The Oxford Dictionary of Food *gives the earliest reference to a Toad in the Hole as 'The dish called toad in the hole, meat boiled in a crust' in 1787. In 1861, Mrs Beeton has steak and kidney cooking in the batter, so neither version was quite the same as today's dish. Never mind – the combination of sausages and crisp, hot batter is irresistible. The cherry tomatoes are my own touch, which adds to the taste and colour of the dish.*

2–3 tablespoons sunflower oil or approximately 25g (1oz) hard vegetable fat
6 large sausages
2–3 cherry tomatoes per portion

FOR THE BATTER
110g (4oz) plain flour
½ teaspoon salt
2 large eggs, well beaten
300ml (½ pint) milk, full cream or semi-skimmed

Serves 4

Sieve the flour and salt into a mixing bowl and make a batter by stirring in the eggs, and making a smooth paste with a little of the milk. Next, beat in the rest of the milk until the mixture resembles unwhipped double cream. At this point leave it to stand for at least 30 minutes, preferably 1 hour. Preheat oven to 220°C/425°F/Gas Mark 7.

You can use either a 20 x 16cm (8 x 6in) roasting tin or individual round tins, whichever is more practical. Add the fat or oil to the roasting tin (or, if using individual tins, put a knob of fat or a little oil in each) and heat in the oven until the fat smokes. Chop each sausage into four and arrange the chunks in the roasting tin or use three chunks per round tin. Intersperse the sausage pieces with cherry tomatoes. Put in the oven for 5 minutes, then pour on the batter and cook for a further 15 minutes. Check to see if the Toad is cooked. The small tins may well be ready at this point, but a large Toad in the Hole will probably require a little longer. The batter should be crisp and golden. Serve piping hot.

Left: Toad in the Hole
Previous page: Roast Duck with Sage and Onion Stuffing and Apple Sauce

Sausage and Apple Plait

A grander version of the sausage roll, this recipe makes good portable picnic fare when cold.

450g (1lb) frozen puff pastry
450g (1lb) sausage meat
1 medium onion, finely chopped
1 leek, chopped
1 eating apple, peeled and chopped
1 tablespoon fresh herbs – a mixture of sage, thyme leaves and parsley, all
    chopped finely, is perfect
1 tablespoon tomato purée
2 teaspoons Worcester sauce
1 egg yolk mixed with a little milk to glaze

Serves 4

Preheat oven to 210°C, 425°F, gas mark 7. Roll the pastry fairly thin, into an oblong approximately 20 x 30cm (8 x 12in). Mix the sausage meat with the chopped onion, leek, apple, herbs, tomato purée and Worcester sauce. Form it roughly into a sausage and lay it on the pastry, leaving a rim around the edge to seal. Brush the edges of the pastry with the egg and milk mixture and pinch the edges of the pastry together to form a roll. Turn the roll over so that the join is underneath. Seal the ends. Cut a cross pattern in the top, brush with beaten egg, lay it on a piece of baking paper on a baking tin (this makes it easier to move later) and bake for 30 minutes. Serve hot, warm or cold.

Pork and Apricot Trelissick Pipkin

The pipkin in this recipe refers to the casserole dish, traditionally a pot that is glazed on the inside and coarse red earthenware on the outside. Old recipes for pork often have fruit in them, the acidity of the fruit contrasting with the rich meat.

3 onions, peeled and chopped
700g (1½lb) diced pork
50g (2oz) dripping or 4 tablespoons sunflower or olive oil
25g (1oz) plain flour
2 teaspoons tomato purée
850ml (1½ pints) chicken or vegetable stock
75g (3oz) dried apricots
½ teaspoon mixed herbs
Salt and pepper to taste

Serves 4

Preheat oven to 190°C, 375°F, gas mark 5. Fry the onions and pork in the dripping or oil, taking care not to burn them. Stir in the flour, then add the tomato purée and stock. Place in a casserole dish with the apricots, mixed herbs, salt and pepper. Cover and cook in the oven for 1½ hours or until tender.

West Country Honeyed Pork Stew

The combination of pork and beans is a winner. Before the Industrial Revolution, everyone had a pig. It was the one animal you did not need to have a licence for. Pigs were the garbage collectors before local councils got lumbered with the job. The pig was not a pet; its time was up at Christmas or some other celebration, and every part of the pig was eaten.

1 tablespoon vegetable oil

450g (1lb) shoulder of pork, diced

50g (2oz) butter beans

1 medium onion stuck with cloves

1 teaspoon mixed herbs

1 tablespoon clear honey

600ml (1 pint) chicken stock

250ml (9fl oz) apple juice

3 medium carrots, peeled and cut into 3cm (1in) sticks

2 celery sticks, chopped

2 leeks, washed and chopped

2 tablespoons Worcester sauce

1 tablespoon tomato purée

Salt and pepper to taste

Serves 4

You will need to start this recipe the day before you cook it by soaking the butter beans.

Heat the vegetable oil in an ovenproof casserole and sauté the pork until nicely browned. Drain the beans and add to the pork together with the onion and mixed herbs. Turn everything for a minute or two in the oil. Then add honey, stock and apple juice. Bring to the boil, reduce the heat, cover the pan and simmer for approximately 1 hour, until the beans are just becoming tender. Add carrots, celery, leeks, Worcester sauce and tomato purée. Simmer for a further 30 minutes, or until the meat is tender and the vegetables are cooked.

Bacon and Egg Pie

This pie is best made on a shallow enamel or ceramic ovenproof pie plate. It is a great picnic dish as it is easy to transport on its plate. You won't need knives and forks as it is quite solid when cool.

450g (1lb) Shortcrust Pastry (see page 54)
Milk, to seal and glaze

FOR THE FILLING
225g (8oz) chopped bacon or lardons
3 tablespoons chopped parsley
6 eggs
Salt and pepper

Serves 4–6

Preheat oven to 170°C, 325°F, gas mark 3. Divide the pastry in half. Roll out the first piece to fit a buttered pie plate. Prick the base. Fill the middle of the plate with the bacon or lardons and chopped parsley. Leave the rim clear for sealing. Season to taste; you probably won't need salt. Make six round indentations in the bacon mixture and crack an egg into each one. Roll out the second piece of pastry to form the lid. Brush the rim of the pie with milk and lay the lid carefully over the top, pressing firmly on the rim to seal it. Trim the lid to fit and use the trimmings to decorate the top of the pie. Make a hole in the middle to let the steam out and glaze the pie with milk. Bake for approximately 1 hour. Serve at room temperature.

Oxtail Stew

Kettners' Book of the Table *suggests that our taste for oxtail was learnt from the Huguenots who settled in Bermondsey, south London. Bermondsey was full of tanneries. The leather workers were sold ox hides with their tails intact, which weren't needed in the process. The Huguenots made the tails into soup so good that its fame spread far and wide. The Oxtail Stew below is spicy and rich. It doesn't take long to prepare, but it needs hours of slow cooking. This is a dish that is even better reheated as it is easier to skim the fat from the surface when it is cold. New potatoes or mash complement the richness of the stew.*

2 pieces of oxtail per person
Plain flour seasoned with salt and pepper
25g (1oz) butter
1 tablespoon olive oil
110g (4oz) bacon, cut into cubes
200ml (7fl oz) red wine
2 onions, stuck with cloves
2 garlic cloves
1 celery stick, chopped
1 large carrot, peeled and chopped
2 small turnips, quartered
1 bouquet garni
2 bay leaves
2 tablespoons tomato purée
600ml (1 pint) vegetable stock
2 large carrots, peeled and cut into chunks
3 leeks, trimmed, sliced and washed

Serves 6

Preheat oven to 140°C, 275°F, gas mark 1. Dust the pieces of oxtail with seasoned flour. Melt the butter and oil. Fry the bacon cubes until they start to brown. Take them out with a slotted spoon and set aside while you brown the oxtail pieces all over. Pour in the wine, let it bubble. Then add the onions, garlic, celery, carrot, turnips, bouquet garni and bay leaves. Mix the tomato purée with the vegetable stock and add it to the casserole. Bring slowly to the boil, then cover the pan and put it in the preheated oven to stew gently for 2–3 hours. If you are going to serve the dish later, let it get cold at this point and skim the cold fat off the surface before you reheat it. Otherwise skim the fat off the hot casserole, add the carrots and leeks and return it to the oven for the final hour's cooking.

Welsh Lamb and Leek Casserole

Two Welsh specialities combined in one dish. Welsh lamb is famous for its flavour – the pure-bred mountain lamb is smaller than its cross-bred cousin but the taste is the best of all. The leek is the vegetable of Wales – tradition says that Welsh warriors wore leeks in their hats to show which side they were on in a victorious battle with the Saxons in the 7th century.

50g (2oz) butter
450g (1lb) neck of lamb, cut into large dice
450g (1lb) leeks, washed and chopped
1 eating apple, peeled, cored and sliced
2 tablespoons plain flour
1 teaspoon mixed herbs or 1 tablespoon fresh mixed herbs, finely chopped
600ml (1 pint) vegetable stock
Salt and pepper to taste
Chopped parsley, for garnish

Serves 4

Preheat oven to 180°C, 350°F, gas mark 4. Melt a quarter or so of the butter in a frying pan. Brown the lamb and transfer to a large casserole. Add the leeks and apple slices to the same pan, fry gently for 5 minutes and add to the lamb. Melt the remaining butter in the pan, stir in the flour and cook gently for 2 minutes or so. Add the herbs and stock. Heat gently, stirring all the time, until the sauce thickens. Season to taste, then pour over the lamb. Cover and cook for approximately 2 hours until the lamb is tender. Sprinkle with chopped parsley and serve with potatoes or rice. It does not need further vegetables.

Irish Stew

'Then hurrah for an Irish Stew/That will stick to your belly like glue.' Irish Stew is a dish that causes arguments. Should it have pearl barley in it or not? Are carrots and/or turnips allowed? The only consensus is that mutton (nowadays, lamb) is the dominant ingredient. This recipe was given to me in Northern Ireland. It makes use of the excellent raw ingredients available there, and tastes delicious. I rest my case! The stew needs no further accompaniment but if you like a piquant relish with it, the recipe for Red Cabbage Pickle on page 292 is perfect.

1 tablespoon vegetable oil
450g (1lb) neck fillet of lamb, cut into chunks
1 large onion, peeled and sliced
2 medium carrots, peeled and cut into short lengths
1 celery stick (optional), chopped
450g (1lb) new potatoes, scrubbed
Approx 1 litre (1¼ pints) vegetable stock
225g (8oz) cooked potato, mashed
Salt and pepper to taste

Serves 4

Preheat oven to 150°C, 300°F, gas mark 2. Heat the oil in a cast-iron casserole and fry the meat and the onions together until nicely browned. Take the casserole off the heat and add the carrots, celery and potatoes. Stir and add the vegetable stock to cover the meat and vegetables. Bring the casserole to the boil and then either simmer very slowly on the top of the cooker or stew gently in the oven until the meat is tender and the vegetables are cooked but still have a little crunch. Stir in the mashed potato to thicken the gravy and season to taste with salt and pepper.

Beef Olives

Beef Olives are nothing to do with olives, but are named presumably because of the shape of these wafer-thin rolls of best beef with a savoury stuffing, braised with vegetables and wine.

675g (1¼ lb) topside of beef, cut in thin slices
2 teaspoons Dijon mustard
300ml (½ pint) vegetable stock
150ml (¼ pint) red wine

FOR THE STUFFING
25g (1oz) butter
2 shallots, peeled and chopped
2 garlic cloves, peeled and chopped (optional)
110g (4oz) chopped bacon or lardons
75g (3oz) white breadcrumbs
2 tablespoons parsley
1 tablespoon other mixed herbs (thyme, tarragon, sage, marjoram are all good)
1 egg
Salt and pepper to taste

FOR THE SAUCE
25g (1oz) butter
1 tablespoon olive oil
2 shallots, peeled and chopped
2 garlic cloves, peeled and chopped
450g (1lb) mixed root vegetables

Serves 6

Preheat oven to 170°C, 325°F, gas mark 3. Put the slices of beef between pieces of clingfilm and beat them very thin. Then trim them so that you have at least two pieces per person about 10cm (4in) square. Spread a little mustard on each slice and season them. Rest them while you make the stuffing.

Continued over page

Melt the butter and fry the shallots and garlic gently for a couple of minutes, add the bacon and continue to cook the mixture for about 5 minutes. Remove from the heat, add the breadcrumbs, herbs and egg, season the mixture and combine all the ingredients. Divide the stuffing, putting about a tablespoonful on the mustard-covered side of each beef slice. Roll them up, tuck the ends over and tie them up with cotton like a parcel. Set them aside while you prepare the vegetable sauce.

Melt the butter and oil and fry the shallots and garlic gently for a few minutes. Add the rest of the vegetables, then turn them so that they are well covered with the butter and oil. Spread the vegetables across the bottom of a shallow ovenproof dish or casserole just big enough to hold everything. Put the beef olives on the top in a single layer. Tip the stock and red wine into the pan that held the vegetables, bubble it up until it is boiling and pour the liquid over the meat. Cover the casserole and cook for 1 hour. After 1 hour, remove the lid, turn the beef olives over and continue cooking with the lid off until they are brown and tender. Snip the cotton off and adjust the seasoning before you serve them. Buttered noodles or mashed potato are good accompaniments.

Beef and Ham Loaf

This is very simple – the English equivalent of a French terrine. It tastes very good with new potatoes.

350g (12oz) best minced beef
350g (12oz) minced cooked ham
50g (2oz) fresh breadcrumbs
1 teaspoon mixed herbs
4 shredded sage leaves
2 eggs, beaten
Salt and pepper to taste

Serves 6

Preheat oven to 180°C, 350°F, gas mark 4. Grease a loaf tin large enough to take all the ingredients, approximately 700g (1½lb). Put all the ingredients except the eggs in a large bowl and mix together evenly. Stir in the eggs and transfer the mixture to the loaf tin, pressing it in well and smoothing the top. Cover with a layer of greaseproof paper and layer of foil and stand the loaf tin in a roasting tin. Fill the roasting tin with water to come half way up the loaf tin. Bake for1 hour. Allow to cool and chill overnight. Unmould onto a serving dish and serve cold.

Shepherd's Pie

Shepherd's Pie probably originated in the north of England or Scotland, where there are large numbers of sheep. In company with its frugal rural traditions, it tastes best when made with leftover chopped or minced lamb. This is weekday fare after Sunday's roast. This well-loved recipe can also be made with beef mince, in which case it is known as Cottage Pie.

2 tablespoons olive or sunflower oil

1 large onion (approximately 225g/8oz), finely chopped

225g (8oz) carrots, peeled and finely chopped

450g (1lb) minced lamb – leftover cooked lamb from a joint is particularly good

1 tablespoon plain flour

300ml (½ pint) beef or lamb stock

1 tablespoon tomato purée

2 teaspoons Worcester sauce

¼ teaspoon dried mixed herbs

Salt and freshly ground black pepper to taste

FOR THE TOPPING

450g (1lb) potatoes, peeled and sliced

25g (1oz) butter

150ml (¼ pint) half cream

Serves 4

Preheat oven to 190°C, 375°F, gas mark 5. Melt the oil in a saucepan and sauté the onion and carrots until the onion is soft but not coloured. Add the minced lamb and cook gently until the meat is browned. Stir in flour and cook for 5 minutes. Gradually stir in the stock, tomato purée, Worcester sauce, herbs and seasoning and bring to the boil. Reduce the heat, cover the pan and simmer for 10 minutes. Turn into an ovenproof dish and allow to cool a little before topping with potato.

Boil the potatoes and drain. Mash them and beat in the butter, together with the cream. Season to taste with salt and pepper. Spread the potato with a fork over the meat. Fork up the top so that there are furrows which will become crisp and golden in cooking. Bake for 20–30 minutes, until the top is golden brown.

Kebob'd Lamb

The earliest picture of grilled 'kebob'd' meat on a shish, or skewer, that I have seen is a part of the Bayeux Tapestry. The scene is a feast at Pevensey, just after the Norman army landed in Sussex. Cooks are preparing chunks of meat and small whole birds, and threading them onto skewers. To their left, William, Duke of Normandy sits down to dine while Bishop Odo says grace. The recipe below is for lamb and vegetable skewers (some of the best lamb in Britain is raised on Romney Marshes, very near Pevensey). Don't thread the pieces onto the skewers too tightly; you want the heat of the fire to penetrate the skewer. Ideally you need to begin this recipe the day before you want to serve it: the longer the lamb marinades, the better it will taste.

900g (2lb) lamb (neck fillet or leg)
1 onion, peeled
2 red peppers
18 cherry tomatoes
12 button mushrooms
12 fresh bay leaves, cut in half

FOR THE MARINADE
150ml (¼ pint) olive oil
150ml (¼ pint) red wine
2 garlic cloves, crushed
1 fresh rosemary sprig, chopped
Salt and pepper to taste

Serves 6 (2 kebabs per person)

Mix all the ingredients for the marinade in a bowl large enough to take the lamb and allow you to stir it. Cut the lamb into 2.5cm (1in) cubes and mix into the marinade, making sure that every piece is well coated. Cover the bowl, refrigerate and leave to stand overnight, if possible, giving it a stir from time to time.

When you are ready to make up the kebabs, cut the onion and peppers into pieces that are about the same size as the cubes of lamb. Oil 12 skewers and thread the meat and vegetables on alternately, interleaving them with the half bay leaves, until you have used up all the pieces. Cook on a barbecue, basting the kebabs with the marinade when you turn them. Serve with couscous or saffron-flavoured rice and a salad. Green Sauce (see page 119) made with mint and parsley is a delicious accompaniment.

Lamb Cutlets Reform

Lamb Cutlets – or Noisettes – Reform was invented for the Reform Club by an Italian, Charles Francatelli, chef to Queen Victoria. He was a pupil of Antoine Marie Carême, the famous French chef to the then Prince Regent (who was later crowned George IV). This recipe is very different from most of the others in this book, but it represents a particular strand of British cooking. The very rich have always employed chefs, many of whom came from France. They have left their mark on our cuisine with recipes that are still cooked today, although their more elaborate confections, including the one below, are something of a curiosity.

The magic ingredient in the sauce used here is the redcurrant jelly. The tart sweetness is perfect with the lamb. Francatelli's original recipe involved frying the cutlets coated in ham and breadcrumbs, and garnishing them with 'reform chips', tiny batons of ham, hard-boiled egg and truffles. I have suggested grilling the cutlets and have simplified the sauce and garnish. Do try it: although it is fiddly, it is still special-occasion food.

12 lamb cutlets
Olive oil, for brushing

FOR THE SAUCE
1 carrot
1 small onion
1 gammon steak
25g (1oz) butter
150ml (5fl oz) white wine vinegar
600ml (1 pint) vegetable stock
150g (6oz) redcurrant jelly
4 cloves
Finely grated nutmeg, to taste
¼ teaspoon dried thyme
2 heaped teaspoons arrowroot

FOR GARNISH
'Reform Chips' – matchsticks of chopped cooked carrots, gherkins, hard-boiled egg whites and ham
A handful of chopped parsley

Serves 6

Continued over page

Finely dice the carrot, onion and gammon. Melt the butter and fry the carrot, onion and gammon until golden brown. Add the white wine vinegar and boil the mixture so that the liquid reduces rapidly. When it is reduced by about one-third, add the vegetable stock, redcurrant jelly, cloves, nutmeg and thyme. Simmer very slowly for 30 minutes. Put the arrowroot in a small bowl, add 1 tablespoon of the sauce and stir until it is smooth. Then stir the mixture into the sauce and whisk or stir until smooth. The arrowroot should thicken the sauce without colouring it. Strain the sauce into a basin and stand it in a pan of boiling water to keep warm while you grill the cutlets. (Alternatively, you can make the sauce ahead of time and reheat it gently when you need it.)

Preheat the grill to high. Alternatively, you can cook the cutlets in a heavy, ridged grill pan over a high heat. Brush the cutlets with oil and grill for approximately 3 minutes on each side. To serve, put a couple of tablespoons of sauce on a heated plate with two cutlets on the top and garnish with the Reform Chips and parsley. Steamed or boiled new potatoes are all that are needed to accompany this classic dish.

Beef and Guinness Casserole

This recipe uses two of Ireland's best-known products – beef and stout. Because they are so good and so complementary to each other there is no need for complex spices and herbs. The recipe is simple, the result delicious. You will find a recipe for Champ – the perfect vegetable accompaniment – on page 136.

1 tablespoon vegetable oil
450g (1lb) steak, cubed
225g (8oz) onions, chopped
425ml (¾ pint) Guinness
225g (8oz) carrots, peeled and cut into fine matchsticks
A little cornflour to thicken the sauce
Salt and pepper to taste

Serves 4

Preheat oven to 150°C, 300°F, gas mark 2. Heat the oil in a cast-iron casserole and fry the steak and the onions until all are nicely browned. Pour over the Guinness – it should cover the meat and the onions, but if it does not, add a little water. Cover the pan and cook in a slow oven until the meat is just tender. At this point add the carrots and cook for a further 45 minutes. Thicken the gravy with a little cornflour – probably about 2 teaspoons creamed with a little water. Season with salt and pepper.

Boiled Beef and Carrots with Parsley Dumplings

'Boiled beef and carrots,' sang music-hall star Harry Champion, 'Keeps you fit and keeps you well.' He's right – and I would add 'keeps you warm'. This is a great dish for a cold day. You will have to plan well ahead though: salt beef is not often available in the supermarket. Most butchers will salt a piece of beef for you, but they need sufficient notice. (My butcher needs a week.) You can't make this recipe in small quantities, but cold boiled beef makes the best sandwiches (mustard or horseradish sauce is a must), and the broth is wonderful soup, so leftovers aren't a problem. I'm suggesting that you use a pig's trotter as this will make the stock even tastier. (Ask your butcher to prepare this for you.) I have included a recipe for Parsley Dumplings, but if you don't like dumplings, double the quantity of new potatoes instead.

1 piece of salted silverside or brisket of beef, at least 1.8kg (4lb)
1 pig's trotter, chopped in half
2 small onions, stuck with cloves
2 small turnips, quartered
2 celery sticks, roughly chopped
1 leek, trimmed, chopped and washed
2 bay leaves
½ teaspoon black peppercorns, lightly crushed
20 baby carrots, scrubbed
225g (8oz) small new potatoes, scrubbed

FOR THE DUMPLINGS
110g (4oz) plain flour
½ teaspoon salt
2 level teaspoons baking powder
25g (1oz) butter
1 egg
A handful of chopped parsley
Milk, to mix

Serves 6–8

Continued over page

Ask your butcher if you need to soak the meat overnight to draw out some of the salt. If not, start by putting it in a large pan or cast-iron casserole. Tuck the trotter, onions, turnips, celery, leek and bay leaves round it and scatter the peppercorns over the meat. Pour water over the meat until it is just covered and bring slowly to the boil. Cover the pan and simmer for about 2 hours.

Remove the trotter and vegetables. Don't throw them away: you can return them to the broth later to enrich it to use for soup. Add the carrots and new potatoes and simmer for a further 20 minutes. This is the moment to make the dumplings, if you are including them.

Sift the flour, salt and baking powder together. Add the butter, chopped into small pieces, and rub it into the flour. (It is very easy to incorporate the butter using a food processor.) Mix the egg with the parsley and add to the flour. Mix with a little milk into a stiff dough. Form into small balls, the size of marbles. Add to the casserole for the final 20 minutes of cooking time. They will puff up to twice their original size.

To serve, lift the meat out onto a serving dish and garnish with the carrots and new potatoes. Carve the meat, add a portion of vegetables and spoon over some of the broth and a couple of dumplings per person.

Right: Boiled Beef and Carrots with Parsley Dumplings
Next page: Lamb Casseroled in Ale with Prunes and Raisins

Lamb Casseroled in Ale with Prunes and Raisins

'Take a piece of Mutton, and cutte it in pieces, and wash it very cleane, and put it in a faire pot with ale…then make it boyle, and skumme it cleyne, and put into your pot a faggot of Rosemary and Time, then some parsley picked fine, and some onions cut round, and lit them all boyle together, and season it with sinamon and Ginger Nutmeggs…so serve it on soppes and garnish it with fruite'. Thomas Dawson in The Good Huswife's Jewel *in 1596. Below is Sara Paston-Williams's tasty adaptation of that old recipe.*

25g (1oz) butter
1 tablespoon vegetable oil
4 lamb leg steaks, approximately 700g (1½lb)
1 large onion, finely sliced
600ml (1 pint) real ale
½ tablespoon fresh rosemary, chopped or ½ teaspoon dried rosemary
½ tablespoon fresh thyme, chopped or ¼ teaspoon dried thyme
2 tablespoons fresh parsley, chopped
½ teaspoon ground allspice
2-3 whole cloves
50g (2oz) raisins
25g (1oz) fresh white breadcrumbs
225g (8oz) prunes, stoned
4 slices wholemeal toast
freshly ground black pepper and salt to taste
orange slices, for garnish

Serves 4

Preheat oven to 180°C, 350°F, gas mark 4. Heat the butter and oil in a heavy casserole dish and brown the lamb steaks quickly on both sides. Remove with a slotted spoon and set on one side. Reduce the heat and cook the onions in the remaining fat until soft. Replace the meat in the casserole and cover with ale. Add the herbs, spices and raisins, then season with salt and pepper. Cover tightly with a lid and place in a moderate oven for 30 minutes. Add the breadcrumbs and prunes and return to the oven for a further 30 minutes, or until the lamb is tender. Check the seasoning and adjust as necessary, then serve each lamb steak on a slice of toast. Pour over the gravy and garnish with slices of orange before serving.

Steak and Kidney Pie

Steak and Kidney Pie has a surprisingly short history for such a national institution. Beefsteak pies and puddings have been around for centuries, but Mrs Beeton gave the first recipe for a pudding with beefsteak and kidney in it in 1859. She also suggested the traditional optional extras of mushrooms or oysters. In her time, the oysters would have been cheaper than the mushrooms. Steak and Kidney Pie is a pub-menu staple and is always available from the ready-meal cabinet at the supermarket, and is even sold in tins. Make your own and it will, I promise, taste much better.

450g (1lb) stewing steak
175g (6oz) kidney
1½ rounded tablespoons seasoned flour
1 large onion, peeled and chopped
25–50g (1–2oz) dripping or 3–4 tablespoons olive or sunflower oil
425ml (¾ pint) beef stock
1 rounded teaspoon mustard powder
Salt and pepper to taste
225g (8oz) shortcrust or puff pastry (see page 54)

Serves 4

Preheat oven to 140°C, 275°F, gas mark 1. Cut the stewing steak and kidney into small pieces and toss in seasoned flour. Fry the sliced onion in the dripping or oil and place in a casserole. Brown the meat lightly in the fat a few pieces at a time and add to the onion. Pour over the stock, cover the casserole and stew gently in the oven for 1–1½ hours. Stir in the mustard powder and correct the seasoning to taste. You can prepare the pie ahead to this point.

Increase the oven temperature to 210°C, 425°F, gas mark 7. Turn the meat and onions into a large ovenproof pie dish. Roll out the pastry and cover the pie, using any trimmings to decorate, and make a slit in the centre. Brush the top with milk and bake for 10–15 minutes. Reduce the heat to 180°C, 350°F, gas mark 4 for a further 20 minutes until the pie is golden. Serve hot with green vegetables, jacket potatoes and mustard.

Beef and Vegetable Pottage with Baked Norfolk Dumpling

'Potage is not so much used in al Christendom as it is used in England. Potage is made of the liquor in which flesh is sodden in with putting-to chopped herbs and salt.' This is a rich man's pottage since it contains meat. See the recipe for Pease Pottage on page 131 for a poor man's version. Pottage was eaten by everyone in the Middle Ages. Notice there are no potatoes in the recipe – they hadn't yet reached Britain.

FOR THE BEEF AND VEGETABLE POTTAGE
900g (2lb) prepared vegetables, roughly chopped
700g (1½lb) shin of beef
Vegetable stock
2 tablespoons fresh mixed herbs or 1 tablespoon mixed dried herbs

FOR THE BAKED NORFOLK DUMPLING
225g (8oz) self-raising flour
Pinch of salt
175g (6oz) shredded suet
Milk

Serves 6–8

Preheat oven to 160°C, 325°F, gas mark 3. Prepare a mix of vegetables of some of the following: leeks, celery, onions, carrots, turnips, cabbage. Chop the meat into large chunks and pack it at the bottom of a large cast-iron casserole. Add the herbs and sufficient vegetable stock to cover the meat and bring to the boil on the top of the stove. Take the casserole off the heat and add all the chopped vegetables in a thick layer on top of the meat and stock. Cover the pan and cook slowly in the oven for at least 2 and preferably 3 hours. Simmer the pot on the top of the stove for the last 30 minutes if you are serving with Norfolk Dumpling (below), so it can bake in a hotter oven. Season with salt if necessary and serve each helping topped with a wedge of dumpling.

For the dumpling, grease a 23cm (9in) flan dish. Mix together the flour, salt and shredded suet with just enough milk to make a soft dough. Knead the dough into a round, approximately 2.5cm (1in) thick, and place in the dish. Make criss-cross lines on the top and brush with milk. Turn the oven up to 190°C, 375°F, gas mark 5 and bake the dumpling for 30–40 minutes. Cut into wedges to serve with the pottage.

Lancashire Hot Pot

Every county in the North has its hotpot. In Cheshire it's called 'Tater 'Ash', in Yorkshire 'Tatie Pot'. There's even a vegetable version that was cooked when the family's breadwinner was laid off and money was scarce – called, logically, 'Fatherless Hotpot'. However, hotpot generally means meat and potatoes in a deep pot, stewed slowly in the oven until tender, with the lid removed at the end of the cooking time to crisp the potatoes. Extras are important: some swear by a layer of black pudding cut into chunks in the middle; others add chunks of stewing beef or lambs' kidneys. Both black pudding and kidney add flavour to the pot and thicken the gravy. Robust root vegetables also add flavour and pad out the (more expensive) meat. Ask your butcher to cut you 'middle and scrag', about 30cm (12in) in thickness, for this dish. This weight should give you two chunks per person. You can make this dish with meat off the bone or lamb chops if these are easier to obtain.

900g (2lb) lamb
2 tablespoons plain flour, seasoned with salt and pepper
25g (1oz) butter
1 tablespoon olive oil
1 onion, peeled and sliced
2 carrots, peeled and chopped
1 turnip, peeled and chopped
110g (4oz) black pudding, skinned and cut into chunks
2 bay leaves
1 bouquet garni
Approximately 600ml (1 pint) vegetable stock
6 large potatoes

Serves 6–8

Preheat oven to 190°C, 375°F, gas mark 5. Dust each piece of meat with seasoned flour. Melt half the butter and the oil in a deep casserole and brown the meat. Take it out and put in the onion. Cook it until it begins to soften. Remove the onion and layer up the casserole as follows. Pack a layer of meat at the bottom. Then put in half the onion, carrot, turnip and black pudding. Next put in a second layer of meat and finish with another layer of vegetables and black pudding. Tuck in the bay leaves and bouquet garni.

Fill the casserole with vegetable stock to just below the top of the vegetables. Peel and slice the potatoes and overlap them in several layers on the top. Melt the rest of the butter and brush it over the potatoes. Bake for at least 3 hours, removing the lid for the last 30 minutes to brown the potatoes.

Kidneys with a Mustard Cream Sauce

We eat less offal than our forebears did. Heads, brains, tongue and sweetbreads are seldom seen in the butchers today and virtually never in the supermarket. Liver and Bacon is still a favourite dish; it hardly needs a recipe. Neither does Grilled Kidneys, once a staple of the breakfast table of the well-to-do. In the 19th century, a version of this dish was often served at the end of the meal as a savoury on toast. I have kept the toast, but like it better as a supper dish. It needs nothing more than a green salad with a light dressing as an accompaniment.

6 lambs' kidneys
25g (1oz) butter

FOR THE SAUCE
2 shallots, peeled and finely chopped
1 tablespoon Dijon mustard
150ml (¼ pint) vegetable stock
1 small glass sherry
1 tablespoon Worcester sauce
2 tablespoons double cream or crème fraîche
Salt and pepper

Serves 2-3

Slice the lambs' kidneys. Heat the butter and gently sauté the kidneys, turning them well in the butter. When they have browned, take them out with a slice or slotted spoon and keep them warm in the oven while you make the sauce.

To make the sauce, sauté the shallots in the pan juices for a minute or two until they begin to soften. Stir in the mustard, then the vegetable stock, sherry and Worcester sauce. Adjust the seasoning; it may already be salty enough. Bring the mixture up to just below boiling point and stir in the cream or crème fraîche. (Don't let it boil; it may curdle.) Pour the sauce over the kidneys, give it a good stir and serve individual portions on toast.

Tripe and Onions

I have specified honeycomb tripe for this dish. This is the most tender variety of tripe, because it has already been prepared before you start cooking, with a long process of soaking and boiling before it even reaches the butcher's slab. Tripe is a very old-fashioned dish and you either like or loathe it. I once cooked a series of dishes for an old couple who were too frail to cook for themselves; they hated the ready meals at the supermarket so I provided ready meals for them. They were particularly ecstatic about my Tripe and Onions – partly because of the taste but mostly, I think, from nostalgia.

450g (1lb) honeycomb tripe
2 large onions
Approximately 600ml (1 pint) full-cream milk
50g (2oz) butter
25g (1oz) plain flour
Salt and pepper
2 rounded tablespoons chopped parsley

Serves 4

Cut the tripe into 2.5cm (1in) pieces and peel and slice the onions. Place the tripe and onions in a heavy-based pan, and pour over the milk. Cover the pan tightly and simmer over a gentle heat for about 2 hours or until the tripe is tender. Strain the liquid through a sieve and set aside about 600ml (1 pint) to make a sauce.

Melt the butter in a small pan, stir in the flour and cook it, stirring all the time, for about 3–4 minutes. Then gradually blend in the cooking liquid. Bring to the boil and season with salt and pepper. Scatter the parsley over the tripe and onions and then mix with the sauce. Reheat and serve immediately.

Casserole of Pheasant with Chestnuts

Pheasants originated in the Near and Far East, but they have been part of the British diet for a long time. There is a recipe for pheasant in the Forme of Cury, *Britain's oldest cookery book, written after the coronation celebrations for Richard II in 1390. The recipe below is inspired by* Constance Spry's Cookery Book, *which was the bible for enthusiastic cooks in the 1950s and 60s. Young pheasants are generally roasted, but if they are older you need to stew them slowly. Pheasant is in season, and readily available, in autumn and midwinter, so chestnuts, which are also harvested in the autumn, seem an appropriate addition.*

1 tablespoon olive oil

25g (1oz) butter

2 pheasants, cut into two, lengthwise

225g (8oz) peeled and skinned chestnuts

225g (8oz) button onions

2 teaspoons plain flour

450ml (16fl oz) stock

Grated zest and juice of 1 orange

2 teaspoons redcurrant jelly

1 glass red wine

1 bouquet garni

Serves 4

Preheat oven to 150°C, 300°F, gas mark 2. Heat the oil and butter in a deep casserole and brown the pheasant joints all over. Remove from the pan. Sauté the chestnuts and onions until they begin to change colour. Remove them from the pan. Mix the flour with the remaining fat and cook for a few moments until it starts to change colour. Add the stock, orange zest and juice, redcurrant jelly, red wine and bouquet garni. Bring to the boil, stirring while the liquid heats. Take off the heat, put in the pheasant pieces, chestnuts and onions and cover with a lid. Cook in the oven for about 2 hours. The meat should be very tender. Sprinkle the casserole with chopped parsley before serving.

Braised Rabbit with Prunes

Tradition says William the Conqueror introduced rabbits into Britain. Certainly in the Middle Ages they were an expensive luxury and cost the equivalent of £20 in today's money. Later, once there was a wild population, rabbits became 'food for free' and farm labourers (who would justify the practice as pest control) trapped and shot them for the pot. Disease decimated the population in the late 20th century and now our rabbits are raised specifically for the pot again. This modern recipe has echoes of medieval cooking with the inclusion of prunes.

2 teaspoons sunflower oil
25g (1oz) butter
8 rabbit pieces (2 per person)
Dijon mustard
20 pickling onions, peeled
110g (4oz) smoked bacon, diced
1 teaspoon dried thyme
Approximately 250ml (9fl oz) dry white wine
2 tablespoons brandy
8 pitted prunes
Salt and freshly ground black pepper to taste

Serves 4

Preheat oven to 180°C, 350°F, gas mark 4. Melt the oil and butter in a frying pan and brown the rabbit pieces on all sides. Remove with a slotted spoon, spread all over with Dijon mustard and put in a casserole. Brown the onions and bacon and add to the casserole with the thyme. Cover with wine, season with salt and freshly ground pepper. Cover the casserole and cook for about an hour, then add the brandy and the prunes. Cook for a further 30 minutes. By this time the rabbit should be really tender.

Chicken or Rabbit Fricassee

Fricassee is a French word which has been used in England since at least the 17th century. It originally meant any meat fried in a pan, but has come to mean white meat, generally chicken or rabbit, served in a savoury white sauce. This recipe is Sara Paston-Williams's reconstruction of an 18th-century recipe. In the original recipe we are told to 'shake or stir it with a spoon till it is thorough hot so serve it up'.

4–6 chicken or rabbit joints
chicken stock or water, to cover
2 medium onions, sliced
1 bouquet garni
50g (2oz) mushrooms
15g (½oz) butter
Salt and black pepper to taste

FOR THE SAUCE
40g (1½oz) butter
2 tablespoons plain flour
1–2 egg yolks
150ml (¼pt) single cream
Squeeze of lemon juice
Slices of lemon, for garnish

Serves 4–6

Put the chicken or rabbit joints in a shallow pan, cover with stock or water and add the sliced onions and bouquet garni. Season well. Cover and simmer for about 40 minutes, or until very tender. Drain off the cooking liquor into a measuring jug, cover the pan again and keep hot. The stock should measure 600ml (1 pint); if it is more, turn into a saucepan and reduce. To prepare the sauce, melt the butter in a separate pan, stir in the flour, cook for a few seconds, without letting the butter brown, then pour on the stock and stir in well. Cook over a gentle heat, stirring all the time until thick. Boil briskly for 3–4 minutes, and then draw aside. At the same time, sauté the mushrooms in butter in another pan. To finish the sauce, mix the yolks with the cream in a bowl, add a little of the hot sauce, then pour the mixture slowly back into the rest of the sauce. Check the seasoning again and add the lemon juice and mushrooms. Pour the sauce over the joints, shaking the pan gently to mix all together. Cover and keep hot for 15 minutes before serving, so that the flavour of the sauce can penetrate the meat. Garnish with lemon slices.

Scotch Collops with Forcemeat Balls

A collop is a small slice of meat. Sara Paston-Williams devised this modern version from several recipes from the late 17th century, one of which began 'Take a legg of Veale and slice it very thin...' It was served at a late-20th-century 'Georgian' dinner at Flatford in Suffolk, and was a great success.

FOR THE COLLOPS
450g (1lb) veal escalope
50g (2oz) butter
25g (1oz) plain flour
300ml (½ pint) beef stock
1 glass white wine
1 teaspoon chopped fresh thyme
Thinly cut zest of 1 orange
Shredded zest of ½ lemon

FOR THE FORCEMEAT BALLS
200g (7oz) fresh white breadcrumbs
50g (2oz) shredded suet
50g (2oz) lean bacon
1 tablespoon chopped parsley
1 tablespoon chopped thyme
Grated zest of ½ lemon
1 egg, beaten
Salt and pepper to taste
25g (1oz) butter for frying

Serves 4

Warm a large serving dish in the oven while you are preparing this dish. Cut the veal into strips 6mm (¼in) thick and approximately 13 x 5cm (5 x 5in). Melt the butter in a large frying pan and fry the collops for a few minutes on each side until evenly brown. Transfer to a large shallow pan or sauté pan. Stir the flour into the frying-pan juices and cook for a few seconds, then add stock together with the wine, thyme and orange zest. Bring to the boil so the sauce just thickens a little, and pour over the collops.

Now prepare the forcemeat balls. Mix together the breadcrumbs, suet, bacon, parsley and thyme, lemon zest and seasoning. Stir in the beaten egg and form into small balls about 4cm (1½in) in diameter. Melt the butter in a frying pan and fry the forcemeat balls until brown. Add to the collops and sauce. Cover and simmer gently for about 10 minutes.

Transfer to the warmed serving dish. Extract and discard the orange zest and garnish with shredded lemon zest.

Cornish Pasties

Pasties – also known as tiddy-oggies – are made all over Cornwall. Originally they were portable meals, taken to work by the tin miners and farm labourers, and had vegetables and meat at one end and a sweet filling for pudding at the other. Forfar Bridies, Priddy Oggies, Yorkshire Mint Pasties and Bedfordshire Clangers are pasties from other parts of Britain, with many different fillings.

225g (8oz) shortcrust pastry (see page 54)
200g (7oz) potato, peeled and chopped
100g (3½oz) raw turnip, chopped
60g (2½oz) onion, chopped
250–300g (9–10½oz) steak chuck or skirt, finely chopped (don't use minced beef)
Milk or egg to glaze

Makes 2 large pasties

Preheat the oven to 200°C, 400°F, gas mark 6. Roll out the pastry to 5mm (¼in) thick and cut two dinner-plate-sized rounds. Mix the vegetables and use to cover half of each piece of pastry. Season the meat well and cover the vegetables. Wet the edges of the pastry, fold each piece in half and crimp the edges; brush with milk or beaten egg to glaze. Bake on a lightly greased tray or on baking paper, starting in a hot oven. After 15 minutes, lower the heat to 180°C, 350°F, gas mark 4 and cook for another 45 minutes.

Faggots

A prettier name for these meaty parcels is 'Savoury Ducks', and they are one way of dealing with some of the less glamorous bits of pig, typical of South Wales and south-west England. Caul is a thin membrane with a lacy pattern of fat, which lines the stomach cavity of the animal; it wraps the mixture neatly, adds flavour and looks pretty. Not all butchers sell caul; you may have to ask around. Laura Mason found this recipe in Glamorgan, and like many Welsh variants it uses only liver and includes apple.

200g (7oz) onion, peeled and cut in chunks
200g (7oz) cooking apple, peeled and cored
200g (7oz) pig's liver, cut in chunks
200g (7oz) breadcrumbs
50g (2oz) suet
20 sage leaves, shredded
1 teaspoon salt and some pepper
1 pig's caul
Stock

Serves 4

Mince or process the onion, apple and pig liver. Mix with the breadcrumbs, suet, sage, salt and pepper. Soak the caul in a bowl of warm water. After a few minutes it should be soft and easy to spread out. Using scissors cut 12 neat squares from it, avoiding the fattest bits. Divide the liver mixture into 12 and wrap each in a piece of the caul. Place in a greased ovenproof dish and add a little stock. Bake at 180°C, 350°F, gas mark 4 for about an hour.

Pork Pie

Laura Mason in Farmhouse Cookery *writes: 'In the past pork pies showed local variations in recipe and method and a good pie was a source of pride to a housewife or local butcher. Skilled pie-makers raised the crust entirely by hand, giving it a slightly baggy appearance, or shaped the pastry over a cylindrical form which was removed to leave space for the filling. Using a cake tin gives more certain results, even if the pie loses a hand-made appearance. Melton Mowbray in Leicestershire still produces a distinctive pie, and this recipe incorporates elements of that tradition – anchovy essence as a flavouring, and fresh meat instead of brined. The pastry recipe, from Derbyshire, is unusual in the combination of fats. Lard is the usual choice, and can be used for the total weight of fat in this recipe if desired. The method for the jellied stock was worked out by Jane Grigson as a better alternative to the gelatine-fortified stock now used by many makers. The stock can be made in advance, but the pastry should be as fresh as possible.'*

FOR THE STOCK
2 pig's trotters, bones, skin or trimmings from the pie meat
1 bay leaf
2–3 sprigs thyme
4 peppercorns
1 onion, stuck with cloves
3 litres (5¼ pints) water

FOR THE FILLING
1kg (2¼lb) pork, a quarter of which should be fatty, the rest lean; I use a mixture of shoulder and belly
1 teaspoon salt
1 teaspoon anchovy essence
6–8 sage leaves, chopped
Pepper to taste

FOR THE PASTRY
450g (1lb) plain flour
½ teaspoon salt
50g (2oz) lard
50g (2oz) butter
25g (1oz) suet
1 egg, beaten

An 18–19cm (7½in) round, sprung cake tin with a removable base

Makes 1 large pie, which will serve 10

Place the stock ingredients in a large pan and bring to the boil. Skim well and simmer, covered, for about 3 hours. Strain the liquid into a clean pan and discard the debris. Boil the stock to reduce it to around 500ml (18fl oz). Leave to cool and jellify.

Cut a quarter of the leanest pork into cubes 1cm (½in) across. Mince the rest coarsely – this is best done by hand with a sharp knife, as a mincer tends to compact the meat. Add the seasonings and turn well so they are evenly distributed.

Put the flour in a large bowl and add the salt. Measure the water into a pan and add the fats. Heat the pan, stirring, until the water has come to the boil and all the fat has melted. Remove the pan from the heat and stir the mixture into the flour. Use a wooden spoon at first, then, as it cools slightly, knead to make sure it is all incorporated properly. Cover the bowl and keep it in a warm place.

To raise the pie, take three-quarters of the pastry, still warm, and shape it into a disc. Put it in the cake tin and quickly raise it up the sides to the top, making it as even as possible and trying not to get the pastry too thick. The dough should be malleable – if it flops, it is too warm. Once the pastry is raised, pack the filling into it. Roll out the remaining quarter to make a lid and brush the edges with beaten egg. Trim any excess and crimp the edges. Make a small hole in the middle and cover it with a pastry rose. Cut leaves from the trimmings and use them to decorate the top of the pie. Brush with beaten egg.

Bake at 200°C, 400°F, gas mark 6 for 30 minutes, then lower the heat to 170°C, 325°F, gas mark 3 and bake for another 1½ hours. Some gravy may bubble out of the pie, but don't worry too much about this – some recipes cite this as an indication that the pie is cooked.

At the end of cooking time, remove the pie from the oven and allow to stand for 20 minutes. If the jellied stock has cooled off, reheat to boiling. Ease off the pastry rose and pour in as much hot stock as the pie will hold. Replace the rose and allow the pie to cool. Wait 24 hours before cutting.

Northumbrian Hodgepodge Pie

'Gees in Hoggepot' and 'Goos in hochepot' are medieval ancestors of the Hodgepodge pie. It is a close relative of the Hot Pot (see page 100). Where it differs is that several different meats are included in this one dish. Where it agrees is in the slices of crisp, golden potato that top it. There are several different regional hodgepodge pies: Scottish Hodgepodge has mutton and peas in it. This Northumbrian version is thickened with pearl barley. All hodgepodges make a filling one-pot meal in a cold climate.

900g (2lb) stewing veal, pork and lamb in equal quantities
Dripping (if you don't have any dripping you can use untraditional olive or
**   sunflower oil)**
225g (8oz) onions, sliced
225g (8oz) carrots, sliced
600–850ml (1–1½ pints) hot water mixed with 1 teaspoon Worcester sauce
2 tablespoons plain flour
2 tablespoons pearl barley
1 teaspoon mixed herbs
450g (1lb) potatoes, thinly sliced
50g (2oz) grated cheese
Salt and pepper to taste

Serves 6

Preheat oven to 160°C, 325°F, gas mark 3. In a large frying pan brown the meat, a few pieces at a time, in the dripping or oil. Transfer the meat to a wide casserole dish. Next fry the onions and carrots for a few minutes. Stir in the flour to soak up the juices, then gradually add the hot water, stirring all the time until the liquid is smoothly blended. Pour the contents of the frying pan over the meat in the casserole – sprinkle in the pearl barley and mixed herbs and season to taste with salt and pepper. Arrange the potato slices on top in an overlapping pattern. Cover with a lid and cook in the oven for 1½ hours. Remove the lid, scatter over the grated cheese and cook for a further 50 minutes. If the top is not browning sufficiently, turn up the oven heat for the last 15 minutes or finish under the grill.

Right: Northumbrian Hodgepodge Pie

Venison Casseroled with Apricots

The Romans first fenced game parks in Britain to raise and hunt deer and wild boar. Venison has been prized as a meat ever since. During the 16th century, it was even sent as a love token. Henry VIII wooed Anne Boleyn, his second wife, with the gift of a haunch of venison. Now we value it because the meat is virtually fat-free and the deer herds, even when farmed, are raised humanely with space to roam and graze. Juniper is the traditional flavouring for game.

50g (2oz) dried apricots
75g (3oz) butter
2 medium onions, peeled and sliced
450g (1lb) venison cut into large cubes
2 tablespoons plain flour
2 teaspoons crushed juniper berries
300ml (½ pint) apple or apricot juice
300ml (½ pint) red wine
Salt and pepper to taste

FOR GARNISH
Chopped parsley
Greek yoghurt

Serves 4

Soak the apricots in cold water overnight. Preheat oven to 160°C, 325°F, gas mark 3. In a sauté pan, melt the butter and sauté the sliced onions until soft and golden. Take out with a slotted spoon and place in a casserole. Now sauté the venison until brown and add to the onions with any cooking juices from the sauté pan. Mix the flour with the crushed juniper berries and salt and pepper to taste. Sprinkle over the meat and onions and turn them well in the flour mixture. Place the casserole in the oven for 10 minutes to cook the flour. Meanwhile heat the juice and wine gently. Remove the casserole from the oven and add the juice, wine and apricots. Stir and return to the oven. Cook gently for at least 2 hours, or until the meat is tender. This may take longer if the venison was wild rather than farmed. To serve, sprinkle with parsley and hand round a bowl of yoghurt separately for guests to add if they wish.

Left: Venison Casseroled with Apricots

Game Pie

Game pie, historically, would only be made on wealthy farms or estates with large amounts of land on which the men could shoot. It can be made in the same way as Pork Pie (see page 110) with hot-water crust and jellied stock, using 450g (1lb) meat from game and the same from pork. This version is a bit of a hybrid between a raised pie and a more standard short-pastry version.

FOR THE FILLING
50g (2oz) butter
450g (1lb) venison, cubed
450g (1lb) assorted other game, cut off the bone (for example, pheasant, pigeon, partridge, rabbit, hare; cooked game can be used)
400–500g (14oz–1lb 2oz) good pork sausage meat, divided into 10–12 balls
2 level tablespoons plain flour
100ml (3½fl oz) red wine
300ml (½ pint) stock, made from the bones and trimmings of game birds cooked with an onion and 1 bouquet garni
Salt and pepper to taste
Nutmeg

FOR THE PASTRY
Shortcrust pastry made from 450g (1lb) plain flour
100g (3½oz) butter
110g (4oz) lard
1 teaspoon salt
100ml (3½fl oz) water

Egg, for sealing and glazing

A circular cake tin 20–22cm (8–9in) in diameter, preferably with a loose bottom; line the base with greaseproof paper.

Serves 10 easily

Make the sauce first. Melt the butter in a large frying pan. Brown the cubed venison, the sausage meat and the other game if it is raw. Remove, leaving as much fat as possible in the pan. Stir in the flour. Add the wine, scraping the bottom of the pan to pick up all the residues from the game. Pour in the stock and simmer gently for about 20 minutes. Taste, and add salt, pepper and a scrape of nutmeg. The sauce should be well seasoned. Turn into a basin and allow to cool to tepid.

Roll three-quarters of the pastry into a large circle and place in the tin, spreading the pastry so it drapes over the sides. Ease it over the base, into the edges and up the sides, trying not to stretch it. You will have to make small pleats in places. Roll the remaining quarter ready to make the lid. Distribute the venison over the base and top with the other game. Add the sausagemeat balls. Pour in the sauce. Cover with the pastry lid, sealing with beaten egg.

Trim, crimp the edges decoratively and add decorations of pastry flowers and leaves. Game pies should be very ornamental. Glaze with beaten egg. Place on a heated baking tray in a preheated oven, 220°C, 425°F, gas mark 7, for 20–30 minutes (watch to see it doesn't brown too quickly), then turn the temperature down to 170°C, 325°F, gas mark 3 and cook for a further 1½ hours. Remove the pie from the oven. Allow to cool in the tin overnight.

Fidget Pie

Fidget – or Fitchett – Pie is made throughout the Midlands. I have found recipes for this dish in various cookbooks, including one in Farmhouse Fare: Recipes from Country Housewives collected by The Farmers Weekly, *published in 1950. This seemed particularly appropriate since it was a popular dish with harvesters, as it could be eaten hot or cold. It always contains pork or gammon, apples and onions. I have chosen a recipe associated with Shropshire, where they add potatoes, which makes the pie very sustaining and perfect for hearty appetites. By the way,* fidget *is a local name for a polecat – the pie was supposed to smell very strong (like a polecat) when cooking!*

450g (1lb) potatoes, peeled and thickly sliced
350g (12oz) lean gammon
2 large onions, sliced
2 large cooking apples, peeled and sliced
2 teaspoons sugar
4 sage leaves
300ml (½ pint) consommé or jellied fresh stock
225g (8oz) shortcrust pastry (see page 54)
Milk, to glaze
Salt and pepper to taste

Serves 4

Preheat oven to 180°C, 350°F, gas mark 4. Put a layer of sliced potatoes in a 1.2 litre (2 pint) pie dish. Dice the gammon and put a layer on top of the potatoes, cover this with onion and apple slices. Sprinkle with 1 teaspoon of the sugar. Shred the sage leaves and sprinkle half of them on top of the onion and apple. Repeat the layers until the dish is full, ending with a layer of gammon. Sprinkle the top layer with the rest of the sugar and sage. Pour just enough stock over the pie to cover the filling. Roll out the pastry to make a fairly thick pie crust and cover the top of the dish. Brush the top with milk and bake for 20 minutes, then reduce the heat to 160°C, 325°F, gas mark 3 and bake for a further 45 minutes. If you think the pastry is getting too brown, cover it with foil for the last 15 minutes of the cooking time.

Savoury sauces

Pork without Apple Sauce, lamb without Mint Sauce, beef without Horseradish? Unthinkable! There are ten sauces, with variations, in this short but important section on traditional British sauces. White Sauce, a close relation to France's Bechamel, is here, with Cheese Sauce, Caper Sauce and Parsley Sauce all based upon it. Butter or Dutch Sauce and Mayonnaise are hot and cold versions of the same thing. Apple Sauce and Gooseberry Sauce are made with fruit and they are sharp, acid accompaniments, perfect with rich meat and fish, as are Horseradish Sauce and Cumberland Sauce. As for Mint Sauce, it is unknown outside this country. Onion Gravy compliments the excellent meaty sausages available today (by the way, a recipe for a classic gravy is included in the section on Roasting on page 317).

White Sauce

White Sauce is not only the basis for many other savoury sauces, but is also an accompaniment in its own right. Traditionally, it was used for coating vegetables, such as cauliflower and carrots. Bland and comforting, it was also considered perfect for invalids. Below, I have given the recipe for a basic white sauce, followed by recipes for some of the sauces for which a white sauce is the basic ingredient. You will notice that I have given an alternative for the liquid base. My preference is for half stock, half milk as it intensifies the flavour, but traditionally full-cream milk alone was used.

300ml (½ pint) full-cream milk or 150ml (¼ pint) milk and 150ml (¼ pint) vegetable, fish or chicken stock
1 bay leaf
1 shallot, chopped
A dash of freshly grated nutmeg
25g (1oz) butter
25g (1oz) plain flour
Salt and pepper to taste

Makes 300ml (10fl oz)

Put the milk (and stock, if using) with the bay leaf, shallot and a dusting of nutmeg in a pan and bring slowly to the boil. Remove from the heat, cover and leave to infuse for 15 minutes.

In a clean, heavy-based pan, melt the butter, stir in the flour and cook for 3 minutes. Strain the liquid through a sieve and gradually blend it into the flour and butter. Bring the mixture to the boil, stirring continuously. It should have thickened a little by now. Turn down the heat and cook it gently, still stirring. The harder you stir, the smoother the sauce. Adjust the seasoning and serve. You can make a white sauce ahead of time and reheat it, but you need to beat it well during reheating.

VARIATIONS
Cheese sauce: Add ½ teaspoon mustard powder and a pinch of cayenne pepper to the flour before making the sauce. Beat in 75g (3oz) finely grated mature Cheddar cheese after the sauce has thickened, until smooth.
Parsley Sauce: Add 2 level tablespoons finely chopped parsley to the sauce just before serving.
Caper Sauce: Add 1 tablespoon lemon juice to the stock before making the sauce. Add 1 tablespoon capers just before serving.

Mayonnaise

When making mayonnaise it is important that all the ingredients are at room temperature, to allow the eggs and oil to emulsify. Warning: recipes containing raw eggs are unsuitable for pregnant women or young children.

2 egg yolks
½ teaspoon Dijon mustard
300ml (½ pint) olive or sunflower oil
1 tablespoon lemon juice
1 tablespoon wine vinegar
Salt and pepper

Makes 300ml (½ pint)

Put the egg yolks and mustard into a bowl and mix thoroughly. Whisk in the oil drop by drop. (This is easiest with an electric mixer or a food processor, but you can do it by hand.) When you have blended in half the oil, add the lemon juice and the vinegar. Then beat in the rest of the oil. Season to taste.

VARIATIONS
Tartare Sauce: Add 1 tablespoon chopped chives, 1 tablespoon chopped parsley, 1 tablespoon chopped gherkins and 1 tablespoon chopped capers to the finished mayonnaise.
Green Sauce: Add 150ml (5fl oz) full-fat yoghurt or crème fraîche, the grated zest and juice of 1 lemon, 2 chopped garlic cloves, 4 tablespoons finely chopped fresh parsley and 4 tablespoons of one of the following herbs, finely chopped: French tarragon, chives, dill, basil or mint.
Dill Mayonnaise: Add 4 tablespoons fresh chopped dill.

Horseradish Sauce

Horseradish Sauce is addictive. Addicts can't eat beef without it. The part of the horseradish used for the sauce is the peeled and grated root. Horseradish has been a staple of the British diet since the 15th century.

Juice of ½ lemon
2 teaspoons caster sugar
¼ teaspoon mustard powder
4 tablespoons freshly grated horseradish
300ml (½ pint) double cream

Makes 300ml (½ pint)

Mix the lemon, sugar and mustard powder into a paste. Stir the paste into the grated horseradish. Whip the cream until thick, but not too stiff. Fold in the other ingredients, add a little salt and chill well.

Cumberland Sauce

This sauce needs to be prepared 24 hours before serving – so some advance planning is needed.

1 orange
1 lemon
225g (8oz) redcurrant jelly
125ml (4fl oz) ruby or tawny port
2 heaped teaspoons arrowroot
1 teaspoon mustard powder

Serves 4–6

Thinly peel the orange and the lemon and cut the skin into shreds. Bring a pan of water to the boil, add the peel and boil for 3 minutes. Drain and cover with cold water for 1 minute, drain again and set aside. Squeeze the juice from the orange and the lemon, pour into a small pan, add the jelly and bring slowly to the boil. Simmer for 5 minutes, then add the port and bring the sauce back to the boil. Remove from the heat. Mix the arrowroot and mustard powder to a paste with a little cold water and stir the paste into the mixture. Return the pan to the heat, bring the sauce back to the boil and cook for a further minute. Add the blanched peel and leave the sauce to stand for 24 hours before using.

Mint Sauce

'The smell of mint does stir up the minde and the taste to a greedy desire of meat,' wrote John Gerard in his Herball *in 1633. No wonder we love mint sauce with roast lamb.*

1 large pack fresh mint leaves (20g)
1 tablespoon sugar
2 tablespoons boiling water
White wine or cider vinegar, according to taste

Makes 125ml (4fl oz)

Strip the mint leaves from their stems. Pile them on a chopping board and spoon over the sugar. Using a large, straight-bladed sharp knife, chop the mint very finely. You will find that the sugar helps to stop the leaves scattering all over the place. Every so often, scrape the mixture up into a pile again. When the mint is very finely chopped, put it into a bowl, spoon over the boiling water and stir until the sugar has dissolved. Top up the bowl with vinegar. (For a less sharp and vinegary sauce, use two-thirds vinegar to one-third water.) Either way, make the sauce at the last minute and the mint leaves will stay green.

Bread Sauce

In medieval European recipes many sauces were thickened with bread. This traditional accompaniment for roast chicken, turkey or pheasant is a direct descendant of those sauces.

1 small onion, peeled and stuck with 6 cloves
2 bay leaves
600ml (1 pint) milk
75g (3oz) fresh white breadcrumbs
25g (1oz) butter
Salt and pepper to taste

Makes approximately 600ml (1 pint)

Put the onion, bay leaves and milk in a pan and bring to the boil. Remove from the heat, cover with a lid and leave to infuse for 15 minutes. Add the breadcrumbs and butter, and simmer uncovered, very gently, for 10 minutes. Remove the onion and bay leaves. Season to taste with salt and pepper.

Onion Gravy

'We never goes home to breakfast till we've sold out; but if it's very late, then I buys a penn'orth of pudden, which is very nice with gravy.'

London Labour and the London Poor, *Henry Mayhew, 1863.*

For this eight-year-old selling watercress in the cold, inhospitable streets of Victorian London, gravy and pudding, bought from a street stall, was one of her few comforts. Gravy is peculiar to the British; to many of us a roast without gravy is unthinkable. There is more information on gravy in the section on roasts (see page 317). This recipe for Onion Gravy, the perfect accompaniment to sausages and mash, comes from Tom Norrington-Davies' Just Like Mother Used to Make. *He emphasises the need to fry the onions gently to extract their full sweetness – don't try to hurry this. You can make the gravy well in advance and reheat it when you want to serve it.*

1 tablespoon olive oil
1 tablespoon butter
3 onions, sliced
4 sage leaves
300ml (10fl oz) red wine
1 teaspoon sugar
1 teaspoon Dijon mustard
Salt and pepper to taste

Serves 4

Heat the oil and butter in a frying pan. Add the onions and fry them gently, giving them a good stir from time to time. Shred the sage leaves and add them after 5 minutes. When the onions are soft and beginning to brown (this should be after about 15–20 minutes) add the wine and sugar and bring the mixture to the boil. Boil the onions and wine for about 5 minutes, then stir in the mustard. Taste and season with salt and pepper. If you aren't planning to serve the sauce immediately, stop cooking at this point and give it a final 5 minutes just before it is needed; otherwise continue to cook for 5 minutes and serve.

Apple Sauce

Apple Sauce is the traditional accompaniment for roast pork or roast duck. In both cases, the tartness of the sauce complements perfectly the richness of the meat. It is important to use cooking apples in the sauce. Bramleys are perfect for the zingy, sharp flavour that you need.

450g (1lb) cooking apples
3 tablespoons water
1 tablespoon cider vinegar
1 tablespoon sugar
25g (1oz) unsalted butter

Makes approximately 300ml (½ pint)

Peel and slice the apples. Put them in a small pan with the water, cover and simmer until the apples are cooked and fluffy. (This will take approximately 10 minutes.) Take the pan off the heat and stir in the cider vinegar, sugar and butter.

Dutch Sauce or Butter Sauce

This sauce – similar to the French Hollandaise – has had an abundance of names over the years. This version was first published by Michael Smith, an expert in British food, in 1973.

110g (4oz) good fresh salted butter
2 level teaspoons fine white plain flour
150ml (¼ pint) milk
1 tablespoon lemon juice or white wine vinegar

Makes approximately 300ml (½ pint)

Cut the butter into small cubes, sprinkle with flour, and, either in the food processor or by hand, work this into a smooth paste. Transfer the paste into a small pan and, over the lowest heat possible, beat it with a wooden spatula until it starts to melt. Gradually beat in the milk without raising the heat. Bring the sauce just to the boil and simmer for 2 minutes, beating all the time. Add the lemon juice or vinegar.

Gooseberry Sauce

Did you know that there have been clubs in England dedicated to growing monster gooseberries for over 200 years? The most well-known, the Egton Bridge Old Gooseberry Society in Yorkshire, still holds an annual competition for the largest berry. It is not a good contest for cooks as the way to achieve success is to strip the bush of all other fruit, leaving just one to grow and grow. The distinctive tart flavour of gooseberries provides the perfect contrast to rich meat such as goose (perhaps that is how they got their name), or oily fish, such as mackerel or salmon. The recipe below is my adaptation of Eliza Acton's recipe in Modern Cooking for Private Families, *first published in 1845.*

450g (1lb) gooseberries
3 tablespoons water
A pinch of ground ginger
1 tablespoon sugar
1 small cube of butter, about 20cm (1in) square

Serves 4

Stew the gooseberries with the water in a small pan until very soft. There is no need to top and tail them since you are going to purée the mixture: rub it through a sieve to get rid of the skin and pips. Return the mixture to the pan, add the ginger, sugar and butter, and heat gently until the sugar is dissolved and the butter has melted. Serve the sauce hot or cold.

Vegetables and Side Dishes

It is not so long ago that the British were the butt of jokes concerning the way we cooked vegetables. Watery cabbage, soggy sprouts, overcooked carrots – this was how the rest of the world saw British vegetable cooking. But there has been a sea change in the last few years, both in the home and in eating out. Today we realise that vegetables are not only good for us, but we can appreciate their flavours and textures, when cooked appropriately.

In fact, vegetables have always played a large part in the diet of both country and town dwellers, at all levels of British society. In *Piers Plowman*, a famous narrative poem written in the 14th century, the food in the cottage of the character Hunger includes parsley, leeks and cabbage. Piers and his neighbours supplement these with peascods, beans, apples, onions and pot herbs. The market gardeners around London sold their produce on the south side of St Paul's Churchyard and, as well as the vegetables mentioned above, they sold turnips, parsnips, beet, radishes, carrots, herbs and fruit.

We know that people made pottage with these vegetables, and ate it daily. Pottage was a broth or stock in which meat and/or vegetables had been boiled, along with herbs and probably pulses and cereals. The result was something between a soup and a stew. Pease Pottage is typical of a pottage that was thick (or 'running'), though some were even thicker (or 'stondyng'), and almost solid enough to slice. For most people, their usual pottage would have been a vegetable one, made with cabbage, lettuces, leeks, onions and garlic. 'White Porray' (leek pottage) was especially popular, and during Lent, when meat-eating was restricted, the rich ate it thickened with ground almonds. 'Green Porray' was also popular, flavoured with parsley and other herbs. There are two modern pottage recipes in this chapter: Pease Pottage, a thick, winter-warming purée from a single vegetable, and Spiced Bean Pottage, a spicy vegetable casserole that provides a main course for the hungry – continuing an old tradition. There are also some less substantial descendants of pottage in the chapter on Soups.

'Pot-herbs' had a slightly different meaning in the past. Today we take it to mean herbs – like parsley, sage rosemary, thyme, or tarragon – that can literally go in the pot. But in the Middle Ages 'pot-herbs' meant 'vegetables for the pot' and, as well as herbs, included onions, carrots, leeks and cabbage, and also salad vegetables like lettuce. Incidentally, carrots were not just orange, a colour developed by the Dutch in the Middle Ages, but also came in purple, yellow and white. Probably we have less choice of vegetables now today than people had in 1500: it has been calculated that over 100 varieties of vegetables were available to grow at that time.

Salads in medieval cookery were simple green leaves, including some – like groundsel and pimpernel – that we no longer eat today. They were decorated with edible flowers, a custom I think we should revive. Primroses, chive flowers, borage flowers, nasturtiums and violas all taste good and look even better. I haven't provided a recipe for oil and vinegar dressing, but I can't do better than quote Robert Evelyn in his *Acetaria*, published in 1699 and entirely devoted to salads. Evelyn defines a *sallet*, as he calls it, thus: 'a particular Composition of certain Crude and fresh herbs, such as usually are, or may be safely eaten with some Acetous Juice, Oyl, Salt etc. to give them a grateful Gust and Vehicle.' He calls his salad dressing an *Oxoleon* – although it's a strange word, the proportions work well, three centuries later: 'Take of clear, and perfectly good *Oyl-Olive*; three parts; of sharpest *Vinegar …Limon* or Juice of Orange; one Part; and therein let steep some Slices of Horse-Radish, with a little salt.' Don't worry about including the horseradish, since the dressing is perfect without it. If you like to experiment, there are two historic salads, or *sallets*, in this chapter. The second rejoices in the wonderful name of Salamongundy – or 'Salmagundi', or even 'Sallid Magundi'.

Naturally there is no mention of potatoes in medieval recipes. The first Europeans to come across potatoes, in 1537 in Colombia, South America, actually called them 'truffles'. And this is exactly how they were treated to begin with – as a rare, delicate luxury. They arrived in the British Isles some sixty years later, in the 1590s, probably brought back by Sir Francis Drake after one of his transatlantic voyages. Potatoes thrive in cool, damp climates, and by 1650 they were the staple diet of the Irish, so much so that the disastrous potato blight of 1845 caused widespread famine in Ireland. Irish potato recipes included here include Champ and Colcannon. Lancashire and Northumbria also grow excellent potatoes. Pan Haggerty, potatoes layered with onion and cheese and cooked in a 'pan' on the fire, is a dish from northern England, as is Leek and Potato Hotpot. Leeks are a favourite everywhere, but particularly in Northumbria, home of the largest leek competition. Leek Pudding (a leek roly-poly), and Leek, Cheese and Bread and Butter Pudding both come from Wallington, an elegant classical house set in the beautiful Northumbrian moors. The leeks there are grown in the kitchen garden, sheltered in a fold of the rolling hills. The Potato Pudding is a modern adaptation by Sara Paston-Williams of a Georgian recipe from Somerset where the potato is flavoured with spices and sugar, and served in puff pastry.

Britain produces excellent hard cheese, which is particularly good for cooking. Macaroni Cheese and Cauliflower Cheese are both old favourites. A modern version of a very old recipe for Cheese Pudding, thickened in the old way, with breadcrumbs rather than flour, also contains beetroot and carrot. And there are some recipes for potting cheese.

In earlier centuries, fresh vegetables were in short supply by the middle of winter. During the colder months, people had to rely on root crops and what could be salted or pickled. Today we are much luckier, with vegetables available all year round, coming from all over the world. By and large the recipes in this chapter do not use exotic vegetables – they use the ones we grow best. And, by the way, the Vegetable and Nut Greate Pye, with its exotic filling of cabbage, mushrooms, dates and nuts, is a surprisingly recent invention, from Norfolk. It was made to serve 20th-century vegetarians at an 'Elizabethan banquet'.

A Salad of Herbs and Flowers

This recipe for an Elizabethan salad comes from The Good Huswife's Jewell *by Thomas Dawson, published in 1596. At Oxburgh House, a fortified manor dating back to the 15th century, this salad was made as part of an Elizabethan banquet held in the spring. It consisted of Welsh onions, shallots, sage, rosemary, thyme, parsley, chives and bay garnished with cowslips, primroses and violets, all from the garden. Only the eggs were not home-produced!*

'Take your herbs and pick them very fine into fine water, and pick your flowers by themselves and wash them clean, then swing them in a strainer, and when you put them into a dish, mingle them with cucumbers or lemons pared and sliced, also scrape sugar, and put in vinegar and oil, then throw the flowers on the top of the salad, and of every sort of the aforesaid things and garnish the dish about, then take eggs boiled hard, and lay about the dish and upon the salad.'

Previous page: Spiced Bean Pottage
Right: A Salad of Herbs and Flowers

Salamongundy

More of a concept than a recipe – in 1747 Mrs Hannah Glasse wrote, 'You may always make Salamongundy of such things as you have, according to your fancy.' She added, 'If it is neatly set out it will make a pretty figure in the middle of the table, or you may lay them in heaps in a dish; if you have not all these ingredients, set out your plates, or saucers with just what you have.'

Salamongundy is basically an English composite salad, similar to the Mediterranean Salade Niçoise. Originally it consisted of cold meats combined with lettuce, grapes and anchovies, but there are many variations. Mrs Glasse refers to plates and saucers. If you want to reproduce the old effect, use a large salad plate and build up the different salads in different-sized bowls and plates. When I was a caterer, we produced a Georgian buffet for a baroque dance group and our Salamongundy consisted of bowls of different brightly coloured salads, beetroot, chopped hard-boiled egg, chopped grapes, chopped ham and chopped cucumber. We tried to keep to foods we knew were in the diet in 1700. Modern Salamongundys can range far and wide, but for authenticity keep each bowl to one colour.

In this vegetarian version the base consists of a mixture of colourful and tasty leaves such as curly endive, cos, lollo rosso, oakleaf, young dandelion leaves and spinach – whatever is available. A layer is placed on a large flat dish, then other vegetables are layered or piled on top to make a colourful display. You can use: leeks and mushrooms cooked 'à la grecque' in a little vinegar and olive oil and cooled; tiny new potatoes cooked and dressed with walnut oil and mint; raw carrot with a poppy-seed dressing; blanched green beans, etc. Hard-boiled eggs can also be added and there should always be a fruit element such as chopped red apples or grapes.

Place the dish in the centre of the table and let your guests help themselves. Served with a good selection of bread and a bottle of Alsace Gewurztraminer, it makes a perfect summer lunch or supper.

Pease Pottage

In the Middle Ages, 'pottage', a semi-liquid dish eaten with a spoon, was consumed by everyone. Vegetable pottages like this were for the poor; the rich enjoyed spicy meat or fish pottages. This modern recipe using frozen peas makes a good 'winter warmer'. It also makes an excellent vegetable accompaniment to poached gammon (see page 80) or Fish and Chips (see page 62), if you don't fancy mushy peas.

450g (1lb) frozen peas
110g (4oz) butter
1 tablespoon fresh mint
Salt, pepper and sugar to taste
Swirl of cream, to serve

Serves 4

Defrost the peas and put them in a saucepan with the butter. Put the lid on and cook very slowly until they become mushy. This will take up to 45 minutes. Season with salt, pepper and a teaspoon of sugar and stir in the fresh mint chopped very finely. Serve with a swirl of cream.

Jugged Peas

This recipe is for fresh peas, especially if you have a glut, they have all ripened at once and you aren't keeping up with eating them plain. Laura Mason suggests that they will 'go with all that lovely Devon lamb; this is good even for end-of-season, slightly-past-their-best peas'. The herbs transform the dish into something to suit 21st-century taste.

1kg (2¼lb) peas in the pod, or 250g (9oz) shelled peas
25g (1oz) butter
1 teaspoon sugar
1–2 tablespoons water
2 mint sprigs
Pinch of salt

TO FINISH
10 green coriander sprigs
12 mint leaves
Green chilli, seeded

Serves 4

Put the peas, butter, sugar, salt, water and the sprigs of mint in a small casserole or a pudding basin that will hold them comfortably. Cover with a lid or some foil and place the arrangement in a saucepan of water. Bring this to a gentle boil and simmer for 30 minutes. At the end of this time, the peas should be tender and well flavoured. Chop the coriander, mint leaves and the chilli finely and stir in just before serving.

Braised Red Cabbage

Cabbage has been valued as a food since the Egyptians. The Romans considered that it was healthy and warded off drunkenness. This is the perfect vegetable to serve at Christmas, when it won't ward off drunkenness, but it can be made in advance and tastes just as good when reheated – and it is healthy.

900g (2lb) red cabbage
1 medium-sized onion, sliced
50g (2oz) butter
1 crisp eating apple (Cox is good)
1 large cooking apple
150ml (¼ pint) cheap red wine, or stock
1 teaspoon salt
1 tablespoon wine vinegar
6 whole cloves
½ teaspoon grated nutmeg
1 level tablespoon soft brown sugar
freshly ground black pepper, to taste

Serves 6

Remove the cabbage's outer leaves, white root and larger pieces of white pith, cut into quarters and shred finely. Place in a large bowl and cover with water. Drain after a minute.

Soften the onions in the melted butter in a large heavy pan, but do not brown. Peel, core and slice thickly the apples, and add to the pan with the wine or stock, salt, vinegar, cloves, nutmeg, plenty of black pepper and finally the cabbage. Combine and cover the pan tightly. Cook gently, stirring occasionally, for about 45 minutes; the cabbage is nicest if it still has a little bite to it. Stir in the sugar and serve.

This loses none of its flavour if reheated the following day.

Leek Pudding

Appropriately, this recipe came from Northumbria. Leeks are serious business in the North. There's a National Pot Leek Society and members compete to produce the world's largest pot leek. The World Leek Challenge offers a prize of more than £1000 for the largest pot leek in the world assessed over four years' production. One of the leeks entered achieved 284.21 cubic inches. Don't choose these monsters for cooking; smaller and tender leeks are what you want.

225g (8oz) self-raising flour
½ teaspoon salt
110g (4oz) vegetarian suet
About 125ml (4fl oz) water
600g (1¼lb) leeks
2 tablespoons of one or more of the following: chopped parsley,
   marjoram and tarragon
Salt and pepper to taste

Serves 4

Preheat oven to 350°C, 180°C, gas mark 4. Mix together the flour, salt and suet. Add enough water to produce a light, elastic dough and knead gently until smooth. Roll into a rectangle approximately 6mm (¼in) thick. Chop the leeks and sprinkle onto the pastry, leaving a margin round the edges. Sprinke the herbs over the leeks and season with salt and pepper. Roll up like a Swiss roll and seal the ends with your fingers.

Lightly butter a piece of foil or use a large piece of baking paper to wrap up the roll, not too tightly to allow for expansion. Bake in the oven for approximately 1½ hours, or until the pastry is golden and cooked through. This is delicious served with a vegetable stew.

Spiced Bean Pottage

This is one of the modern versions of the medieval staple, pottage, in this book. Using pulses, this is extremely nutritious. It provides quite a considerable portion of the protein required daily in our diet, so it's a good bet if you are feeding vegetarians. Originally invented by Sara Paston-Williams for a feast, it tastes every bit as good as it reads.

110g (4oz) chickpeas, washed and soaked overnight
175g (6oz) dried haricot beans, washed and soaked overnight
6 tablespoons oil, sunflower or olive
2 red onions, diced
2 garlic cloves, peeled and finely chopped
1 teaspoon of each of the following: ground coriander, turmeric, cumin
1 fresh chilli, de-seeded and finely chopped (optional; leave it out if you prefer a
    less 'hot' dish)
Juice and zest of 1 lemon
2 red peppers, diced
225g (8oz) spinach, washed, stalked and shredded
50g (2oz) pine nuts
Salt and pepper to taste

Serves 4

NB: This recipe must be started the previous day.

Soak the beans and chickpeas overnight, drain.

Heat 5 tablespoons of the oil and sauté the onions and garlic for a couple of minutes. Then add the spices and the chilli. Cook for a further 2–3 minutes and add the lemon juice and zest and the drained haricot beans and chickpeas. Cover with water, bring to the boil, cover the pan and simmer until the beans and peas are tender. This will take about 3 hours. Heat the remaining oil and fry the peppers until tender. Add to the mixture with the spinach and pine nuts. Season with salt and pepper to taste. Serve piping hot with lots of crusty bread.

Champt

Champ is Irish. My recipe comes from Northern Ireland. There are many regional names for Champ –
Bruisy, Cally, Goody and Pandy are some of them. There are also many stories surrounding the
dish because it was prepared specially for Hallowe'en (31 October). It was customary to offer Champ
to the fairies then. A bowl would be left out under a hawthorn bush on Hallowe'en or All Souls' Night
(1 November).

675g (1½lb) potatoes
250ml (9fl oz) buttermilk
6 spring onions, finely chopped
50g (2oz) butter
Salt and pepper to taste

Serves 4

Peel, boil and drain the potatoes. Heat the buttermilk gently in a pan and mash the potatoes with
the buttermilk until they are very smooth. Season with salt and pepper and stir in the chopped
spring onions which can either be fresh or blanched for a more delicate flavour. Put a mound of
champ on each plate. Make a well in the centre and fill it with a knob of butter. Serve immediately.

Bubble and Squeak or Colcannon

Bubble and Squeak and Colcannon are, respectively, English and Irish versions of the same dish. The Irish cooked it first and, traditionally, Colcannon is flavoured with leeks or shallots, and is served in individual bowls topped with a knob of butter. Bubble and Squeak, however, was made from leftover cooked cabbage and potatoes, fried in dripping, but it is such a good dish, it's worth making on its own account. The added twist to the recipe below is that the Bubble and Squeak is cooked in the oven in butter. I owe this idea to Tom Norrington-Davies' Just Like Mother Used to Make *– and I think it is inspirational. The taste is utterly delicious, and you have the time and space while it is cooking to fry the eggs, which are the perfect accompaniment.*

3 waxy-fleshed potatoes, cut into small dice
2 tablespoons butter
1 tablespoon olive oil
2 onions, chopped
Approximately half of a Savoy cabbage, cored and chopped
Salt and pepper to taste

Serves 4

Preheat oven to 200°C, 400°F, Gas Mark 6 and warm a baking dish large enough to take all the ingredients. Boil the potatoes. (This will take approximately 10 minutes.) Drain them and put them in a large mixing bowl. Set to one side.

Heat half the butter with the olive oil in a large frying pan. Fry the onions for 5 minutes, stirring to stop them catching. Then add the cabbage and fry until it wilts. Take the pan off the heat and add the contents to the potatoes in the mixing bowl. Give them a good stir and season with salt and pepper. Take the baking dish out of the oven and melt the rest of the butter in it. Add the rest of the ingredients and return it to the oven for approximately 20 minutes. The top of the Bubble and Squeak should be golden brown when cooked.

Ragoo of Mushrooms

A ragoo is a stew, originally of meat and vegetables. I wanted to include this as Mushroom Stroganoff, though it is not traditional. However, picking and cooking mushrooms has been a country occupation for centuries and this is a particularly good way of cooking them. So for the purposes of this book, I've called Mushroom Stroganoff 'Ragoo of Mushrooms'. By the way, the original recipe isn't authentically Russian either, since the main ingredient should be steak.

50g (2oz) butter
1 tablespoon sunflower oil
1 medium onion, finely chopped
3 celery sticks, finely chopped
Pinch of thyme and a crumbled bay leaf
450g (1lb) button mushrooms
1 tablespoon wholemeal flour
150ml (¼ pint) vegetable stock
2 tablespoons medium sherry
2 tablespoons Greek yoghurt or crème fraîche
Salt and pepper to taste

FOR GARNISH
Chopped parsley
Paprika

Serves 4

Heat the butter and oil together and sauté the chopped onion and celery with the thyme and bay leaf until soft. Chop the mushrooms into halves or quarters and add to the pan. Add the flour and turn the vegetables so that they are well coated. Cook gently for 5 minutes, then add the stock and the sherry. Cook for another 5 minutes, taste to ensure that the flour is cooked and stir in the yoghurt or crème fraîche. Adjust the seasoning. Reheat gently, stirring all the time so that the sauce does not separate. Serve immediately on a bed of rice garnished with chopped parsley and paprika.

This is a surprisingly rich dish and only needs a green salad as an accompaniment.

Potato Pudding

Potatoes, like carrots, spinach and artichokes, were often made into sweet puddings in the 18th century. They would be served with the first course of meat and fish. The original recipe for this modern adaptation is as follows: 'Take 12oz of Potatoes, pound them very fine in a Mortar. 12 yolks of Eggs, 4 Whites, 12oz sugar, 12oz butter, some Mace and Cynnamon dry'd and powdered – a Spoonful or two of Brandy as you please. A Quarter of an Hour will bake it, put it in puff paste – round the rim.'

175g (6oz) shortcrust pastry (see page 54)
1 tablespoon brandy
150ml (¼ pint) single cream
2 eggs
½ teaspoon cinnamon
450g (1lb) potatoes (preferably Désirée) cooked, peeled and diced
25g (1oz) butter, cut into dice
Salt and pepper to taste

Serves 4

Preheat oven to 180°C, 350°F, gas mark 4. Line a 23cm (9in) flan dish with the pastry and bake blind for approximately 15 minutes. Beat the brandy, cream, eggs and cinnamon together for a minute or two. Stir in the diced potato, mix well and fill the flan case with the mixture. Dot the top with the butter and put back into the oven for approximately 30 minutes, until the top is nicely brown.

Cheese Pudding

This tasty dish is a Norfolk adaptation of Michael Barry's modern version of a recipe dated 1818, originally noted at Goudhurst in Kent. An example of how inspiration travels down the centuries and across counties! This is a beautiful dish, golden, light and speckled with carrot and beetroot; it makes a very good light meal for two with a salad. Serve with a spoonful of Frances's Spicy Apple and Onion Chutney (see page 291) as a relish.

300 ml (½ pint) milk
250g (9oz) soft white breadcrumbs
200g (7oz) melted butter
175g (6oz) mature Cheddar cheese, grated
4 eggs, separated
50g (2oz) grated beetroot
50g (2oz) grated carrot
2 tablespoons fresh parsley, finely chopped
Salt and pepper to taste

Serves 2

Preheat oven to 190°C, 375°F, gas mark 5. Butter a 20cm (8in) china soufflé or gratin dish. Pour the milk onto the breadcrumbs in a bowl large enough to take all the ingredients. Stir in the melted butter, grated cheese and egg yolks together with the grated beetroot and carrot. Whisk the egg whites until they are nicely frothy, about 5 minutes, and fold them into the mixture together with the parsley. Season to taste. Pour into the buttered dish and bake for about 20 minutes. Serve immediately.

Pan Haggerty

Is Pan Haggerty a Lancashire or a Northumberland speciality? Both counties lay claim to it. Haggerty comes from the French hacher *– to chop or slice. Traditionally, it is always served in its cooking dish, so if you want to be traditional leave the mixture in the frying pan to brown at the end. Be sure it can take the grill, though.*

450g (1lb) potatoes
225g (8oz) onions
1 tablespoon butter
110g (4oz) Lancashire cheese, grated
Salt and pepper to taste

Serves 2

Slice the potatoes and onions very thinly. You may find this easiest in a food processor. Heat the butter in a large non-stick frying pan and put in the potatoes and onions with the grated cheese in layers, seasoning each layer lightly with salt and pepper. Fry it all gently until cooked. Place in an ovenproof casserole dish and brown under a grill. This makes a delicious supper dish served with a crisp, green salad.

Potted Stilton

This is an excellent way to extend the life of the Christmas Stilton, which may be becoming a little dry in January. It keeps well in the refrigerator for up to 2 weeks.

275g (10oz) Stilton cheese
50g (2oz) softened butter
Pinch of mace
Pinch of cayenne pepper
2 tablespoons port or milk
50g (2oz) clarified butter

Fills 4 small ramekins

Blend the Stilton, softened butter, mace and cayenne together with the port or milk to make a smooth spreadable paste. Pack into small ramekin dishes. Melt the clarified butter very gently and pour over the Stilton to seal the ramekins, taking care to leave behind the milky sediment. Chill until required.

Potted Cheese

Another recipe for frugal housewives. Here the potting with cream and herbs complements the texture and flavour of the cheese. These little pots should be eaten within a couple of days of mixing.

150g (5oz) Stilton cheese
150g (5oz) Cheddar cheese
2 teaspoons mixed herbs
About 150ml (¼ pint) single cream
Chopped parsley, for garnish

Fills 4 small ramekins

Finely grate the Stilton and Cheddar cheeses. Beat in the mixed herbs together with enough single cream to give a smoothish paste – I prefer this with a little texture to it, but a food processor can be used to make a very smooth paste. Pack into four individual pots garnished with parsley. Serve with savoury shortbread, toast or herb scones as a snack or light lunch.

Almondines

Almondines are part of the European tradition of grand cooking. They are included here, partly because English cooking has been influenced by France, and partly because we have such a love affair with the potato and almondines are a wonderful example of the many different ways you can treat mashed potato. Snow Potatoes are boiled potatoes put through a ricer and served just as they are. Mixed with egg yolk, they become Duchesse. Formed into rolls dipped in breadcrumbs and fried, Duchesse potatoes become Croquettes. Roll Croquettes in almonds, and they become Almondines. And we love them all.

900g (2lb) potatoes
25g (1oz) butter
1 egg, beaten
2 teaspoons chopped fresh herbs
Salt and pepper to taste
110–175g (4–6oz) flaked almonds

Makes about 16 Almondines

Preheat oven to 190°C, 375°F, gas mark 5. Peel the potatoes and chop them roughly. Cook them in salted water until tender, drain and mash with the butter. Add the ground almonds, egg, herbs and salt and pepper to taste. Form into small balls, about the size of small plums, and roll in the flaked almonds. Chill for about 30 minutes in the fridge.

Place the almond balls on a lightly greased baking sheet and bake in the preheated oven for 15–20 minutes until they are lightly golden.

Right: Almondines
Next page: Macaroni Cheese

Vegetable and Nut Greate Pye

Alison Sloane invents delicious modern versions of historic recipes. This is a small version of the truly 'great pyes' that were so popular in the Middle Ages and later. They were large enough for practical jokes: when a pie was cut into, birds or frogs might jump out, the origin of the nursery rhyme 'Sing a Song of Sixpence/A pocketful of rye/Four-and-twenty blackbirds baked in a pie.'

225g (8oz) Shortcrust Pastry (see page 54)
¾ white cabbage, shredded, cooked and well drained
225g (8oz) sliced raw mushrooms
50g (2oz) vegetarian suet
75g (3oz) pine nuts or walnut pieces
50g (2oz) ground almonds
75g (3oz) chopped dates
½ teaspoon cinnamon
½ teaspoon nutmeg
75g (3oz) Parmesan cheese, grated
Milk or beaten egg, to glaze

Serves 4

Preheat oven to 180°C, 350°F, gas mark 4. Line a 23cm (9in) flan tin with two-thirds of the pastry. Prick the base and chill while you mix all the other ingredients together for the filling. Roll out the remainder of the pastry. Pile the filling into the tin – it should be fairly full – and cover with the pastry lid. Brush with milk or beaten egg to glaze. Bake for approximately 35–40 minutes or until the pastry is golden. The juices from the raw mushrooms flavour the pie as they cook during baking.

Left and previous page: Vegetable and Nut Greate Pye

Homity Pies

Homity Pies originated in the West Country during World War II, when meat was rationed. They were made popular later by Cranks, one of the first successful all-vegetarian restaurants.

FOR THE PASTRY
175g (6oz) plain wholemeal flour
50g (2oz) plain white flour
Pinch of salt
50g (2oz) butter
50g (2oz) vegetarian lard
2 tablespoons cold water

FOR THE FILLING
350g (12oz) potatoes
450g (1lb) onions
3 tablespoons vegetable oil
25g (1oz) butter
1 tablespoon parsley, chopped
110g (4oz) Cheddar cheese, grated
2 garlic cloves, crushed
1 tablespoon milk
Salt and pepper to taste

Serves 6

Preheat oven to 220°C, 425°F, gas mark 7. First make the pastry. In a large bowl, mix together the flours and salt. Cut the fats into pieces and then, using your fingers, rub the fats until the mixture resembles breadcrumbs. Add the water and gently gather the pastry together into a ball. Knead lightly, then wrap the pastry ball in clingfilm and chill in the fridge for 30 minutes. Roll out the pastry and line six 10cm (4in) individual tins – Yorkshire pudding tins are ideal. Boil or steam the potatoes for the filling until tender. Chop the onions, sauté in the oil until soft but not coloured. Then combine the potatoes and onions, add butter, parsley, half the cheese, garlic, milk and salt and pepper to taste. Cool, then use to fill the cases. Sprinkle with the remaining cheese and bake in the oven for 20 minutes, until golden.

Macaroni Cheese and Tomato Bake

Britain has always had an affection for maccheroni, *pasta tubes. We even anglicized its name to* macaroni. *At the beginning of the 19th century, our dandies were called 'macaronis' because they wore wigs with white curls that were supposed to resemble macaroni. Macaroni Cheese has long been a supper standby. Combining cheese sauce with basil and tomatoes makes this dish especially appetising.*

225g (8oz) dried macaroni
1 medium onion, chopped
1 tablespoon oil
800g (1¾oz) tinned tomatoes, drained
4 teaspoons tomato purée
Fresh basil
75g (3oz) butter
50g (2oz) plain flour
1 teaspoon mustard powder
425ml (¾ pint) milk
225g (8oz) cheese, grated
Salt and pepper to taste

Serves 4

Preheat oven to 200°C, 400°F, gas mark 6. Boil the macaroni in the usual way according to the instructions on the packet and drain well.

Fry the chopped onion gently in the oil and add the drained tomatoes, tomato purée and plenty of basil. Cook together for a few minutes, breaking the tomatoes with a wooden spoon and adding salt and pepper to taste. Make a cheese sauce: melt the butter in a saucepan, stir in the flour with the mustard and cook for a minute before pouring in the milk. Stirring all the time, bring to the boil and add 175g (6oz) of the grated cheese.

Stir the tomatoes into the cooked macaroni and spoon either into individual baking dishes or one large dish. Cover each dish or the large dish with the cheese sauce and sprinkle the remaining grated cheese on top. Bake in the oven for 20 minutes or until golden brown.

Leek and Potato Hot Pot

This Leek and Potato Hot Pot comes from Lancashire. It's a Fatherless Pie. Vegetarian hotpots were made when the earner of the family was out of work and money was short. The Lancashire plain was full of market gardens and potato fields, so the leeks and potatoes were plentiful and good value. A pity this excellent dish was viewed as second best. Now we can appreciate it in its own right.

450g (1lb) leeks
1 tablespoon sunflower oil
50g (2oz) butter
25g (1oz) plain flour
150ml (¼ pint) milk
1 teaspoon mustard powder
175g (6oz) Cheddar cheese, grated
450g (1lb) new potatoes, cooked
Finely chopped parsley, to serve

Serves 4

Preheat oven to 160°C, 325°F, gas mark 3. Trim, slice and wash the leeks in a colander. Sauté gently in the sunflower oil until soft but not mushy. Make a cheese sauce: melt the butter, and stir in and cook the flour for a couple of minutes. Gradually add the milk, stirring all the time, until the mixture comes to the boil and a thick sauce is made. Add the mustard and cheese and heat gently until melted into the sauce. Arrange half the potatoes in the bottom of each dish, then the leeks, then cover with the cheese sauce. Arrange the balance of the potatoes on top, brush with a little extra oil and bake uncovered in the oven for 20 minutes. Serve with a scattering of chopped parsley.

Vegetable Cobbler

Inventive and tasty, this dish has a particular flavour thanks to the addition of fennel.

3 medium carrots, peeled and sliced
¼ small cauliflower, separated into florets
75g (3oz) butter
8 small leeks, thickly sliced
2 small heads of fennel, sliced
25g (1oz) wholewheat flour
425ml (¾ pint) vegetable stock
2 tablespoons fresh parsley

FOR THE TOPPING
25g (8oz) self-raising flour
1 teaspoon mixed herbs
1 teaspoon mustard powder
2 tablespoons fresh chopped parsley
50g (2oz) vegetarian lard
1 egg
Milk to mix
75g (3oz) cheese, grated
Salt and pepper to taste

Serves 4

Preheat oven to 180°C, 350°F, gas mark 4. Cook the carrots and cauliflower for 5 minutes in boiling, salted water and then drain. Place in a casserole. Melt half the butter and fry the leeks and fennel over a moderate heat for 3–4 minutes. Add to casserole. Melt the rest of the butter in a small pan, add the wholewheat flour and cook gently for a few minutes. Gradually add the vegetable stock and season if necessary. Simmer for a minute or two, add the parsley and pour over the vegetables. Cover the casserole and bake for 30 minutes. To make the topping, sieve the flour with the mixed herbs, mustard powder and salt and pepper. Rub in the lard until the mixture resembles coarse breadcrumbs. Mix the egg with a little milk and combine to make a springy dough. Roll out to about 2cm (¾in) thick and cut into round scones with a biscuit cutter. Arrange scones on top of the vegetables round the edge of the casserole and sprinkle with the grated cheese. Increase the oven heat to 230°C, 450°F, gas mark 8 and bake the casserole for a further 15 minutes. Serve at once.

Cauliflower Cheese

The secret of this recipe for a well-loved old favourite is the amount of cheese. There is a lot of protein in this dish. Eat this as a main course not as a vegetable accompaniment to meat. The contrast of the rich sauce to the chunks of slightly crisp cauliflower is perfect.

1 cauliflower
1 level tablespoon cornflour
300ml (½pint) milk
40g (1½oz) butter
450g (1lb) mature Cheddar cheese, grated
Sprinkling of cayenne pepper
Salt and pepper

Serves 3-4

Preheat oven to 210°C, 425°F, gas mark 7. Boil or steam the cauliflower until just tender. Drain, cut into large chunks and put in an ovenproof dish. It also looks good made in individual ovenproof dishes if you have them. In a non-stick pan cream the cornflour with a little cold milk, pour in the balance of the milk and add the butter. Bring to the boil stirring continuously until the sauce has thickened. Add two-thirds of the cheese, season to taste with salt and pepper and simmer gently for 5 minutes, or until the cheese has melted. Pour over the cauliflower, sprinkle the top with the remainder of the cheese and dust with cayenne pepper. Cook in the oven, uncovered, until the top is golden brown – approximately 15 minutes.

Leek and Cheese Bread and Butter Pudding

Bread puddings, savoury and sweet, are part of our heritage. This recipe from Northumberland uses the superlative local ingredients to good effect.

2 tablespoons vegetable oil
4 medium leeks, trimmed, washed and finely sliced
8 slices herb-flavoured bread, sliced and buttered (if unavailable add
   1 teaspoon dried mixed herbs to the leeks when sautéing)
6 eggs, well beaten
600ml (1 pint) milk
300ml (½ pint) double cream
1 tablespoon finely chopped fresh chives (use chive flowers when in season)
225g (8oz) Northumberland cheese, grated
Salt and pepper to taste

Serves 6

Preheat oven to 180°C, 350°F, gas mark 4. Butter a large ovenproof dish. Heat the oil and gently sauté the leeks until soft. Lay the bread in the dish interspersed with the softened leeks. Whisk together the eggs, milk and cream, stir the chives and grated cheese into the mixture and season to taste. Bake for approximately 50 minutes until golden and set but still wobbly in the middle. Serve at once with a green salad.

Parsley and Lemon Stuffing

This recipe is my own favourite basic stuffing. I like a light stuffing and I prefer to cook it separately from the meat or poultry, either rolled into balls or pressed into a well-buttered china dish or tin and cut into squares or slices to serve. I nearly always add extra ingredients such as herbs, nuts or fruits to this stuffing and I have listed some variations to the basic method. This recipe is also the basis for the Sage and Onion Stuffing recipe on page 74.

50g (2oz) butter
1 small onion, peeled and finely chopped
2 celery sticks, chopped
Zest and juice of 1 unwaxed lemon
150g (6oz) fresh white breadcrumbs
Large handful of fresh parsley, chopped
1 large egg, well beaten

Serves 4

Preheat oven to 180°C, 350°F, gas mark 5. Melt the butter in a medium-sized pan. Fry the chopped onion and celery for about 5 minutes or until slightly softened but not coloured. Take the pan off the heat and stir in the lemon zest and juice, breadcrumbs and parsley. Mix well, season with salt and pepper to taste and bind together with the beaten egg. Either press the mixture into a buttered ovenproof dish or make it into patties the size of a golf ball. Put these on a baking tray lined with baking parchment.

Bake for 30 minutes. The top of the mixture or the patties should be golden brown.

VARIATIONS
Tarragon and Apple Stuffing: Add a large handful of chopped French tarragon and a finely chopped crisp apple to the mixture at the same time as the breadcrumbs.
Almond and Oregano Stuffing for Turkey: When making stock from turkey giblets, keep back the liver and use it for this stuffing. Chop the liver and fry it with 25g (1oz) of flaked almonds and the chopped onion and celery. Add 1 tablespoon of chopped fresh oregano or marjoram at the same time as the breadcrumbs. You can also add a handful of fresh cranberries at this point.

Welsh Rarebit

There are at least three basic versions of this toasted cheese dish. This is one of the more elaborate ones. I like the use of beer in it: ale and cheese complement each other beautifully.

200g (7oz) strong cheese, Cheddar or a good Cheshire, grated
25g (1oz) butter
1 level teaspoon mustard powder
2 teaspoons plain flour
4 tablespoons beer
Pepper to taste
4 slices of bread, toasted on one side only

Serves 4

Put everything except the bread in a saucepan. Stir well and heat gently until all is melted and well amalgamated. Spread over the untoasted side of the bread and brown under the grill.

Yorkshire Pudding

In Yorkshire, pudding was always served at the beginning of the meal – with gravy – to take the edge off the appetite and enable the cook to serve smaller helpings of expensive meat. It may be called Yorkshire, but batter puddings (or 'pudden') were eaten everywhere. Nor is gravy the only accompaniment. Sugar, vinegar, jam, golden syrup and mustard were all eaten with pudding. It was sold on street stalls in London during the 19th century (with gravy). Northerners often accuse Southerners of not being able to make a good Yorkshire pudding. This may simply be a difference in taste. Northerners like their puddings very crisp, while Southerners prefer a slightly softer pudding. Two essentials when making it: you must let the batter stand before using and the fat in the pan must be smoking hot.

2 eggs, well beaten
175g (6oz) plain flour
Water to mix
300ml (½ pint) milk
Salt and pepper to taste
Approximately 25g (1oz) hard vegetable fat

Serves 4–6

In a mixing bowl, stir the eggs into the flour and add sufficient water to make a smooth paste. Beat in the milk until the consistency of the mix is similar to unwhipped double cream. Leave to stand for 30 minutes.

Preheat oven to 220°C, 450°F, gas mark 7. You can use either a 20 x 16cm (8 x 6in) oblong tin, or individual pudding tins. Put a knob of fat in the tin or tins and heat in the oven until the fat smokes. Divide the mixture among the tins and bake for 15 minutes, until risen and golden brown. If cooking one large pudding this will probably require an extra 5 minutes.

Essentials for a good Yorkshire Pudding are very hot fat, not too much of it and a good hot oven.

Hot Puddings

Queen of Puddings, Sussex Pond Pudding, Chocolate Fudge Pudding, College Pudding, Christmas Pudding, Treacle Tart – even the names conjure up pictures of sweet indulgence. With your hunger already assuaged by the previous courses, the only real justification for eating pudding is pleasure. And a memorable pleasure too: the chances are that any childhood memory of a delicious meal is going to feature pudding. Steamed puddings, both savoury and sweet, are a British speciality – one that amazed sophisticated 17th-century European visitors. Monsieur Misson de Valberg's ecstatic comments on puddings, in 1690, must be the most-quoted culinary comment on this particularly British food: 'Blessed be he that invented pudding! For it is manna that hits the palates of all sortes of people, better even than that of the wilderness. Ah! What an excellent thing is an English Pudding! To come in pudding-time is as much as to say to come in the most lucky moment in the world.'

The *Oxford Companion to Food* agrees that 'Pudding may be claimed as a British invention', but how did it all start? Certainly the British were already enjoying milk puddings such as syllabubs, possets, flummeries and fools by the reign of Elizabeth I. And they were already baking tarts, pies and puddings – both sweet and savoury – in bread ovens, in large houses and cookshops. But that British speciality, the steamed pudding (actually a descendant of savoury faggots, haggis and sausages) came into its own at the beginning of the 17th century, with the invention of the pudding cloth. A 1617 recipe for sweet Suet Pudding, also called College Pudding, proclaims: 'Let your liquor boil and throw your pudding in, being tied in a fair cloth; when it is boiled enough, cut it in the midst, and so serve it.'

There are seven steamed puddings in this chapter, including a modern version of College Pudding, and a recipe for Christmas Pudding that I have been making for Christmas since I was given it eleven years ago. Cooks have been known to compete to make the best version of a particular recipe. Sussex Pond Pudding is a steamed suet crust enclosing butter, sugar and a whole lemon. Cut into it and it releases a delicious rich lemon syrup. But add currants and it becomes Kentish Well Pudding, a slightly different variation.

I did not ask my donors where their recipes came from, but I am willing to bet that more than a few had the same sort of history as Gerty's Treacle Pudding. When I was compiling this book, my eldest daughter said 'you must put in the treacle pudding that Granny used to cook'. My mother had cooked it for me as a child, too, and I had often watched her make it – a suet roly-poly pudding, spread with golden syrup and then baked in milk in the oven. We ate it with clotted cream on Sundays, as a final treat at the end of roast lunch, and it remains a culinary high spot in my memory. My mother told me that she was given the recipe by Gerty, her parents' cook, back in the 1920s in Norfolk. To my knowledge, the recipe had never been written down, but I found the almost identical Hollygog Pudding in *Traditional Puddings*, a collection of British recipes by Sara Paston-Williams. Many of the recipes in this and the next chapter come from this invaluable book. The author has not only researched the recipes, she has gone further and tracked down the village or county where these puddings were first tasted. Hollygog Pudding was written down in Oxfordshire, so I wonder how it managed to reach Norfolk? As far as I know, Gerty had never travelled out of the county.

Fritters, or Fritours, are some of the earliest puddings, pre-dating the invention of the pudding cloth, and fried directly over an open fire. They have been found in menus from medieval banquets. The recipe here is for Apple Fritters, but parsnip and carrot fritters were also popular. Pancakes date from the same time. Today we prefer them wafer-thin, but they were originally a thick round of fried batter flavoured with herbs and spices. Since they were made with eggs and milk, and fried in butter, they could not be eaten during Lent, the forty-day fast before Easter when meat and dairy products were forbidden. Today, some people still make pancakes on Shrove Tuesday, the day before Lent, but they do so because they are delicious, and fun to make, rather than to use up the 'illegal' ingredients. Some recipes seem very old, but are actually quite recent: I wonder who, accidentally or on purpose, first tipped sweet pastry ingredients – mixed but not yet kneaded – on top of fruit, then baked the result and found it good? It seems extraordinary that Fruit Crumble may only have been around for sixty years or so.

Sugar, milk or cream and eggs are the ingredients necessary for a true custard. Forget using ready-made custard powder – it doesn't take long to make the real thing, and is well worthwhile (and the recipe is at the end of this chapter). The filling for Sweet Egg Pie, popular since Elizabethan times, is a version of custard. Add breadcrumbs and you have the base for the wonderful Queen of Puddings, an 18th-century English recipe that was hijacked by Charles Francatelli, 'maître d'hôtel and chief cook in ordinary' to Queen Victoria, and renamed in her honour. To the French, custard is known as Crème Anglaise, and you can indeed serve it, hot or cold, as an alternative to cream. There are also recipes for Fruit Sauce, and for Brandy Butter (a hard sauce made from spirits, sugar and butter), that essential accompaniment to Christmas Pudding or Mince Pies.

Nobody could dispute the fact that the British make a great variety of very good puddings. Indeed there are so many puddings that there are two separate chapters in this book, for hot and cold versions. But these hot puddings, and their sauces, are certainly hard to beat.

Abbot's Fruit Pudding

Abbot's Fruit Pudding is named after the Abbot of the Cistercian monastery at Buckland Abbey in the far west of Devon. It was given to Sally Whitfield, the Head Gardener there, by an old lady who was already 90, and it had been handed down to her. Sally gave it to me. So many pudding recipes are handed down by word of mouth.

25g (1oz) sago
150ml (¼ pint) milk
225g (8oz) breadcrumbs
225g (8oz) mixed fruit
175g (6oz) dark brown sugar
1 teaspoon bicarbonate of soda
1 teaspoon mixed spice

Serves 4–6

Soak the sago overnight in the milk. Butter a 1.25 litre (2 pint) pudding basin. In a bowl large enough to take all the ingredients, dissolve the bicarbonate of soda in a little extra milk, add all the rest of the ingredients, mix well and put in the pudding basin. Cover with a layer of greaseproof paper and foil and steam for 2 hours. Serve with an Egg Custard Sauce (see page 188).

Fruit Crumble

Whenever I cook this recipe for guests from abroad, they are very enthusiastic and very surprised when told how simple the recipe is. Fruit Crumble is an essentially British dish. Its history probably does not go back further than sixty years, according to the Oxford Companion to Food, *but it is well established now in the British canon of puddings.*

700g (1½lb) of fruit – apples, plums and rhubarb are all good choices. You can also use a mixture of fruit; blackberries and apples is a particular favourite.
Sugar to taste

FOR THE CRUMBLE TOPPING
110g (4oz) plain flour
1 teaspoon mixed spice
110g (4oz) butter
110g (4oz) brown sugar
50g (2oz) chopped walnuts or almonds

Serves 6

Preheat oven to 200°C, 400°F, gas mark 6. Layer the fruit in an ovenproof dish with sugar (the amount depending on the sharpness of the fruit).

Sieve the flour with the spice. Rub the butter into the flour with your fingers until the mixture is the texture of fine breadcrumbs. (You can also do this in a food processor.) Mix in the sugar and the nuts and sprinkle in a thick even layer over the fruit. Bake in the oven for 30–40 minutes. Serve hot with pouring cream or yoghurt.

Right: Fruit Crumble
Next page: Almond, Orange and Lemon Tart

Steamed Ginger Sponge Pudding with Ginger Sauce

By the 18th century, every region had its own recipe for gingerbread. This one is from Cornwall.

FOR THE PUDDING
110g (4oz) butter
110g (4oz) caster sugar
2 eggs
175g (6oz) self-raising flour
50g (2oz) stem ginger, finely chopped
3 tablespoons golden syrup

FOR THE GINGER SAUCE
300ml (½ pint) full cream milk
1 tablespoon fresh ginger, grated
25g (1oz) butter
25g (1oz) plain flour
50g (2oz) caster sugar

Serves 4

Butter an 850ml (1½ pint) pudding basin. Cream together the butter and sugar until pale and fluffy. Beat in the eggs, adding one spoonful of flour with each egg. Fold in the remaining flour and the chopped ginger. Spoon the syrup into the bottom of the pudding basin, then the pudding mixture on top. Smooth the top. Cover with a layer of greaseproof paper and foil and steam for 1–1½ hours.

While the pudding is steaming, make the sauce. Bring the milk to the boil with the ginger. Let the mixture stand for at least 30 minutes to infuse, then strain off the milk. Melt the butter slowly and stir in the flour, cook gently for 2–3 minutes, add the milk gradually, stirring all the time. Bring the sauce to the boil and simmer for at least 5 minutes, stirring constantly. Add the sugar and stir until dissolved.

Turn the pudding out and serve the sauce separately. Serve both warm – there is no need to burn tongues, the gentle spiciness will add its own heat.

Left: Steamed Ginger Pudding with Ginger Sauce   Previous page: Custard Tart or Sweet Egg Pie

Baked Jam Roll

This pudding is also known as Jam Roly Poly. It used to be boiled, in a cloth or even the sleeve of a shirt, but nowadays it is generally baked. Baking gives the pudding a crisp, golden-brown crust – a good contrast to the hot, sweet, jammy interior.

225g (8oz) self-raising flour
Pinch of salt
110g (4oz) shredded suet
About 7 tablespoons cold water
450g (1lb) pot of jam (strawberry, apricot, blackcurrant, etc)

Serves 4

Preheat oven to 190°C, 375°F, gas mark 5. Grease a 450g (1lb) loaf tin or line it with baking paper. Sift the flour and salt in a bowl, then sprinkle in the suet and mix lightly with your hands to distribute evenly. Add enough cold water to give a light, elastic dough and knead gently until smooth and the mixture leaves the sides of the bowl clean. Roll out into an oblong about 12mm (½in) thick. Spread evenly with jam and roll up. Trim the edges, use any pastry trimmings to decorate the top, and place in the greased loaf tin. Brush the top with beaten egg and milk and bake for approximately 30 minutes until a pale golden brown. Serve hot with Egg Custard Sauce (see page 188).

Custard Tart or Sweet Egg Pie

Also known as Transparent Pudding, this pie has been popular since Elizabethan days when the filling was made with vegetables or fruit, eggs, thick cream and lots of spices. Originally the pastry case was literally to provide a 'coffyn', or container, in which to cook the custard.

FOR THE PASTRY
175g (6oz) plain flour
75g (3oz) unsalted butter
50g (2oz) caster sugar
1 egg yolk
1–2 tablespoons ice-cold water

FOR THE FILLING
3 eggs
1 level teaspoon cornflour
425ml (¾ pint) single cream or milk
1 vanilla pod, pierced
Grated nutmeg or ground cinnamon for sprinkling

Serves 4–6

Preheat oven to 190°C, 375°F, gas mark 5. Sieve flour into a mixing bowl. Rub the butter into the flour using fingertips. Stir in 10g (½oz) of the sugar. Beat the egg yolk with cold water and add to the flour and butter mixture. Collect into a dough, knead very lightly and set aside in a cool place to chill for 30 minutes. Then roll out on a lightly floured board and line a 20cm (8in) deep flan tin. Chill again. Bake blind for 15–20 minutes until the pastry is almost cooked. Remove from the oven, empty, and leave to cool while you make the filling. Lower oven to 150°C, 300°F, gas mark 2.

Beat eggs and mix in cornflour and remaining sugar. Beat until sugar granules have dissolved. Heat the cream or milk with the pierced vanilla pod until it reaches boiling point. Pour onto the egg mixture, whisking continuously. Remove the vanilla pod. Strain through a sieve into the flan case and sprinkle with grated nutmeg or ground cinnamon. Bake in the centre of the oven for about 45 minutes or until the custard is set (test with a fine skewer, which should come out clean). Remove from the oven when set and leave to cool a little before removing from the flan tin. Serve warm or cold, decorated with a few fresh flowers.

Exmoor In and Out

This Devon recipe is essentially a spiced apple pudding with an almond sponge topping.

900g (2lb) cooking apples (preferably Bramleys)
50g (2oz) demerara sugar mixed with 1 teaspoon cinnamon
4 tablespoons apple juice mixed with a few drops of almond essence

FOR THE TOPPING
110g (4oz) butter
110g (4oz) demerara sugar
2 eggs
110g (4oz) self-raising flour
50g (2oz) ground almonds
A handful of flaked almonds

Serves 6

Preheat oven to 180°C, 350°F, gas mark 4. Peel and slice the apples into an ovenproof dish and drizzle the sugar, cinnamon and apple juice over the apples. Cover with a damp cloth while mixing the topping. Beat the butter and demerara sugar together until light and beat in the eggs gradually (this can be done in a food processor). Then fold in the flour and ground almonds. Spread on the apples and scatter over the handful of flaked almonds. Bake until golden brown – about 40 minutes.

Gingerbread Pudding

Gingerbreads, popular over many centuries, always spiced with ginger and sometimes containing chunks of preserved ginger, vary enormously throughout Britain. Many towns had their own specialities. Ashbourne in Derbyshire has a 'white' gingerbread, Ormskirk a 'dark' one. Grasmere gingerbread is like a shortbread. This gingerbread recipe comes from Warwickshire, so presumably it is local to that county.

110g (4oz) butter
75g (3oz) sugar
225g (8oz) golden syrup
1 tablespoon orange marmalade
1 large egg
150ml (¼ pint) milk
225g (8oz) self-raising flour
1 teaspoon ground ginger
1 teaspoon ground cinnamon
1 teaspoon bicarbonate of soda

Serves 6

Preheat oven to 160°C, 325°F, gas mark 3. Grease a 20cm (8in) square tin. Put the butter, sugar, golden syrup and marmalade into a saucepan and heat until the sugar has dissolved. Leave to cool. Beat the egg with the milk and add to the syrup mixture. Sift the flour with the ginger, cinnamon and bicarbonate of soda, pour into the mixture and beat until smooth. Turn into the prepared tin and bake for 45 minutes, or until firm. Serve hot with cream.

Apple Pie

Everyone has their favourite apple pie. I like the sharpness of the filling here, the use of the citrus fruits and the spice. It tastes delicious.

350g (12oz) shortcrust pastry (see page 54)
700g (1½lb) Bramley apples, peeled and thinly sliced
25g (1oz) soft brown sugar (use more if you like a sweeter filling)
Grated zest and juice of half an orange and half a lemon
¼ teaspoon ground cloves
½ teaspoon ground cinnamon
Milk to glaze
Caster sugar for decoration

Serves 4–6

Preheat oven to 200°C, 400°F, gas mark 6. Roll out a little more than half the pastry and line a 23cm (9in) enamel pie plate, pressing it gently and firmly all round. Cover the pastry shell with the sliced apples, sprinkling in the brown sugar, zests, ground cloves and cinnamon between the layers. Pour over the juices when finished. Roll out the other half of the pastry to form a lid. Dampen the bottom layer of pastry round the edge with milk, then fix the lid in position, pressing it very firmly all round. Cut slits in the top crust to release steam. Brush with milk and sprinkle with a little sugar before baking for 40 minutes. Serve warm with cream or yoghurt.

Dolbury Pudding

This steamed pudding recipe comes from the restaurant at Killerton, a delightful house set in the rich green countryside of East Devon. The person who named it thought the pudding shape reminded them of Dolbury Hill, which rises behind the house.

110g (4oz) butter
25g (1oz) lard
150g (5oz) soft brown sugar
3 eggs, beaten
200g (7oz) chopped apples
200g (7oz) mincemeat
225g (8oz) self-raising flour
A little milk if necessary

Serves 4–6

Grease a 1.2–1.5 litre (2–2½ pint) pudding basin well and put a round of greased greaseproof paper in the base. Cream together the fat and sugar until pale and fluffy. Add the beaten eggs, a little at a time, and beat well after each addition. Stir in the apples and mincemeat and gently fold in the flour. If necessary pour in a little milk to give a dropping consistency – the mixture should be moist. Cover the basin loosely with a double layer of greaseproof paper or a piece of foil and secure with string. Place in a pan of boiling water (which should come halfway up the pudding basin) and steam for 2 hours. Serve with any sort of fruit sauce, custard or cream.

Christmas Pudding

Plum Pudding, as this used to be called, has been associated with Christmas only since Prince Albert, Queen Victoria's husband, introduced it. The making and the eating of Christmas pudding has become thick with tradition. It should be made on Stir-Up Sunday, the Sunday before Advent, and all the family should give it a stir and make a wish. Silver coins – these used to be silver threepenny pieces – are cooked with the pudding, as are charms. The various charms have significance. A ring means marriage; a horseshoe is good luck.

225g (8oz) raisins
175g (6oz) sultanas
175g (6oz) currants
50g (2oz) candied peel
25g (1oz) flaked almonds
25g (1oz) flour
1 teaspoon mixed spice
1 teaspoon cinnamon
½ teaspoon nutmeg
110g (4oz) caster sugar
110g (4oz) fresh white breadcrumbs
Grated zest and juice of 1 lemon
25g (1oz) butter
2 eggs
150ml (¼ pint) orange juice

Makes 2 puddings serving 6 or 1 large pudding serving 12

In a large bowl mix together the raisins, sultanas, currants, candied peel and almonds. Sieve the flour with the mixed spice, cinnamon and nutmeg. Add to the fruit, together with the sugar and breadcrumbs, grated zest and juice of the lemon, and the diced butter. Mix thoroughly. Beat the eggs well with the orange juice and stir into the mixture. Leave to stand overnight. The next day, pack the mixture into pudding basins. There is probably sufficient mixture for one large or two medium-sized basins. Leave at least 2.5cm (1in) at the top for expansion. Cover with greaseproof paper and foil and tuck it down round the rim. Stand the basins on top of upturned saucers in a pan. Fill the pan with water to halfway up the basins and simmer for at least 3 hours.

The puddings will then keep for as many months as you want. They taste just as good even a year later. On Christmas Day, re-cover with fresh paper and foil and steam for an hour before serving.

Baked Almond Pudding

Sweet almonds arrived here with the Romans. The nuts have been great favourites in British cooking every since. Marchpane, which was used in medieval banquets to sculpt wonderful table decorations known as 'subtleties', is made from ground almonds and sugar. Macaroons, large almond biscuits that are crispy and sticky at the same time, are also traditional (see page 268).

25g (1oz) butter
300ml (½ pint) single cream
300ml (½ pint) milk
Grated zest of 1 lemon
1 piece of cinnamon stick
1 blade mace or 1 pinch of powdered mace
75g (3oz) caster sugar
175g (6oz) fresh white breadcrumbs
110g (4oz) ground almonds
110g (4oz) almond biscuits, broken into small pieces (use Amaretti or
    something similar with a good flavour)
4 eggs
¼ teaspoon grated nutmeg
Pinch of salt

Serves 6

Preheat oven to 190°C, 375°, gas mark 5. Butter a 23cm (9in) gratin dish. Bring the cream and milk to the boil, reduce the heat and add the lemon zest, cinnamon stick, mace and sugar. Stir well and simmer for 10 minutes. Mix the breadcrumbs, ground almonds and almond biscuits in a large bowl and pour in the milk and cream mixture through a sieve. Mix thoroughly and allow to cool to lukewarm. Beat the eggs until foamy, add nutmeg and salt and stir into the almond mixture. Pour into the gratin dish and bake for approximately 45 minutes until firm. Serve warm from the oven.

Almond, Orange and Lemon Tart

This has a subtle, unusual flavour. It is an adaptation of an old recipe from the Common Place Book *kept by Mrs Margaretta Ackworth, who lived with her husband Abraham in London during the 18th century. Her book records all kinds of 'receipts', not only for eating, but also cleaning and simple remedies. This tart is an unusual mixture for today's cooking, but do try it – it looks beautiful and tastes delicious.*

175g (6oz) shortcrust pastry (see page 54)
450ml (¾ pint) whipping cream
Lemon slice
75g (3oz) caster or granulated sugar
75g (3oz) ground almonds
¼ teaspoon almond essence
¼ teaspoon orange-flower water
1 tablespoon candied peel
3 large egg whites
2 small unwaxed lemons
2 small unwaxed oranges

Serves 6

Preheat oven to 160°C, 325°F, gas mark 3. Roll out and line a 25cm (10in) deep flan dish with the shortcrust pastry. Bring the cream up to the boil with a slice of lemon zest. Take off the heat and allow to cool. In a bowl large enough to hold all the ingredients, mix the sugar, ground almonds, flavourings and candied peel. Whisk the egg whites until stiff and gently fold into the cooled cream, then fold the egg whites and cream into the rest of the ingredients. Pour into the pastry case. Slice the oranges and lemons thinly and cover the whole of the top of the flan with the slices. Scatter the top with a little extra sugar and bake for 1–1¼ hours or until just set. Serve warm or cold.

Apple Hat

Sara Paston-Williams wrote this recipe, a sweet version of Steak and Kidney Pudding. She lives in Cornwall, where clotted cream is good and available. This also tastes very good without it though.

225g (8oz) self-raising flour
pinch of salt
110g (4oz) shredded suet
6–8 tablespoons cold water
700g (1½lb) cooking apples, peeled, cored and sliced
50g (2oz) raisins or sultanas
75g (3oz) brown or white sugar
3 cloves
Pinch of ground cinnamon
Pinch of ground ginger
Grated zest and juice of ½ lemon or 1 orange
50g (2oz) unsalted butter
1 tablespoon clotted cream (optional)

Serves 6

Butter well a 1.2 litre (2 pint) pudding basin. Sieve the flour with salt into a mixing bowl. Stir in the suet and mix with sufficient cold water to make a soft, light dough. Knead lightly and roll out on a floured board about 6mm (¼in) thick. Use two-thirds of the pastry to line the prepared basin. Fill the lined basin with layers of apples, raisins or sultanas, sugar and spices. Add lemon or orange zest and juice and the butter, cut into small pieces. Cover the basin with the reserved piece of pastry, dampening the edges and pressing together firmly. Cover with a piece of pleated, well-buttered greaseproof paper followed by a piece of buttered foil with a pleat in the centre, at right angles to the greaseproof paper to allow room for the pudding to rise. Tie down securely with string. Steam for 2–2½ hours, topping up with boiling water as necessary. Turn out onto a warmed serving plate and remove a square of the pastry from the top of the pudding. Pop in a tablespoon of clotted cream.

VARIATIONS
Apple and Bramble Hat: Use 450g (1lb) cooking apples and 225g (8oz) blackberries. Omit raisins.
Apple and Marmalade Hat: Replace the grated zest and juice of lemon with 1–2 tablespoons orange or quince marmalade, and omit raisins.
Apple and Golden Syrup Hat: Use 3 tablespoons golden syrup instead of brown sugar.

Apple Cake

Apple cakes are a speciality of the West Country, where orchards cover the rolling hills. Some cakes also contain cider. I chose this example because I like the idea of eating it warm first as a pudding.

175g (6oz) self-raising flour
1 teaspoon mixed spice
225g (8oz) sugar
225g (8oz) butter
700g (1½lb) cooking apples
2 eggs, beaten

Serves 6

Preheat oven to 190°C, 375°F, gas mark 5. Grease a 23 x 23cm (9 x 9in) tin. Sift the flour and mixed spice together and put into a bowl with the sugar. Roughly chop in the butter but do not rub in or cream. Peel the apples and slice into the mixture. Add the beaten eggs and enough milk to make a fairly stiff batter. Bake in the tin for about 1½ hours – until golden brown. This can also be made with pears or plums. It is delicious served hot with thin cream; any left over can be eaten as cake.

Apple Fritters in Ale Batter

'Frutours' or 'fritours' were a great favourite on medieval menus. They usually appeared as part of the last course and were dusted with sugar. Sweet root vegetables such as parsnips, as well as almonds and edible flowers, were also battered and fried. This recipe was researched by Sara Paston-Williams for A Book of Historical Recipes *(National Trust)*.

4 medium cooking or crisp, tart eating apples
1 tablespoon lemon juice
caster sugar

FOR THE BATTER
110g (4oz) plain flour
½ teaspoon ground cinnamon
2 tablespoons sunflower oil
150ml (¼ pint) pale ale, or still, dry cider
2 egg whites
oil for deep-frying
caster sugar and ground cinnamon for sprinkling

Serves 4

Make the fritter batter first so that it has time to rest for at least 30 minutes before using. Sieve the flour and cinnamon together into a bowl. Make a well in the centre and pour the oil into this, followed by the pale ale or cider. Gradually beat the liquids into the dry ingredients, to make a smooth creamy batter. Set aside for 30 minutes.

When ready to cook, heat the oil for deep-frying to 190°C (375°F). Peel, core and slice the apples into 5mm (¼in) thick rings and sprinkle with lemon juice and caster sugar. Whisk the egg whites until stiff and fold them into the batter to make it extra light. Make the fritters in small batches, three or four at a time. Pat the apple slices with kitchen paper to mop up any excess lemon juice, dip them into the batter using a skewer or kitchen tongs, then shake off any excess batter. Lower carefully into the hot fat and fry for about 4 minutes or until golden brown and crisp. Drain well on kitchen paper and keep hot in a single, uncovered layer in a cool oven until all are cooked. Serve piping hot, sprinkled with caster sugar and cinnamon.

Bread and Butter Pudding

This is an everyday version of this old favourite – served hot or warm from the dish. A good sauce to go with it is the Fruit Sauce on page 188.

8 slices of white bread, buttered
2 tablespoons demerara sugar
110g (4oz) sultanas
4 eggs
700ml (1¼ pints) milk
Freshly grated nutmeg

Serves 6

Preheat oven to 180°C, 350°F, gas mark 4. Grease a 1.2–1.5 litre (2–2½ pint) ovenproof dish. Cut the buttered bread slices in half and arrange, buttered side up, in layers in the ovenproof dish, sprinkling the layers with the sugar and sultanas. Finish with a layer of bread and sugar. Whisk the eggs lightly and add to the milk. Pour the whole lot over the bread, sprinkle some freshly grated nutmeg on top and bake for 30–40 minutes until set and lightly brown. Serve warm.

Apricot Bread and Butter Pudding

This is a grander, richer affair. Not only is cream half the liquid in the pudding, but the pudding is turned out and served with its own hot sauce. The apricots add a welcome tang.

175g (6oz) dried apricots
75g (3oz) sultanas
450g (1Ib) medium-sliced white bread, lightly buttered
Grated nutmeg or powdered cinnamon
225ml (8fl oz) milk
225ml (8fl oz) single cream
6oz (175g) caster sugar
Vanilla essence
3 eggs, lightly beaten
1-2 teaspoons lemon juice

Serves 6

Preheat oven to 180°C, 350°F, gas mark 4. Soak the apricots in 600ml (1 pint) water overnight. Generously grease a 1.5 litre (2½ pint) soufflé dish. Soak the sultanas in hot water for 10 minutes, drain and mix with 50g (2oz) apricots. (Retain the rest of the apricots and their liquid to use for the apricot sauce.) Remove the crusts from the buttered bread and cut into triangles. With the buttered side up, line the sides of the soufflé dish and place the rest in the soufflé dish, layered up with the sultanas and apricots and a sprinkling of nutmeg or cinnamon. In a saucepan heat together the milk, cream and caster sugar to boiling point. Take off the heat and add a few drops of vanilla essence and stir in the well-beaten egg yolks. Pour the custard over the bread mixture and wait a few minutes for it all to be absorbed. Cover the dish with foil and bake in a bain-marie for 50 minutes or until the pudding is set and firm. Remove from the oven and allow to cool a little so that it can firm up slightly before turning out onto a serving dish.

To make the sauce, put the remaining apricots and the soaking liquid into a saucepan and simmer for around 15 minutes. Add the balance of the sugar and lemon juice and stir until dissolved. Blend in a liquidiser or food processor and serve separately in a jug.

Chocolate Fudge Pudding

The first chocolate in the form of a drink reached Britain soon after the restoration of Charles II to the throne in the 1660s. However, there are few recipes using chocolate until the 20th century. Even Mrs Beeton has just one steamed pudding and a soufflé. We have made up for it since then. This is a magical recipe where the sauce is poured over the sponge mixture, the pudding is baked and – to my endless astonishment – the sauce is underneath and the sponge is on top.

FOR THE PUDDING
110g (4oz) butter
110g (4oz) caster sugar
2 eggs
175g (6oz) self-raising flour
2 level tablespoons cocoa
A little milk if necessary

FOR THE CHOCOLATE BASE
300ml (½ pint) water
75g (3oz) brown sugar
3 level tablespoons cocoa

Serves 4

Preheat oven to 180°C, 350°F, gas mark 4. Butter an ovenproof dish, approximately 10cm (4in) deep and 20 x 23cm (8 x 9in) in diameter. Cream the butter and sugar until pale and fluffy. Beat in the eggs, adding one spoon of the flour with each egg. Fold in the remaining flour and cocoa, sifted together. If the mixture seems too stiff, fold in a little milk until it is a suitable mixture to spread in the dish.

Gently heat the water, brown sugar and cocoa in a saucepan until the sugar is dissolved and the mixture resembles a thinnish sauce. Pour the sauce over the pudding mixture and bake for 45–60 minutes, until the top is crisp and brown.

Serve warm. The pudding will have risen through the sauce, combining a rich, dark, moist base with a crisp top. For total indulgence serve with extra pouring cream.

Right: Chocolate Fudge Pudding

Pears in Red Wine Syrup

Pears were very popular in the Middle Ages. The pear most available then was called a Warden. Wardens were large, hard and responded well to poaching. I prefer to use small pears, which are easier to poach, and allow two per serving. Sara Paston-Williams developed this from a recipe dated around 1430.

About 450ml (16fl oz) dry red wine
110g (4oz) caster sugar
¼ teaspoon ground cinnamon
Pinch of ground ginger
12 small pears, ripe or unripe
Red food colouring (optional)
Small bay leaves to decorate

Serves 6

Put the wine, sugar and spices in an enamel-lined or stainless-steel saucepan just large enough to hold pears standing upright. Heat gently until the sugar has dissolved, then bring to the boil and simmer for 5 minutes.

Meanwhile, peel the pears as thinly as possible, leaving the stalks on. Put the pears into the hot syrup, cover and simmer very gently for 20–30 minutes, or until just tender, basting them occasionally with the syrup. Transfer the pears to a serving dish with a slotted spoon. Taste the syrup and stir in a little more sugar to taste, then boil rapidly without covering until reduced by half and of a coating consistency. Cool a little, then spoon over the pears to give them an attractive reddish gleam. If the colour of the syrup does not seem bright enough, intensify it with 2 or 3 drops of red food colouring. Continue to baste the pears with the syrup until cold, then chill until ready to serve. Decorate with bay leaves stuck into the stalk ends of the pears.

Left: Pears in Red Wine Syrup

Rice Pudding

This unusual rice pudding is made on top of the stove and takes far less time than a baked rice pudding. It is also made with long-grain rice, as used in savoury dishes. Try making it with the best basmati – it will have a delicious flavour.

350g (12oz) long-grain rice
1–1.5 litres (1¾–2½ pints) milk
Knob of butter
110g (4oz) sugar
Pinch of salt
½ teaspoon ground nutmeg
125ml (4fl oz) single or double cream

FOR GARNISH
Jam
Freshly grated nutmeg

Serves 6

Put the rice in a heavy-bottomed pan. Add the milk, butter, sugar, salt and nutmeg, bring to the boil and simmer very gently, stirring frequently, for 30–40 minutes or until the rice is soft. If your stove is rather fierce the rice may tend to stick. Should this happen, change the pan halfway through to a clean one. Just before serving, stir in the cream and pour into individual bowls. Add a swirl of jam and a dusting of nutmeg. A very unusual method, but it works beautifully.

Old English Baked Rice Pudding

For me, the best part of a rice pudding is the golden skin that forms on the top as it cooks slowly, so slowly in the oven. You can't hurry a baked rice pudding; best make the other pudding here if time is short. This recipe is based on one from 1685.

50g (2oz) raisins
2 tablespoons brandy (optional)
50g (2oz) butter
50g (2oz) caster sugar
110g (4oz) pudding or short-grain rice
700ml (1¼ pints) full-cream milk
300ml (½ pint) single cream
1 vanilla pod
Thinly sliced zest of 1 lemon
Freshly grated nutmeg

Serves 6

Preheat oven to 160°C, 325°F, gas mark 3. Soak the raisins in the brandy while you are preparing the pudding. This part of the recipe is optional; you can stir in the raisins straight from the packet if you prefer.

Melt the butter in a pan and dissolve the sugar in it. Add the rice and boil up until the mixture is golden and bubbly. Pour on the milk and cream and heat gently. Split the vanilla pod. Add to the mixture with the lemon zest and stir well until just boiling. Remove from the heat, stir in the raisins (and the brandy, if using) and pour into a shallow earthenware dish. Grate some fresh nutmeg over the top. Bake for 2 hours. By this time, the mixture should be almost set and there will be a golden skin on the top. Serve warm or at room temperature.

Spicy Ground Rice Pudding

This recipe, from Traditional Puddings *by Sarah Paston-Williams, is based on one by Eliza Acton, one of the best known of the 19th-century cookery writers. Eggs are added to make a richer pudding. Pies and puddings were often 'iced' or topped with egg whites as in this recipe.*

40g (1½oz) ground rice or semolina
600ml (1 pint) full-cream milk
Strip of lemon zest
1 vanilla pod
1 bay leaf
Pinch of ground nutmeg
25g (1oz) caster sugar or ½ tablespoon honey
2 eggs, separated
25g (1oz) butter
Grated nutmeg or ground cinnamon for sprinkling
110g (4oz) caster sugar

Serves 4–6

Preheat oven to 180°C, 350°F, gas mark 4. Butter well a 1.2 litre (2 pint) ovenproof dish. Mix ground rice or semolina to a smooth paste with a little of the milk in a basin. Boil the rest of the milk with the lemon zest, vanilla pod, bay leaf and pinch of nutmeg. Pour onto the ground rice or semolina, stirring continuously. Rinse the pan in which the milk was boiled and leave a film of cold water on the bottom. Return the rice and milk and bring slowly to the boil again, stirring all the time, so that it does not burn on the bottom of the pan. Cook gently for 10 minutes. Add the sugar or honey. Beat the egg yolks and beat into the rice. Remove the vanilla pod, bay leaf and lemon zest. Pour into the prepared pie dish. Dot with the butter and sprinkle with nutmeg or cinnamon. Bake in the centre of the oven for about 25 minutes. Whisk the egg whites until stiff and whisk in 50g (2oz) of the caster sugar. Fold in the remaining caster sugar. Pile the sweetened egg whites on top of the pudding and bake for a further 20 minutes until the meringue is crisp and lightly browned. Serve hot with pouring cream and a fruit sauce.

Baked Apples

Baked apples, often cooked in cider or wine, have been a country favourite for centuries. They can be filled with any dried fruit and topped with sugar, honey, jam or marmalade. The secret of a good baked apple is to use a good-quality cooking apple, preferably a Bramley. These apples were first grown in Nottinghamshire by Matthew Bramley, an innkeeper and butcher from Southwell. The Bramley is a late cropper and is large with a shiny green skin. This recipe comes from Sara Paston-Williams's Traditional Puddings.

6 Bramley cooking apples
50g (2oz) chopped dates
50g (2oz) sultanas
50g (2oz) raisins
25g (1oz) chopped almonds or hazelnuts
Grated zest and juice of 1 orange
75g (3oz) soft brown sugar
1 level teaspoon ground mace or mixed spice
40g (1½oz) butter
150ml (¼ pint) sweet sherry or Madeira

Serves 6

Preheat oven to 180°C, 350°F, gas mark 4. Wash and core apples. Score skin around the middle of each apple to prevent it bursting during baking and stand close together in a well-buttered ovenproof dish. Mix the chopped dates, sultanas, raisins and nuts with the orange rind and juice. Pack the centres of the apples with this mixture. Top with a knob of butter. Pour the sherry or Madeira around the apples and bake in the centre of the oven for 45 minutes, basting occasionally. Serve hot or warm with pouring cream.

Queen of Puddings

Queen of Puddings, or Queen's Pudding, is an 18th-century milk, breadcrumb and egg pudding. It was given this particular name by the chef Charles Francatelli at Buckingham Palace during the reign of Queen Victoria. You can make it in a large dish, but I prefer to use small ramekins, so I have given instructions for both.

75g (3oz) fresh white breadcrumbs
600ml (1 pint) full cream milk
175g (6oz) caster sugar
Zest of 1 lemon, grated
3 eggs, separated
3 tablespoons raspberry jam

Serves 6

Preheat oven to 180°C, 350°F, gas mark 4. Butter generously either a 1.2 litre (2 pint) shallow ovenproof dish or 6 ramekins. Sprinkle the breadcrumbs in the bottom of the dish or dishes. Put the milk, butter and lemon zest in a pan and bring slowly to the boil. While it is heating, whisk the egg yolks and 50g (2oz) of the sugar in a bowl until they are pale and thick. Take the milk off the heat, let it cool a little, then whisk in the egg yolks. Strain the custard over the breadcrumbs and leave to soak for 15 minutes. Stand the dish or dishes in a roasting tin and fill with water halfway up the dish or dishes. Bake in the oven until set. This will take about 25 minutes. Allow to cool slightly.

Turn the oven temperature down to 150°C, 300°F, gas mark 2. Warm the jam and spread over the top of the pudding(s). Whisk the egg whites until very stiff, then whisk in the remaining sugar, a little at a time. Pile the meringue mixture on top of the jam. Sprinkle with a little extra caster sugar and bake for a further 15 minutes until the meringue topping is crisp and lightly browned.

Pancakes

Pancakes have been part of our diet since the Middle Ages. Cooked in a pan, no oven required, they could be made in even the simplest household. Pancakes are always eaten on Shrove Tuesday, the day before Lent begins. One particular tradition is the Pancake Race and the oldest of these is held in Olney, Buckinghamshire. Only local housewives can take part, they must make the pancake themselves, they must wear an apron and a scarf or hat, and they must toss the pancake three times before the finish. The prize is a prayer book.

300ml (½ pint) milk
2 eggs
20g (¾oz) caster sugar
Pinch of salt
Grated zest of ½ lemon
110g (4oz) plain flour
20g (¾oz) melted butter
oil for frying
caster sugar for dusting

Serves 4

Place the milk, egg, sugar, salt and grated lemon zest in a liquidiser and switch onto maximum for 10–20 seconds. Sieve the flour and add to the liquidiser. Continue liquidising for a further 15 seconds. Switch off. If any flour remains sticking to the sides of the liquidiser, scrape it into the batter with a plastic spatula. Liquidise for a further 10 seconds, then pour the batter into a bowl. Let it rest for at least 30 minutes – the starch cells will swell and the batter will thicken.

Just before the batter is required, stir the melted butter into it. (Butter adds a richness to the pancake batter.) Pancakes need a fierce heat, so heat an omelette (or crêpe) pan with a little oil until the oil smokes. Do not use butter as the frying agent – it will burn at too low a temperature. Pour off the oil into a dish and keep it for the next pancake. Hold the pan at 45° and add 1 full tablespoon of batter. The batter will quickly run over the bottom of the pan. Swirl the pan around so that the pancake is paper thin. The pancake should be golden brown on the bottom within 30 seconds. Quickly turn the pancake over with a spatula and cook on the other side. Turn out onto a plate and dust with caster sugar. Eat with a squeeze of lemon juice and sugar, syrup or jam.

Bread Pudding

Bread Pudding was and still is made in bakeries to use up yesterday's bread. The difference with a bread pudding made at home is that you can make up your own mix of dried fruit. I think it should always contain some candied peel, but how about crystallised ginger, chopped prunes and dates? Or halved crystallised cherries and dried apricots? Try it and see.

425ml (¾ pint) milk
150ml (¼ pint) cold strong tea
110g (4oz) butter, melted
1 tablespoon mixed spice
3 eggs, well beaten
350g (12oz) mixed dried fruit
450g (1lb) fresh breadcrumbs

Serves 6

Preheat oven to 180°C, 350°F, gas mark 4. Either grease a tin 5cm (2in) deep and 20 x 28cm (8 x 11in) wide or line it with baking paper. Combine the milk, tea, melted butter, mixed spice, beaten eggs and dried fruit and mix well. Mix in the breadcrumbs and leave to soak for at least an hour or overnight if you wish. Spread the mixture into the prepared tin and bake for 1¼ hours. Cool and serve cut into squares.

Sussex Pond Pudding

Sussex and Kent extend their rivalry to puddings – the most famous being Sussex Pond Pudding and Kentish Well Pudding. The former consists of a suet crust enclosing butter, brown sugar and a whole lemon, and in the latter currants are added. Either way, when the pudding is cut open, a rich, sweet syrup – the well or pond – oozes out. This recipe first appeared in Traditional Puddings.

225g (8oz) self-raising flour
Pinch of salt
25g (1oz) caster sugar
110g (4oz) shredded suet, grated
Zest of 1 large lemon
6–8 tablespoons cold water
2–3 cloves
1 large thin-skinned lemon
110g (4oz) unsalted softened butter
110g (4oz) soft dark brown sugar

Serves 6

Sieve the flour and salt together into a mixing bowl. Stir in the sugar. Add the suet and 1 teaspoon grated lemon zest. Add just sufficient water to mix to a soft, but not sticky, dough using a palette knife. Roll out on a lightly floured board. Well butter a 1.2 litre (2 pint) pudding basin and line with the suet crust, reserving about one-third for the lid. Sprinkle the remaining lemon zest into the bottom of the basin. Press the cloves into the lemon (it is essential that your lemon is juicy and thin-skinned to get the full flavour). Prick the lemon all over with a darning or trussing needle. Pat the softened butter around the lemon and roll in the dark brown sugar. Place the coated lemon in the lined basin and pack any remaining butter and sugar around it. The basin should be full. (If the lemon is a bit large you may have to cut the end off.) Dampen the pastry edges and fit the lid. Seal well by pressing the edges together. Cover with buttered kitchen foil, making a pleat across the centre to allow the pudding to rise. Tie down securely with string. Steam for 3–3½ hours or until the suet is cooked and well risen. Allow to rest for a few minutes before turning out onto a warmed serving plate. When cut, the delicious buttery 'pond' flows out.

VARIATION
Kentish Well Pudding: Add 110–175g (4–6oz) currants to the pudding when you put in the lemon. Pack the currants round the lemon.

Gerty's Treacle Pudding

This recipe was passed down to me by my mother. She was given it by her mother's cook, Gerty, who was born, brought up and lived in Fakenham, Norfolk. Until today, no one, as far as I know, has written it down. It was passed on by word of mouth. Sara Paston-Williams, in Traditional Puddings, *says Hollygog Pudding, which is very similar, was first made in Kiddington in Oxfordshire. I would love to know how many times the recipe was passed on before it arrived in Norfolk.*

225g (8oz) self-raising flour
A pinch of salt
2 tablespoons caster sugar
150g (6oz) butter, cut into small pieces
Golden syrup
Milk, for baking and glazing

Serves 4–6

Preheat the oven to 200°C, 400°F, Gas Mark 6. Sift the flour, salt and sugar together and rub the butter into the flour. Mix with a little water to make a stiff dough. Roll out the dough to make a rectangle, roughly 300 x 200cm (12 x 8in). Spread the dough thickly with golden syrup to within 2.5cm/1in of the edge. Brush the edges with milk and roll up to form a sausage. Butter a deep pie or gratin dish and lay the sausage in it, with the join underneath. Brush the top with milk and scatter a little sugar over it. Pour in sufficient milk to come approximately halfway up the pudding. Bake uncovered for 30–45 minutes, until the pudding is golden brown. Serve hot with cream.

College Pudding

Also called Cambridge Pudding, this is reputed to have been the first pudding boiled in a cloth rather than in animal guts or a vegetable container. It was served to students at Cambridge University in 1617. Nowadays, it is easier to cook this pudding in a basin. It should be dark and spicy. This recipe is also from Traditional Puddings.

75g (3oz) self-raising flour
75g (3oz) fresh white or brown breadcrumbs
1 teaspoon mixed spice
75g (3oz) shredded suet
Pinch of salt
75g (3oz) raisins
50g (2oz) currants
25g (1oz) chopped candied peel
50g (2oz) brown sugar
1 egg
6 tablespoons milk

Serves 6

Well butter a 1.25 litre (2 pint) pudding basin. Mix together all the dry ingredients in a bowl. Beat the egg and add to the dry ingredients with enough milk to produce a soft dropping consistency. Spoon into the prepared basin, cover with buttered kitchen foil, making a pleat across the centre to allow the pudding to rise. Tie the foil firmly in place with string, making a handle across the top so that you can lift the pudding easily. Steam for 2–2½ hours, topping up with boiling water when necessary. Remove from the heat and allow to shrink slightly before turning out onto a warmed serving plate. Serve very hot with Egg Custard Sauce (see page 188).

Egg Custard Sauce

Our own sweet sauce, which is known in France as Crème Anglaise. *An essential ingredient of the Trifles on pages 207 and 208, it is also a wonderful accompaniment to a variety of tarts, puddings and pies.*

600ml (1 pint) full cream milk
2 large eggs
1 level tablespoon caster sugar
110g (4oz) cornflour
Drops of vanilla essence

Serves 6–8

Heat the milk in a pan to almost boiling. Whisk the eggs, sugar and cornflour together while the milk is heating. Add a couple of drops of vanilla to the mixture. Then whisk in the hot milk. When it is blended, wash out the pan and return the mixture to the pan. Heat very gently (stirring hard all the time) until the sauce has thickened. Serve hot with puddings or cool for a trifle. The custard will develop a skin as it cools, but this can be whisked smooth when the sauce is needed.

Fruit Sauce

I make this fruit sauce to serve instead of cream with chocolate puddings or cakes, or sliced ripe fruit, such as mangoes or peaches. It is also delicious with ice cream. It is an essential ingredient in Peach Melba, the grand and delicious pudding invented by Georges Escoffier, the great chef at the Savoy Hotel, as a tribute to Dame Nellie Melba, the Australian opera diva.

225g (8oz) raspberries (fresh or frozen)
100g (4oz) fresh strawberries
75g (3oz) caster sugar
Juice of 1 lemon

Makes 300ml (½ pint)

Heat the fruit, sugar and lemon juice gently, stirring continuously until they come to the boil. Remove from the heat, press through a sieve and leave to cool. Refrigerate until you need it.

Brandy Butter

As a small girl I didn't really like Christmas Pudding, but I ate it because I adored Brandy Butter and was allowed to have a teaspoonful with the pudding (but not without), and because I might be lucky enough to find a silver charm or threepenny piece in my portion.

Brandy butter can be made a week ahead of use and will keep for a couple of weeks in the fridge. It must be well sealed as it easily picks up other flavours, which will spoil its delicate taste. It is an essential accompaniment for Christmas Pudding (see page 168). Try a small teaspoon on the top of warm mince pies – absolutely delicious! (There's a recipe for Mince Pies on page 283.)

75g (3oz) unsalted butter, softened
75g (3oz) icing sugar
Grated zest of ½ orange
2–3 tablespoons brandy

**Provides a spoonful for six with the Christmas pudding plus
leftovers for mince pies**

Either put the butter, about half of the sugar and the orange zest in a food processor and process until the mixture is smooth and creamy, or beat half of the sugar and the orange zest into the butter by hand, with a wooden spoon. Stir in the brandy, then beat in the rest of the sugar. The mixture should be soft enough to spoon, but stiff enough to stand up in peaks when you fork it into a bowl for serving.

Cold Puddings

Perfect for warm summer days, the names of these puddings slip off the tongue almost as easily as the puddings themselves go down. Syllabub and Snow, Flummery and Fool, Tart and Trifle, Posset and Blancmange. Many of these delights are direct descendants of the sweets served as the dessert, or 'banqueting course', at great Tudor feasts. As the last part of a feast, the puddings were special, and only the host or hostess's closest, most important guests were invited to eat this course, which used the richest, most expensive ingredients.

Syllabubs would have been one of the delicacies offered on such occasions. Traditionally, a country syllabub was made by milking the cow directly into a punchbowl containing ale or cider that was already sweetened and spiced. The warm milk and alcohol formed honeycomb curds and alcoholic whey, and the syllabub was served in a special 'syllabub pot', that allowed you to drink the whey from the spout, and eat the curds with a spoon. I have included one Syllabub recipe that uses red wine and ale, a very old combination. My other recipe is a complete contrast, made with white wine and flavoured by bruising and steeping lemon-geranium leaves in lemon juice.

Fine Almond Blancmange is a very old recipe – versions of it probably even predate the Tudor banqueting course – while, over the centuries, the recipes for the traditional fools, flummeries, creams, snows and possets have all merged a little. Those I have been given are all light concoctions, made from different fruit purées combined with eggs, sugar and varying amounts of cream.

Tarts have definitely been on the menu quite as long as syllabubs. Tafferty Tart is an apple lattice tart – sadly, I don't know the origin for the delightful name. The recipe for Border Tart was provided by the curator of the Wordsworth House at Cockermouth, in Cumberland – the birthplace of the great poet, and an area with an interesting history. In the 18th century, Whitehaven, the nearest port, had a thriving trade with the West Indies, and imported rum, dried fruits and spices. Local housewives created 'receipts' that used this exotic tropical bounty, and these became traditional Cumberland fare. Border Tart, with its currant and brown sugar filling, is a typical example. The original recipe for Maids of Honour Tarts may have originated in the kitchens of Hampton Court, where these little cakes are said to have been a favourite of King Henry VIII. The 'official' recipe is a closely guarded secret, but here is one of the many unofficial recipes, a Victorian version collected by Laura Mason.

On the colder side, there are three recipes for Ice Cream. We British have always preferred ice cream to water ices, or sorbets, unlike our neighbours the French. A few ice-cream recipes appear as far back as the 18th century, such as Damson Ice Cream. The first recipe for Brown Bread Ice appeared in 1772, while Vanilla Ice Cream is essential for making Peach Melba – so I really couldn't leave it out.

The pudding course has always provided an opportunity for chefs to show off their talents, and then name their creation in honour of a place or famous person. Eton School and Clare College, Cambridge are probably still arguing over who first mixed strawberries, cream and crushed meringues together, and then flavoured them with orange liqueur. Is it Eton Mess or Clare College Mush? Either way, it is scrumptious. Boodles Orange Fool was first eaten by the members of Boodles gentlemen's club, and Peach Melba was the invention of the great French chef, Escoffier, who created it at the Savoy Hotel, in honour of Dame Nellie Melba, the famous Australian opera singer.

Finally, with some trepidation, I have included two trifle recipes. I could not leave it out – after all, in his book on trifles, Alan Davidson calls it 'Britain's supreme contribution to the dessert tables of the world'. But everyone has a favourite recipe that they believe is the 'right' trifle, and they are all different! The contributions here are an 18th-Century Trifle – Sara Paston-Williams has researched and rewritten a trifle recipe from its golden age – and Sherry Trifle, my own recipe. For many years I cooked for parties, and this particular trifle was our recipe of choice: I happen to think it is the best in the world.

Apricot, Honey and Rosemary Mousse

This is a modern recipe using ingredients that were popular in the Middle Ages, even before Henry VIII's gardener brought the first apricot tree to Britain in 1542. Dried 'apricocks' feature in much earlier recipes. Honey was the universal sweetener before sugar, while rosemary, a Mediterranean herb, was brought here by the Romans.

50g (2oz) butter
450g (1lb) semi-dried apricots
Water
75g (3oz) honey
2 fresh rosemary sprigs
1 tablespoon gelatine
300ml (½ pint) double cream

FOR DECORATION
Rosemary sprigs
Chopped apricot

Serves 6

Melt the butter in a pan, add the apricots and turn in the butter. Add water just to cover the fruit, bring to the boil, reduce the heat, simmer until tender, then purée. Heat the honey so it can be measured in a measuring jug, and add to the purée. Add the rosemary and leave in the purée to infuse while it cools.

When the purée is completely cold, remove the rosemary. Melt the gelatine in a little hot water and stir into the purée. Whip the cream and fold into the purée. Pile into glasses and garnish with a tiny sprig of rosemary and a little chopped apricot.

Previous page: Blackcurrant and Rum Posset
Left: Apricot, Honey and Rosemary Mousse

Baked Quinces in Honey

The quince is a relative of the apple and pear. It is usually large, yellow and knobbly. It is also very hard and is nearly always cooked. It has an extraordinary subtle and special flavour, for which it is highly prized. If you are offered quinces, which are seldom in the shops, take them. Not only will they taste delicious, but they also turn a delicate pink when you cook them.

275g (10oz) honey
300ml (½ pint) orange or grapefruit juice
6 quinces, peeled, cored and quartered

Serves 6

Preheat oven to 160°C, 325°F, gas mark 3. Mix the honey into the fruit juice. Lay the quince quarters in a casserole or gratin dish and pour over the liquid. It should well cover them. Put in the oven and bake until the quinces are tender which will take about 2 hours. Check the dish after an hour or so and if they are getting too dry, add a little water and cover the dish with a lid or foil for the rest of cooking time. Allow to cool and serve cold. The grainy texture of the quinces provides a good contrast to the sweet syrup.

Lemon Geranium Syllabub

Syllabubs are in cookery books from the 16th century onwards. They are always confections of cream, lemon and alcohol – wine, ale or cider. What makes this syllabub special is the lemon-geranium leaves, which impart a very unusual flavour. Note: some people can be slightly allergic to geraniums.

8 lemon-geranium leaves
Juice of 1 lemon
6 tablespoons white wine
3 tablespoons caster sugar
300ml (½ pint) thick double cream

FOR DECORATION
Zest of lemon
Fresh lemon-geranium leaves

Serves 6

Bruise the lemon-geranium leaves and infuse them in the lemon juice, white wine and sugar. Chill for at least 30 minutes in the fridge (if the infusion is very cold it will whisk more easily with the cream). Discard the leaves and stir the cream into the infusion. Whisk until thick. This can take some time; it depends on the weather! If it is hot and thundery, whisk gently and gradually to prevent the mixture curdling. When thick, pile into glasses and decorate with lemon zest and lemon-geranium leaves. This is the most delectable flowery syllabub.

Summer Pudding

Quintessentially English, this pudding was known as Hydropathic Pudding in the 19th century, when it was served at health resorts where pastry was forbidden. This recipe is for a large pudding. A tip: don't make the pudding in the basin too liquid; it might collapse when you unmould it. You can always add liquid once it is safely on its dish.

7–8 medium slices of white bread, with the crusts cut off
700g (1½lb) prepared mixed soft fruit (ie blackcurrants and redcurrants,
    stripped from their stems; strawberries; blackberries; raspberries;
    gooseberries, topped and tailed)
300ml (½ pint) water
About 150g (5oz) caster sugar
Thick double cream to decorate

Serves 6

Lightly butter a 900ml (1½ pint) pudding basin. Line the base and sides of the pudding basin with the bread, making sure that there are no gaps between the slices. Reserve two slices for the top. Put the fruit in a pan, cover with water and simmer until the fruit is tender. Gooseberries and blackcurrants need 5 minutes or so; strawberries, blackberries and raspberries just need to be brought up to the boil and then removed from the heat immediately. Lift the fruit into the bowl with a slotted spoon. Add the sugar to the juice and reheat it to make a syrup. The amount of sugar may vary according to the mixture of fruits and your taste. Then pour over the syrup so that it comes just below the top of the bowl. This should leave you with a small amount of extra juice. Cover the top with the reserved bread slices. Put a small plate or saucer over the pudding (one that fits inside the rim of the bowl), place a weight on top and chill overnight.

Unmould by holding a serving dish with a rim (a china quiche dish works well) over the top and turning the pudding over. Use the reserved juice to spoon over and soak any bits of bread that still look white. Serve cut into slices with some thick cream. Best made in season, but try it with frozen fruit for a taste of summer in the winter.

Summer Fruit Moulds

These are essentially individual summer puddings. Mixing the bread and fruit together makes them firmer and easier to turn out.

450g (1lb) prepared fresh soft fruit (ie blackcurrants and redcurrants, stripped from their stems; strawberries; blackberries; raspberries; gooseberries, topped and tailed)
6 thick slices of milk loaf
300ml (½ pint) water
Sugar
2 tablespoons cassis or elderflower cordial

TO DECORATE
Extra fruit
Fresh mint or lemon-balm sprigs

Makes 6 ramekins

First put a piece of baking paper, cut to size, in the base of each ramekin. This will make them easier to turn out.

Try to use at least two varieties of soft fruit. Cut the crusts off the bread and cut the slices into large dice. Put the fruit in a pan, cover with the water and simmer until the fruit is tender. Gooseberries and blackcurrants need 5 minutes or so; strawberries, blackberries and raspberries just need to be brought up to the boil and then removed from the heat immediately. Remove the fruit from the juice with a slotted spoon and add sufficient sugar to the juice to make a syrup. This will vary according to the fruits and taste. Bring the syrup to the boil and simmer for 5 minutes. Allow to cool and add the cassis or elderflower cordial. Mix the fruit and bread together. Put a little syrup in the bottom of each ramekin, then pack in the fruit and bread pressing the mixture down well. Spoon a little syrup over the top of each ramekin. Chill until required.

To serve, run a knife round the inside of each ramekin and unmould onto a dessert plate. Take off the paper and pour over the rest of the juice and decorate with more fresh fruit and fresh mint or lemon-balm sprigs.

Blackcurrant Flummery

The name Flummery originally came from the Welsh llymru, *a dish of oats cooked until they were almost solid, eaten with honey or a sweet sauce. Later it became a jelly or blancmange, sometimes made in elaborate moulds for table centres, such as a flummery in the shape of fish in a pond of jelly. I think this modern recipe is borrowed from its American cousins, where the name means a thickened berry dessert. Warning: recipes containing raw eggs are unsuitable for pregnant women or young children.*

450g (1lb) blackcurrants
300ml (½ pint) double cream
225g (8oz) caster sugar
1 egg white
Whipped cream for decoration

Serves 6

Make a thick sieved purée of the blackcurrants, stewed with a little water. Allow to cool. Whip the cream with the caster sugar. Whisk the egg white separately and fold into the cream. Gently stir the cream mixture into the purée so as to give a marbled effect and serve in individual glasses garnished with a rosette of whipped cream. Chill before serving. This is also excellent made with gooseberries.

Treacle Tart

Treacle Tart is now not made with black treacle (otherwise known as molasses) but with golden syrup. I found different recipes using oats and no breadcrumbs and recipes involving nuts. I have chosen a recipe given to me by the chef in the Regatta Café at the National Maritime Museum in Greenwich. I particularly liked the inclusion of grated apple or pear. Not because it makes the tart any healthier – one of the guilty treasures of Treacle Tart is its sweetness – but because I think it introduces just a hint of a different taste and texture.

350g (12oz) shortcrust pastry
225g (8oz) golden syrup
Zest and juice of 1 lemon
225g (8oz) fresh white breadcrumbs
1 crisp apple or pear, peeled and grated
1 teaspoon mixed spice
1 egg yolk beaten with a little water
Pouring cream, crème fraîche or yoghurt, to serve

Serves 6–8

Preheat oven to 180°C, 350°F, gas mark 4. Roll out the pastry. Grease a 25cm (10in) flan dish and line with the shortcrust pastry, reserving a quarter for the top. Warm the syrup and lemon in a pan. Stir in the breadcrumbs, the grated fruit and the mixed spice, then pour into the uncooked pastry case. Use the last quarter of the pastry to cut into strips to make a lattice on top. Crimp the edge of the tart with a fork, pressing the lattice strips on firmly. Brush the lattice on top with beaten egg yolk and water. Bake for approximately 35 minutes or until set. Serve with pouring cream, crème fraîche or yoghurt.

Elderflower and Gooseberry Fool

The earliest record of a cultivated gooseberry is said to be a fruiterer's bill from the court of King Edward dated 1276. Elderflowers have been used in our cookery since medieval times. The two have a perfect affinity, the one enhancing the taste of the other. The name Fool comes from the French fouler, *to crush. Fools have been made for many centuries, always from stewed fruit because people feared that only cooked fruit was 'safe'. Early recipes were much more elaborate and involve eggs, cream, spices and wine. The simple fruit purée and cream fool that we enjoy today has been a favourite since the 19th century.*

700g (1½lb) fresh gooseberries
175g (6oz) sugar
2 tablespoons elderflower cordial
300ml (½ pint) double or whipping cream
Fresh mint leaves, egg white and caster sugar for decoration (optional)

Serves 6–8

Wash the gooseberries and put them into a pan without any extra water (the juice running out of the gooseberries will provide all the liquid you need). Simmer for approximately 15 minutes, or until cooked and squashy. Add the sugar. Pour into a blender or food processor and purée. Then sieve the purée to remove the pips etc. Allow to cool, then stir in the elderflower wine or cordial. Whip the cream until it is thick but not stiff and fold gently into half the gooseberry purée. Spoon the two mixtures in layers into individual glasses, starting with a layer of the gooseberry and cream mixture, then the rest of the gooseberry purée in another layer and then the remainder of the gooseberry and cream mixture. Chill before serving.

For a special occasion you could decorate the glasses with frosted leaves. Beat a little egg white, paint it on each of the mint leaves and coat with caster sugar. Leave to dry on a paper towel until crisp before decorating.

Old English Syllabub

This recipe harks back to Elizabethan times, when ale was used far more in cooking than it is now. It is a very good idea to chill all the ingredients for at least an hour before making the syllabub.

300ml (½ pint) double cream
100ml (3fl oz) red wine
100ml (3fl oz) light ale
50g (2oz) caster sugar
Tot of whisky (optional)
Grated nutmeg
Boudoir biscuits or small shortcake biscuits, to serve

Serves 6

Whip the cream, wine, ale and sugar until thick. Do not worry if the cream separates – it will taste just as good. Fold in the whisky if used. Pour into serving glasses and put into the fridge to chill for approximately 1 hour. Sprinkle with grated nutmeg and serve with boudoir biscuits or small shortcake biscuits.

Blackcurrant and Rum Posset

The earliest form of posset was milk, lightly curdled by adding wine, ale or lemon or orange juice. Later, possets became more solid. By the 19th century, the posset had become closely related to the fool or syllabub. Rum and blackcurrant work well together – today you can order a rum and blackcurrant cordial at a bar. Warning: recipes containing raw eggs are unsuitable for pregnant women or young children.

225g (8oz) blackcurrants
50g (2oz) caster sugar
2 tablespoons water
2 tablespoons rum
600ml (1 pint) whipping or double cream
3–4 egg whites

Serves 6–8

Place the blackcurrants and sugar in a pan and stew lightly with the water. Sieve the cooked fruit, saving a few whole blackcurrants, and add the rum. Whip the cream and fold into the blackcurrant purée. Whisk the egg whites until stiff and gently fold into the cream and fruit mixture. Spoon into individual glasses and decorate with a few whole blackcurrants. Serve well chilled.

Border Tart

A Cumbrian recipe which uses the dried fruits that came from the Caribbean in the ships that docked in ports on the north-west coast of England. Serve this rich and sweet tart with yoghurt.

225g (8oz) shortcrust pastry (see page 54)
175g (6oz) currants
50g (2oz) walnuts, chopped lightly
50g (2oz) butter
50g (2oz) brown sugar
2 eggs

FOR THE ICING
75g (3oz) icing sugar
Lemon juice

Serves 6

Preheat oven to 200°C, 400°F, gas mark 6. Grease and line a 20cm (8in) flan tin with the pastry. Wash the currants and put in a pan with the walnuts, butter and sugar. Melt, gently, stirring all the time, then turn the mixture into the flan case and spread evenly all over the base. Beat the eggs well and pour over the flan filling. Bake for 25–30 minutes until set, then take the tart out and leave to cool. In the meantime mix the icing sugar with enough lemon juice to make a pouring water icing. Dribble this over the flan filling and leave to set.

Toffee and Apple Crumble Tart

A tart with an apple crumble and toffee sauce filling. Total self-indulgence.

FOR THE PASTRY
225g (8oz) plain flour
4 tablespoons caster sugar
110g (4oz) butter
4 egg yolks

FOR THE FILLING
900g (2lb) cooking apples
50g (2oz) butter
50g (2oz) sugar
75g (3oz) soft brown sugar
150ml (¼ pint) golden syrup
150ml (¼ pint) double cream
2 drops vanilla essence

FOR THE CRUMBLE
75g (3oz) butter
110g (4oz) flour
110g (4oz) porridge oats
75g (3oz) soft brown sugar

Serves 4

Preheat oven to 180°C, 350°F, gas mark 4. First make the pastry as follows. Sift the flour with the sugar, rub in the butter and stir in the egg yolks to bind the dough. Roll out, line a greased 25cm (10in) flan tin and prick the bottom. Chill while you prepare the filling and the crumble. Peel and slice the apples thinly. Arrange on the bottom of the pastry case. Melt the butter and dissolve the sugars and the syrup over a very low heat in a saucepan. Cook very gently, stirring well for 5 minutes. Remove the pan from the heat and stir in the cream and the vanilla. Beat well until the sauce is smooth. Let it cool to lukewarm, then pour it over the apples. To make the crumble, rub the butter into the flour and oats until the mixture is crumbly, stir in the sugar and spread the mixture evenly over the filling. Bake for approximately 30–40 minutes. The top should be golden and crunchy. This is also delicious made with pears.

Fine Almond Blancmange

I can't do better than quote Sara Paston-Williams's short history and recipe from her book Traditional Puddings. *She writes: 'Although its actual name is undoubtedly of French origin, blancmange has been known in Britain for many centuries. It is mentioned in some of the oldest cookery books as 'Blewe Manger' or 'Blank Mange' or 'white food'. Chaucer, in* The Canterbury Tales, *describes it as a mixture of 'minced capon with flour, cream and sugar'. In fact, it was made with any white meat stewed with rice, dried fruits, almonds and spices. Exactly when the meat was omitted is not known, but by Elizabethan times the dish had become a mixture of cream, sugar and rose-water, thickened with egg yolks. The English blancmange of the 18th century was a kind of jelly, stiffened with isinglass or hartshorn and flavoured with almonds and rose-water. By the early 1820s, arrowroot was being exported to Britain from the West Indies and became the thickening agent. Boiling milk, sweetened and seasoned with cinnamon, mace and lemon peel, was poured onto a solution of arrowroot. It was set in elaborate moulds – and here was the true forerunner of our modern cornflour blancmange. Try experimenting with different flavourings like chocolate, coffee, lemon, orange, brandy or other liqueurs, and vanilla.'*

40g (1½oz) cornflour
300ml (½ pint) milk
300ml (½ pint) single cream
1 bay leaf
Strip of lemon zest
2 tablespoons caster sugar
4–5 drops almond essence
25g (1oz) toasted flaked almonds

Serves 4–6

Mix the cornflour to a smooth paste with a little of the milk. Heat the rest of the milk and cream in a pan with the bay leaf and lemon zest and gradually blend in the cornflour mixture. Bring to simmering point and cook for about 3 minutes, stirring continuously until thickened. Remove from the heat and sweeten to taste. Stir in the almond essence. Pour into a fancy 600ml (1 pint) mould, rinsed out with cold water. Put in the fridge to set. Unmould onto a plate, decorate with toasted almonds and serve with Fruit Sauce (see page 188).

Maids of Honour

Tradition says these little sweet cheese tarts are named after the ladies-in-waiting to Queen Caroline, wife of George II, who reigned from 1727 to 1760. She lived in a palace in Richmond, Surrey, where, on Richmond Green, a terrace of lovely houses still stands called Maids of Honour Row. Not far down the road, Newens, the last of the famous Kew tea rooms, still sell Maids of Honour, made to a secret recipe. This not-so-secret 19th-century recipe comes from Laura Mason's Farmhouse Cookery.

500ml (18fl oz) whole milk
Pinch of salt
Rennet
100g (3½oz) butter at room temperature
2 egg yolks
2 teaspoons brandy
12 almonds, blanched and chopped
25g (1oz) sugar
1 teaspoon ground cinnamon
Juice and zest of ½ lemon
4 tablespoons currants
250g (9oz) puff pastry

Makes about 24

The day before you want to bake the Maids of Honour, heat the milk to blood temperature, stir in a pinch of salt and add rennet as directed on the bottle. When the curd has set and cooled, transfer it to a clean square of muslin or a jelly bag and allow the whey to drip out overnight. Next day, rub the curd through a sieve with the butter. Beat in the egg yolks and brandy, then stir in the almonds, sugar, cinnamon and the lemon juice and zest.

Next day, preheat oven to 220°C, 425°F, gas mark 7. Roll the pastry out very thinly and cut into rounds with a plain cutter. Using a fork, prick the centres of the rounds lightly a few times, otherwise your maids may go head-over-heels in the oven. Line the patty tins with the rounds and put a generous teaspoon of mixture in each. Scatter a few currants on top of each one. Bake for 7 minutes, until the pastry is risen and nicely browned.

An 18th-century Trifle

Sara Paston-Williams devised this trifle using a recipe from an ancient cook book. Pre-18th-century trifles were more like a cooked cream or a fool, but this recipe has biscuits, wine, custard and whipped cream.

FOR THE BASE
18 boudoir biscuits or sponge fingers
3–4 tablespoons medium-dry sherry or white wine

FOR THE CUSTARD
300ml (½ pint) double cream
3 large egg yolks
1 level teaspoon cornflour
25g (1oz) caster sugar

FOR THE TOPPING
Finely grated zest and juice of 1 lemon
4 tablespoons medium-dry sherry or white wine
1 teaspoon orange-flower or rose-water
50g (2oz) caster sugar
300ml (½ pint) double cream
Redcurrant or blackcurrant jelly, to decorate
Finely shredded orange, lemon or citron zest, to decorate

Serves 6–8

Prepare the topping several hours in advance. Put the lemon zest and juice, sherry or wine, orange-flower or rose-water and caster sugar into a bowl. Cover with clingfilm and leave for a few hours to let the oils from the zest impregnate the liquor. Meanwhile make the custard. Heat the cream in a small non-stick pan. Beat the egg yolks with the cornflour and sugar in a small basin until smooth, then pour on the hot cream, stirring all the time. Return the custard to the pan and stir it with a wooden spoon over a low heat until thick. Place the pan on a cold surface or in a bowl of cold water to remove any heat that might curdle the custard. Leave to cool while you prepare the base. Break the biscuits in half and place in the bottom of a shallow glass or china dish. Sprinkle over the sherry or wine, then pour over the custard. Cool completely. To make the topping, strain the prepared liquor into a clean bowl and stir in the cream, gradually beating it with a whisk until it stands in soft peaks. (Be careful not to overbeat or the syllabub will separate.) Decorate with small blobs of jelly and zest.

Sherry Trifle

Trifle is one of those dishes for which no one can agree on the correct recipe. Grown men remember with affection the trifle made by their mothers and grandmothers and come to blows over whether or not jelly and/or jam should be ingredients. Alan Davidson and Helen Saberi's book, Trifle, *traces the recipe back to 1596, and includes versions from as far afield as Laos and India. The recipe below is for a modern trifle that features neither jelly nor jam, includes fruit (non-traditional) and has given pleasure to many over the years.*

Crème pâtissière or Egg Custard Sauce (see page 188)
6 trifle sponge cakes
4 tablespoons whisky or sherry
1 small ripe pineapple
1 small punnet of strawberries
1 small punnet of raspberries
8 ratafia biscuits or small macaroons
300ml (10fl oz) double cream
25g (1oz) flaked almonds

Serves 8

Make up the crème pâtissière or custard. Leave it to cool while you continue making the trifle. Break up the sponge cakes and use them to fill the bottom of a large glass fruit bowl. Spoon the whisky or sherry over the sponge base. Peel the pineapple, then core and dice the fruit; hull and quarter the strawberries. Scatter the pineapple dice, the strawberries and the raspberries over the sponge base, interspersed with the ratafia biscuits or crumbled macaroons.

When the custard is cool, spoon it over the trifle and smooth the top. Whip the cream and spread it over the custard. Toast the almonds until golden, cool and scatter on the top of the trifle. Chill until required.

Right: Sherry Trifle

Claret Jelly

Cooks have been setting liquids with gelatine, isinglass and hartshorn since the Middle Ages. These early jellies sometimes contained meat and they were often highly spiced, and also sometimes sweetened and flavoured with rosewater. They are the ancestors not only of sweet jellies but also of the vegetable, fish and meat terrines and mousses still made today.

Dessert jellies often contain fruit but this is very different. Jellies made with wine or port were very popular with the Victorians. I often make wine jellies in individual glasses, so you can pour a little thin cream on top and eat the jelly through the cream. Delicious.

600 ml (1 pint) claret
Zest and juice of 1 lemon
20g (¾oz) powdered gelatine
75–110g (3–4oz) sugar

FOR DECORATION
Black grapes
Egg white
Caster sugar

Serves 6

Place 4 tablespoons of the claret and the lemon juice in a small basin and stir in the gelatine. If you wish to serve your wine jelly in glasses, 15g (½oz) gelatine will be sufficient, but if you wish to turn it out of a fancy mould, add an extra 15g (½oz) to make certain, but do check quantities on the packet, because different brands can vary in strength. Leave for 5 minutes until swollen and soft, then stir this into half the remaining claret in a pan. Add the sugar and lemon zest, then bring slowly almost, but not quite, to the boil, stirring all the time. Strain into a bowl and gently stir in the remaining claret. Pour into glasses, a wetted mould or a pretty bowl and leave to set in a cool place. Serve slightly chilled. Decorate with small bunches of black grapes which have been frosted with egg white and caster sugar. A little thin cream poured on top of the jelly is a perfect accompaniment.

Left: Claret Jelly

Damson Ice Cream

Ice creams have been part of our diet (at least in rich households) since long before refrigeration. The ice-cream syrup in this recipe can be used for most fruit purées. Damsons are tart and their deep red flesh produces a sharp-tasting, beautifully coloured ice cream.

FOR THE ICE-CREAM SYRUP
700ml (1¼ pints) water
425g (15oz) sugar
Juice and thinly pared zest of 1 lemon
2 drops vanilla essence

FOR THE ICE CREAM
1 litre (1¾ pints) hot ice-cream syrup
600g (1¼ pints) damsons
150ml (¼ pint) whipping or double cream

Serves 6–8

Make the ice-cream syrup as follows. Bring the water and sugar to the boil in a heavy-bottomed pan. While the mixture is heating up, add the lemon zest. When at boiling point, leave the syrup to bubble for exactly 1 minute. Remove from the heat, add the lemon juice and vanilla essence, then pour into a cold container and leave to cool. When cold, strain. Cover and store in the fridge, where it will keep for up to 2 weeks.

Poach the damsons in the syrup for about 10 minutes until the fruit is soft. Leave to cool overnight. When cold, strain, remove the stones and liquidise the pulp to a fine purée. Set to freeze. After 1 hour, remove, whip the cream until stiff and add to the mixture. Beat thoroughly and replace in the freezer. Repeat until the mixture hardens into ice cream. The process will take about 4–5 hours.

Brown Bread Ice Cream

Ice creams became popular in the 18th century. Country houses of this period were designed with ice houses, insulated brick vaults where ice was stored. The ice was used not only to prolong the life of fish and meat but also to make iced desserts. The first recipe for Brown Bread Ice *was given by Mary Smith in 1772. It became very popular in late Victorian and Edwardian days, when it was served as a country weekend treat. Warning: recipes containing raw eggs are not suitable for pregnant women or young children.*

75g (3oz) wholemeal breadcrumbs
50g (2oz) unsalted butter
75g (3oz) caster or soft brown sugar

FOR THE ICE CREAM
4 eggs, separated
115g (4oz) caster sugar
2 tablespoons rum, brandy or Madeira
425 ml (¾ pint) double or whipping cream

Serves 6–8

Preheat oven to 180°C, 350°F, gas mark 4. Spread the breadcrumbs on a baking tray lined with baking paper. Add the melted butter and sprinkle with the sugar. Bake for about 30 minutes or until crisp. Cool and then crush.

To prepare basic Ice Cream, beat the egg yolks with the sugar and the brandy, rum or Madeira. Whip the cream until it holds its shape and add to the egg mixture. Whisk the egg whites until stiff and fold into the cream and egg mixture. Freeze in a lidded container for about 1 hour and then stir in the prepared breadcrumbs. Freeze again.

Remove from the freezer and place in the fridge at least 30 minutes before serving. Scoop into glasses.

Killerton Chocolate Pot

Recipes using chocolate usually date from no earlier than the 20th century. However, chocolate puddings are now part of our tradition. I like the concentration of flavour that these little pots provide. You could also make the cocoa-and-sugar paste with strong instant coffee for a change, and stir in a tablespoon of rum or Tia Maria.

4 tablespoons cocoa, the best quality you can find
225g (8oz) soft brown sugar
Boiling water to mix
1 tablespoon Grand Marnier or Cointreau
600ml (1 pint) double cream
Grated orange zest, to garnish
Thin cream, to serve

Serves 4

Mix the cocoa and sugar into a thick paste with boiling water. Leave to cool, then chill in the fridge until really cold. Put the liqueur and cocoa mixture into a mixing bowl. Using an electric rotary whisk, beat in the cream slowly, being careful not to overbeat the mixture. When all is combined, fill small ramekins with the chocolate mixture and garnish with grated orange zest. This is very rich and creamy and keeps excellently for a day or two in the fridge. Serve with a jug of thin cream to pour on top of the pots.

Tafferty Tart

This is a modern version of a 16th-century recipe.

350g (12oz) shortcrust pastry

FOR THE FILLING
8 large cooking apples, thinly sliced
150g (5oz) sugar blended with the grated zest of 1 lemon
**   and the lemon pulp, finely chopped**
25g (1oz) butter

FOR THE TOPPING
110–175g (4–6oz) icing sugar
1 tablespoon milk
1 tablespoon lemon juice

Serves 6

Preheat oven to 200°C, 400°F, gas mark 6. Butter a 25cm (10in) pie plate. Roll out two-thirds of the pastry and line the plate, pressing it gently and firmly into place. Arrange the thinly sliced apples in layers, sprinkling each layer with the lemon and sugar mixture. Dot with butter and cover with the remainder of the pastry arranged in lattice strips. Place in the oven on a baking sheet and bake for 35 minutes.

While warm, drizzle with the topping made by mixing the icing sugar, milk and lemon juice together to produce a pouring consistency.

Eton Mess or Clare College Mush

The original recipe for this traditional pudding is said to have come from Clare College, Cambridge. It is a delicious combination of strawberries, cream and crushed meringues and can be flavoured with an orange liqueur, Kirsch, Framboise, brandy or vanilla.

2 large egg whites
110g (4oz) caster sugar
900g (2lb) fresh strawberries
25g (1oz) icing sugar
3 tablespoons Kirsch or orange liqueur
425ml (¾ pint) double or whipping cream

Serves 6

To make the meringues, whisk the egg whites in a clean bowl, with a balloon, rotary or electric whisk. Be careful not to overbeat. Whisk until the whites are stiff enough not to fall out of the bowl when it is turned over. Add the caster sugar, spoonful by spoonful, whisking in between each addition. With a tablespoon, drop even amounts of meringue mixture onto a lightly greased baking tray. Bake in a very cool oven (130°C, 250°F; gas mark ½) for about 1½ hours, or until the meringues are cream-coloured with a slightly soft chewy centre. Remove from the oven and leave to get cold. Chop up the strawberries roughly or leave whole if small. Save a few perfect berries for decorating. Sift the icing sugar over the strawberries and sprinkle with the liqueur. Chill well for at least 1 hour. Just before serving, whip the cream until it holds its shape. Gently fold in the strawberries and their juices. Crush the meringues into pieces and fold into the cream and strawberry mixture. Taste, and add more sugar if necessary. Pile into a glass bowl or individual glasses and decorate with strawberries.

Boodles Orange Fool

A speciality at Boodles Club, a London club in St James's Street, which was founded in 1762. The idea of combining sponge with fruit fool dates back to the 18th-century version with ratafias. In this pudding, the lemon and orange fool, the cream and juice separate so that the sweet, sharp juice soaks the sponge at the bottom of the pudding.

4 sponge cakes
Grated zest and juice of 1 lemon
Grated zest and juice of 2 oranges
50–75g (2–3oz) caster sugar
600ml (1 pint) double cream

FOR DECORATION
Crystallised orange slices
Crystallised angelica

Serves 4–6

Cut the sponge cakes into 1cm (½in) strips and line the base of a glass serving dish, or individual glass dishes. Mix the zest and juice of the fruit with the sugar and stir until dissolved. Whip half the cream until thick, but not stiff, and beat the juice into the cream slowly. Taste for sweetness. Spoon over the sponge cakes and chill thoroughly for 2–3 hours, until the juice has soaked into the sponge and the cream has set. Whip the remaining cream until stiff, and pipe or spoon on top of the pudding to decorate. Garnish with crystallised orange slices and angelica.

Peach Melba

Peach Melba was invented in the late 19th century by Auguste Escoffier, the chef at the newly opened Savoy Hotel in London's Strand. It was named after Dame Nellie Melba, the Australian opera star and diva. Make it in June or July when peaches are at their best.

1 ripe peach per person

FOR THE RASPBERRY SAUCE
225g (8oz) raspberries
75g (3oz) caster sugar
Juice of 1 lemon

FOR THE VANILLA ICE CREAM
450ml (16fl oz) single cream
1 vanilla pod or a few drops of vanilla extract
3 egg yolks
110g (4oz) caster sugar
150ml (¼ pint) double cream

Heat the single cream with the vanilla pod very gently until it just reaches boiling point. Take off the heat. Beat the egg yolks and sugar together until thick, pale and creamy, then whisk in the hot cream. Return the mixture to the pan and heat very gently until it thickens. It should just coat the back of a wooden spoon. Do not let it boil. Take off the heat, remove the vanilla pod if you are using one or flavour the custard with the vanilla extract, pour the mixture into a bowl and let it cool completely. When it is cold, whip the double cream until it stands in peaks and fold it into the cold mixture. Put the bowl in the freezer. After about an hour take the bowl out and whisk, preferably with an electric whisk, to break up the ice crystals. Return the bowl to the freezer until it is firm.

To make the raspberry sauce, heat the raspberries, sugar and lemon juice gently, stirring continuously, until they come to the boil. Remove from the heat, press through a sieve and leave to cool. Refrigerate until required.

To assemble, first cut a ring round each peach with a knife. Then put them in a deep bowl and cover with boiling water. Leave for 1 minute, then remove from the water and allow to cool. Peel away the skin, slice in half and remove the stone. Put two balls of ice cream in each bowl. Top each ball with half a peach and pour the raspberry sauce on top. Serve immediately.

Burnt Cream or Trinity Pudding

This pudding, also known as Burnt Cream and Cambridge Cream, was traditionally served at dinner during May week at Trinity College, Cambridge. It was brought in on a large silver dish and the caramelised top was cracked with great ceremony. The recipe is said to have been based on an ancient Scottish dish which may have been brought over from France by Mary, Queen of Scots. It is similar to the delicious French Crème Brulée. *There are endless versions of this creamy pudding with different flavourings – lemon rind, vanilla pod or a bay leaf. The sugary top used to be browned by a 'salamander', a flat iron which was heated and passed over the top of the pudding. You can make this custard in one large baking dish or individual ovenproof dishes, and it is best made the day before you want to serve it.*

850ml (1½ pints) double cream
1 vanilla pod
6 egg yolks
75g (3oz) caster sugar
Caster sugar for caramelising
Fresh flowers to decorate

Serves 6–8

Preheat oven to 150°C, 300°F, gas mark 2. Put cream and vanilla pod into a pan and bring very gently to the boil. Leave to cool a little. Remove the vanilla pod, wash and reserve for future use. Cream the egg yolks and sugar together in a basin until almost white. Pour the hot cream onto the yolks in a steady stream, whisking all the time. Strain into a shallow ovenproof dish, or individual dishes, and place in a roasting tin half-filled with hot water. Bake for 1–1¼ hours or until just set. Remove the dish and leave until cold. Chill in the fridge overnight, if possible.

Just before serving, coat the top of the pudding with an even layer about 6mm (¼in) thick of caster sugar, using a sugar dredger. Heat the grill until really hot. Put the pudding in a roasting tin or large dish of ice cubes (this will make sure that your custard does not spoil when you are caramelising the top). Slip until the hot grill and watch carefully, turning if the sugar is browning unevenly. When the sugar has completely melted and is an even caramel colour, remove the tin and leave to cool.

Serve chilled, decorated with a few fresh flowers. Serve with a bowl of fresh cherries, strawberries and raspberries when in season.

Damson Snow

Damsons are small, sharp-tasting plums. They are not an eating variety; they must be cooked but they have an intense, rich flavour unique in the plum family. If you are offered damsons, or see them in the greengrocer, seize them, because they make wonderful jams and jellies, they pickle beautifully, and make delicious puddings like this one.

900g (2lb) damsons
175g (6oz) caster sugar
150ml (¼ pint) cold water
425ml (¾ pint) double cream
2 tablespoons brandy or Marsala
3 egg whites

Serves 6–8

Put the washed and de-stalked damsons into a pan with the sugar and water. Bring slowly to the boil and cook gently for 10–15 minutes or until fruit is tender. Rub through a sieve and leave the damson pulp to get cold. Lightly whip the cream with the brandy or Marsala until thick. Whisk the egg whites until stiff and fold into the cream mixture. Stir in the damson pulp, reserving 1 tablespoon for decoration. Pour into individual glasses and chill well. Just before serving, stir in the reserved damson pulp to give a marbled effect, or just top with damson pulp. Serve with any home-made biscuits.

VARIATION
Edinburgh Fog: Omit the damson pulp and replace the brandy with sweet sherry. Sweeten with 50g (2oz) caster sugar and stir in 50g (2oz) ratafias. Chill well, and serve with a bowl of fresh raspberries or strawberries and sprinkled with toasted flaked almonds.

Marbled Rose Cream

This delicate raspberry cream is flavoured with rose-water, which you can buy at grocers and chemists. It was a favourite flavouring in Tudor and Stuart cookery. Rose bushes, specifically for making rose-water, were grown in the kitchen garden alongside fruit bushes. Any soft fruits can be used in this recipe. It can be frozen and served as an ice cream.

900g (2lb) fresh or frozen raspberries
250g (9oz) caster sugar
2 tablespoons cold water
600ml (1 pint) double cream
2 tablespoons rose-water or Kirsch
Crystallised mint leaves

Serves 8–10

Put 450g (1lb) raspberries into a saucepan with 175g (6oz) caster sugar and the water. Bring gently to the boil and simmer for a few minutes, or until the raspberries start to yield their juice. Push through a sieve and leave to cool. Whip the cream until thick and add the remaining caster sugar gradually. Mash the remaining raspberries, reserving a few of the best berries for decoration. Mix very thoroughly into the whipped cream and stir in the rose-water or Kirsch. Now add the cooked raspberry pulp, stirring just enough to give a marbled effect. Pour into a glass bowl and put into the fridge for at least 3 hours before serving. Decorate with reserved berries rolled in a little caster sugar and crystallised mint leaves.

Breads, Teabreads and Scones

Bread – the staple of life. The finer the flour, the whiter the bread – and the farther up the social scale you were, if you could afford it. For hundreds of years that was the way things were, until the gourmets and the doctors agreed, for once, that bread with the bran left in not only tasted better, but was better for you, too.

The finest bread in the Middle Ages was *paindemaigne* or *manchet*, a pale cream in colour. Middling bread of varying quality was *trete*, *cocket*, or *wastel*, while the brownest bread, made from unbolted flour, was *panisenter* or *tourte*. An English law, known as the Assize of Bread, attempted to standardize loaf prices, fixing a common weight of bread known as a penny loaf, but in general you got more bread for your penny if you bought the lower-quality bread, and prices were by no means fixed. And not all bakers were honest – through the centuries there were prosecutions for adulteration: alum, root vegetables, sand, gravel and dried beans are just some of the substances bakers put in to eke out their flour.

So it was generally much better to bake bread at home, and know exactly what was in it. While only the well-off had hearths that were big enough to house a bread oven, a griddle was within most people's reach. In Scotland, and northern England, a homestead or croft might be far from a baker's shop and, as also in Wales, there is still a tradition of griddle cooking in these areas today. No griddle? Then you would probably have eaten your grain as porridge, *frumenty* or gruel.

There are four recipes for bread in this chapter. One of them comes from Northern Ireland, where bread is taken very seriously. Indeed, throughout Ireland, an ability to bake a good loaf is considered almost as important as a good character (well, perhaps I'm exaggerating a little!). A fresh loaf of Wheaten Bread, buttered with sweet Irish butter, is so good that it is tempting to make a meal of it. And, of course, that's what many people did. Wheaten Bread is raised with baking powder, while Oatmeal Soda Bread is raised with bicarbonate of soda and cream of tartar. These loaves don't keep as well as yeast-based bread, but since they usually disappear so quickly, this doesn't really matter. The Soda Bread recipe comes from Buckland Abbey, in the far west of Devon – again an isolated part of the world where village bakers were few and far between, and a household had to bake for itself if possible. The one yeast-based recipe here is for Granary Bread or Rolls. Granary flour is a modern British flour mix, and the resulting bread – a slightly crumbling, soft brown loaf, speckled with crisp malted grains – is surely one of our better inventions.

How can you tell the difference between a cake and a teabread? Maybe the dictionary definition of a teabread is a little narrow: 'Yeast- leavened baked goods considered suitable for either afternoon tea or high tea in Britain, including many spiced, fruited and enriched breads and buns.' Being yeast-based, Chelsea Buns (see page 236) fit this definition perfectly, but so many of the recipes I've been given were raised in other ways. Besides, I think the home cook often finds yeast complicated and long-winded to use, and the time required for the mix to rest is, so often, unavailable in today's busy world. So my preferred definition for a tea bread is 'food for teatime that tastes best buttered', and I think that covers all the tea breads, scones and griddle cakes here. Bara Brith, or 'Speckled Bread', is probably the most famous teabread of all, and my recipe came from its home, North Wales. Soak the fruit in the best Earl Grey Tea and the resulting loaf will taste subtle and delicious.

Griddle cooking, a method that evolved from the age-old idea of cooking on a flat, hot stone in the fire, is still popular today. By the Middle Ages, large round metal griddles were hung above the fire, and various breads were cooked on them. Welsh Cakes, Pikelets, Staffordshire Oatcakes, Scotch Pancakes and the delightfully named Singin' Hinnies are all griddle-cooked.

Scone recipes are very special, and cooks guard them closely. Perhaps this is because the basic ingredients are so simple – just flour, liquid, fat and a raising agent – so any variations generally come from minute adjustments of quantities. There are recipes here for both savoury and sweet scones. Savoury scones are a speciality in Northumberland, where many people prefer to eat a scone with soup rather than bread. Some scones include local specialities: Old Hannah's Cheshire Potato Cakes, Erddig Apple Scones and Leek and Onion Scones from Souter Lighthouse are three of these.

And I can't write about scones without admitting that my whole writing career started with a scone recipe! Years ago, I was asked to cook a lunch for 125 people, to celebrate the opening of a lovely maritime museum at Cotehele, on the Cornish side of the River Tamar. I was given use of the tea room's kitchen for my preparation. Glancing around this busy kitchen, knowing I was being sized up by the band of local cooks and helpers, I realised that I must get the cook in charge, Mrs Laver, on my side if lunch was going to happen. I'd been given a cup of coffee and a buttered scone, more to keep me out of the way than anything else. The scone was delicious, so I complimented Mrs. Laver and asked for her recipe – the rest was plain sailing. That experience led me to thinking that there must be other good traditional food being cooked in tea rooms right across Britain. Ten years later, my first collection of recipes from National Trust cooks was published.

Finally in this chapter there is Lardy Cake. I remember Lardy Cake as a childhood treat but what I didn't realise, until I started research for this book, was that it was one more gift from the household pig – it is traditionally made from the animal's lard, or dripping.

Erddig Apple Scones

This recipe comes from Erddig, a National Trust house and estate in North Wales. At Erddig, apple scones are served with Welsh cheese. Each year the estate holds an Apple Day, when the head gardener puts on a display of the old apple species grown in the garden. There is a demonstration of cider-making by one of the Bulmer cider family, and cider is available to drink. You can buy apples direct from the growers and original pictures of apples direct from the artists.

450g (1lb) self-raising flour
1 teaspoon salt
110g (4oz) butter
50g (2oz) caster sugar
450g (1lb) dessert apples
Milk to mix

Makes 12 scones

Preheat oven to 200°C, 400°F, gas mark 6. Grease and flour a baking sheet. Sieve the flour and salt into a large bowl. Cut the butter into small pieces and rub into the flour until the mixture resembles coarse breadcrumbs. Stir in caster sugar. Peel and core the apples, grate half and roughly chop the rest. Stir into the mixture. Add sufficient milk to make a soft dough. Turn it onto a floured board. Knead for a couple of minutes, then either cut into 12 or form into two rounds. If you choose rounds, then score each into 6 wedges. Brush the tops with milk, sprinkle with a little sugar and bake for approximately 20 minutes.

Right: Erddig Apple Scones

Ulster Scones

Baking is a huge tradition in Ulster and still very important. Bakers' shops are full of different shapes and sizes of scones, teabreads, tray cakes and soda-bread varieties not seen in the rest of the UK. Ulster bakers swear by buttermilk, and I am glad to say that you can now buy it in most supermarkets. In Ulster you can also buy soda-bread flour, a combination of brown and white. I asked my daughter, who is married to an Irishman, for the proportion she uses, which I have given here, but really it is a matter of taste and what works for you. It is a hotbed of controversy in Ireland, where cooks are assessed on their breads and everyone has a different key to success.

250g (9oz) wholemeal flour
250g (9oz) strong white flour
½ teaspoon bicarbonate of soda
75g (3oz) sugar
50g (2oz) chopped glacé cherries or 50g (2oz) sultanas (optional)
75g (3oz) butter
350ml (12fl oz) buttermilk
1 egg, beaten
Milk, to brush

Makes about 24 scones

Preheat oven to 220°C, 425°F, gas mark 7. Grease or line a baking sheet with baking paper. Sift the two flours together with the bicarbonate of soda and sugar. (If you are making fruit scones, add the cherries or sultanas at this point and mix them in well.) Rub in the butter. Stir in the buttermilk and egg and knead the mixture until it forms a soft dough. *Do not overwork the dough.* Roll the dough out to about 2.5cm (1in) thick and cut the scones into rounds or triangles. This should make about 24. Brush the tops with milk and bake 10–15 minutes, until golden brown and risen.

Left: Erddig Apple Scones

Ulster Cheese Cakes

These buttery little tarts aren't cakes and contain no cheese. Perhaps they did long ago. They now seem most closely related to the Bakewell Tart (see page 254). I was given this recipe at Mount Stewart, a wonderful house on Strangford Lough, south of Belfast.

225g (8oz) shortcrust pastry (see page 54)
Sunflower oil
175g (6oz) butter
175g (6oz) caster sugar
3 eggs, well beaten
175g (6oz) plain flour
Strawberry or raspberry jam
Caster sugar, for dusting

Makes approximately 16

Preheat oven to 160°C, 325°F, gas mark 3. Roll out the pastry and use to line small tartlet tins brushed with sunflower oil. Prick the bottoms and leave to rest while making the filling. Cream the butter and sugar together until light and fluffy. Beat in the eggs gradually, adding a little flour if the mixture should start to curdle. Then fold in the remaining flour.

Place a small teaspoonful of jam on each pastry base and fill with the sponge mix. Bake for approximately 20 minutes, until golden brown. Allow to cool and dust with caster sugar before serving.

Staffordshire Oatcakes

Biddulph Grange is a spectacular garden, with a tearoom where I had an oatcake for lunch. I asked for the recipe and found out that at Biddulph the oatcakes are made by a local baker, whose recipe is a secret. I have adapted this recipe from Elizabeth David's English Bread and Yeast Cookery. *She describes the oatcakes as 'an intensely local delicacy unheard of north of Leek, unimagined south of Banbury'. The tearoom at Biddulph, seven miles west of Leek, serves them for lunch with vegetables. They can also be eaten with butter and honey or with bacon and eggs for breakfast.*

225g (8oz) bread flour
225g (8oz) fine oatmeal
2 teaspoons salt
10g (½oz) bakers' yeast
425ml (¾ pint) warm milk
425ml (¾ pint) warm water
Butter for greasing frying pan or griddle

Makes 16–18 16–18cm (6–7in) oatcakes

Put the flour and oatmeal in a bowl with the salt. Cream the yeast with a little of the warm milk. Stir into the flour, add the rest of the liquid and beat well with a wooden spoon. If it seems too thick add a little more warm water. Cover the bowl and leave to rise for an hour or so.

Heat a griddle or heavy-based frying pan until very hot. Grease sparingly and make the oatcakes as you would pancakes. Put a ladle of mixture into the pan, cook for a minute or two until bubbles appear in the mixture, then flip over and cook for another minute or two. The oatcakes can be kept warm in a folded damp cloth.

Bara Brith

Bara Brith means 'spotted bread'. Recipes for it are traditional in all Celtic communities. This recipe comes from Wales. Use ordinary tea if you don't have any Earl Grey and note that ideally you should begin this recipe the day before you cook it.

225g (8oz) sultanas or mixed dried fruit
175ml (6fl oz) cold Earl Grey tea
225g (8oz) wholemeal flour
2 teaspoons baking powder
1 teaspoon mixed spice
175g (6oz) demerara sugar
Pinch of salt
2 eggs, well beaten

Makes one loaf

Preheat oven to 180°C, 350°F, gas mark 4. Soak the fruit in the cold tea for at least 5 hours or overnight. Grease and line a 900g (2lb) loaf tin. Sift together wholemeal flour and the baking powder, and add the spices, sugar and fruit. Mix well. Stir in the eggs. Spoon the mixture into the tin and bake for approximately 1 hour. Leave to cool in the tin. Keeps well; indeed it even improves.

Wheaten Bread

In Ireland, breadmaking and scone-making is highly esteemed. Characters are assessed through the quality of their bread. Families even fall out over recipes. Wheaten bread sliced warm from the oven and spread with Ulster butter is irresistible.

225g (8oz) wholemeal flour
225g (8oz) strong white flour
1 teaspoon baking powder
110g (4oz) butter
110g (4oz) sugar
350ml (12fl oz) buttermilk
1 egg, beaten
Milk, for brushing

Makes 2 small or one large loaf

Preheat oven to 200°C, 400°F, gas mark 6. Grease either 2 x 450g (1lb) loaf tins or 1 x 900g (2lb) loaf tin. Sift together all the dry ingredients except the sugar. Rub in the butter until the mixture resembles coarse breadcrumbs. Add the sugar and stir well. Make a well in the centre and gradually work in the buttermilk and egg until you have a soft dough. Knead lightly. Form into one large loaf or two smaller ones. Place in the tins, brush with milk and bake until well risen and golden brown. The bread should sound hollow when knocked and a skewer should come out of the loaf clean. For a 900g (2lb) loaf this may take 1¼ hours, but the smaller loaves need a little less time; have a look at them after 45 minutes.

Welsh Cakes

Pice ar Maen *is Welsh for 'cakes on the stone'. It is traditional to cut them into either circles or triangles. Few small houses in rural Wales had an oven, but Welsh cakes could be cooked on a griddle on an open fire. Serve them hot dusted with sugar or cold with butter.*

225g (8oz) self-raising flour
Pinch of salt
Pinch of mixed spice
Pinch of cinnamon
110g (4oz) butter
75g (3oz) caster sugar
75g (3oz) currants
25g (1oz) chopped peel
1 egg
Milk to bind

Makes approximately 12 cakes

Preheat and grease a griddle or heavy-based frying-pan. Sift together the flour, salt and spices and rub in the butter until the mixture resembles fine breadcrumbs. Stir in the sugar and the currants and peel. Mix with the egg and milk to a firm but not dry dough. Roll out to 6–12mm (¼–½in) thick and cut into rounds. Cook the Welsh Cakes on a moderately hot griddle till brown on both sides – about 10 minutes in all.

Leek and Onion Scones

This recipe comes from the Souter Lighthouse on the rugged Northumbrian coast, where a leek scone is served with a steaming bowl of Vegetable Barley Broth (see page 14) to keep out the cold. Northumbrians also eat leek scones, rather than bread or biscuits, with their good local cheese.

1 tablespoon olive oil
1 large leek, cleaned and chopped fine (you can use the whole leek)
1 small onion, finely chopped
Pinch of sugar
450g (1lb) self-raising flour
Salt to taste
110g (4oz) butter
250ml (9fl oz) milk

Makes approximately 24 scones

Preheat oven to 230°C, 450°F, gas mark 8. Either grease a baking sheet or line it with baking paper. Heat the oil and sauté the chopped leek and onion with the pinch of sugar until soft. Sift the flour with salt and rub in the butter until the mixture resembles fine breadcrumbs. Stir in the leek and onion and sufficient milk to form a soft dough. Turn out onto a floured surface and knead lightly. Roll out to approximately 2.5cm (1in) thick. Stamp out 5cm (2in) rounds. Place on the baking sheet and brush the tops with milk. Bake for approximately 12 minutes, or until golden brown.

Singin' Hinnies

Traditionally, Singin' Hinnies are cooked on a griddle or in a heavy-based frying pan. You can also bake them in an oven. Allow about 15 minutes in all, turning and flattening them after 7–8 minutes. Serve warm, split and buttered. Singin' Hinnies are a Northumbrian delicacy. 'Hinnie' is a term of endearment, used especially for children. The fat in the hinnies makes them 'sing' when they are cooking; they are ready to eat when the singing stops. Originally, a Singin' Hinnie was one large scone, but the recipe I have been given is for individual small hinnies.

50g (2oz) butter
50g (2oz) lard
225g (8oz) plain flour
25g (1oz) currants
1 teaspoon baking powder
¼ teaspoon salt
Milk and soured cream to mix

Makes approximately 8–10 hinnies

Preheat oven to 180°C, 350°F, gas mark 4. In a mixing bowl large enough to take all the ingredients, rub the fats into the flour. Add the other dry ingredients. Mix to a soft dough with the milk and soured cream. Roll out and cut into rounds the size of a muffin, about 2.5cm (1 in) thick. Cook for 7–8 minutes each side on the griddle or in the oven.

Cheese and Herb Scones

Another Northumbrian recipe for scones to be served with soup. This recipe comes from Wallington, a classical mansion set deep in the bleak, beautiful Northumbrian moors north of Newcastle.

450g (1lb) self-raising flour sifted
10g (½oz) baking powder
1 teaspoon salt
110g (4oz) mature Cheddar cheese, grated
10g (½oz) mixed dried herbs
50g (2oz) butter
225ml (8fl oz) milk and water mix (half and half)

Makes approximately 20 scones

Preheat oven to 230°C, 450°F, gas mark 8. Either grease and flour a metal baking sheet or line it with baking parchment. Put the flour, baking powder, salt, half the grated cheese and the dried herbs in a large bowl. Rub the butter into the dried ingredients until the mixture resembles breadcrumbs. Make a well in the centre and add the milk and water slowly and knead until you have a soft dough. Roll out the dough and cut into 12 x 7.5cm (3in) rounds. Sprinkle the rest of the cheese on the top of each scone. Bake for approximately 17 minutes. Keep an eye on them: oven temperatures vary and this is very hot.

Wholemeal Sultana Scones

This is a slightly sweet scone to eat buttered, with or without jam. It can also be a part of that great British tradition, the cream tea, which consists of scones, clotted cream and jam, a cake of some kind and a large pot of good tea. Eaten at around 4 to 5 o'clock, it takes care of hunger for several hours.

225g (8oz) wholemeal flour
13g (½oz) baking powder
50g (2oz) lard, diced
25g (1oz) soft brown sugar
38g (1½oz) sultanas
1 egg
50ml (2fl oz) milk

Makes approximately 12 scones

Preheat oven to 220°C, 450°F, gas mark 8. In a large mixing bowl sift the flour and the baking powder – add any bran left in the sieve. Rub in the diced fat with your fingertips until the mixture resembles coarse breadcrumbs. Add the sugar and sultanas and combine evenly. Make a well in the centre and slowly add the egg and milk, beaten together. Stir the mixture with a fork to make a smooth dough. Knead slightly to make a ball and place on a floured board. Roll out to a thickness of not less than 2.5cm (1in) and cut out the scones using a 5cm (2in) cutter. Place on a greased baking tray and, if you like, brush with milk or dust with flour. Bake for 15 minutes.

ALTERNATIVE
Date and Walnut Scones: Omit the sultanas, and substitute 40g (1½oz) chopped dates and 25g (1oz) walnuts.

Pikelets

The current Welsh name for Pikelets is Pice'r Pregethwr, *but they used to be known as* Bara Pyglyd, *which means 'pitchy bread'. Like Welsh Cakes (see page 230), these were cooked on a griddle, but you can use a heavy-based frying pan very successfully. Pikelets are made with a batter similar to the one used for crumpets and look, when cooked, like a cross between a pancake and a crumpet. Originally, the batter was yeast-based, but now many recipes, like this one, are soda-based.*

225g (8oz) self-raising flour
110g (4oz) caster sugar
1 egg, well beaten
Approximately 300ml (½ pint) full-cream milk
50g (2oz) butter
¼ teaspoon bicarbonate of soda
1 teaspoon vinegar

Makes approximately 12 pikelets

Sieve the flour and sugar together. Add the beaten egg and milk and mix to form a thick batter. Melt the butter, add the bicarbonate of soda and vinegar and mix into the batter.

Drop a tablespoon onto a hot, greased griddle or heavy-based frying pan. Cook until bubbles appear and the bottom is brown. Then turn the pikelet over and cook the other side. Serve warm and well buttered.

Chelsea Buns

Chelsea Buns were originally made as a treat for the Chelsea pensioners at the Royal Hospital in Chelsea, London.

225g (8oz) plain flour
2 teaspoons caster sugar
10g (½oz) fresh yeast or 2 teaspoons dried yeast
125ml (4fl oz) milk
15g (½oz) butter
75g (3oz) mixed dried fruit, candied peel, currants or raisins
¼ teaspoon mixed spice
50g (2oz) light soft brown sugar
25g (1oz) melted butter
2 tablespoons honey

Makes 9 buns

Sift 50g (2oz) of the measured flour into a small bowl and add the caster sugar. Crumble in the fresh yeast or spoon in the dried yeast and beat in the milk with a wooden spoon. Leave this yeast mixture in a warm place for about 20 minutes, by which time it should be frothy. Sift together the remaining flour and the salt into a large bowl and rub in the butter with your fingers. Make a well in the centre and pour in the yeast mixture. Using one hand, gradually work in the flour until you have a dough. When it leaves the side of the bowl clean, turn the dough out onto a lightly floured surface and knead it for 10 minutes until it is very smooth. Put it back in the bowl, cover it with a cloth and leave it to rise for 1½ hours. It should double in size.

Knead the dough on a lightly floured surface for a minute, then roll it out with a rolling pin to a rectangle 30 x 23cm (12 x 9in). Mix the fruit, sugar and spice together. Brush the dough with melted butter and spread the fruit mixture on top to within 2.5cm (1in) along the longer edges. Roll up the dough from the long sides and press the join to seal it.

Preheat oven to 220°C, 425°F, gas mark 7. Cut the roll into nine equal slices and pack them cut side upwards, in rows of three in a greased 18cm (7in) square cake tin. Leave to rise in a polythene bag in a warm place for about 30 minutes. Remove the polythene bag. Warm the honey and pour it over the buns. Bake for about 20–25 minutes until a deep golden brown. Test with a skewer to see that it comes out clean from a bun. Cool on a wire rack.

Granary Bread and Rolls

Granary bread is named after the flour used, a British flour composed of mixed brown wheat and rye flour with malted cracked-wheat grains. This recipe comes from the National Trust property Killerton in East Devon. Originally the home of the Acland family, it is a thriving agricultural estate. The bread in the restaurant is famously good and people come some distance to eat it in the elegant dining room of the 18th-century house.

800g (1¾lb) granary bread flour
2 teaspoons salt
25g (1oz) fresh yeast or 1 teaspoon dried yeast
2 teaspoons molasses dissolved in 75ml (3fl oz) of hand-hot water
600ml (1 pint) warm water

Makes 450g (1lb) loaf or approximately 15 rolls

Put the granary flour and salt in a large bowl and warm together in the oven at its lowest temperature for a few minutes. Cream the fresh yeast with molasses and hand-hot water or sprinkle the dried yeast in and mix well. Add the yeast mixture to the warmed flour with 600ml (1 pint) of warm water; combine thoroughly but do not knead. The mixture should be very wet. Spoon into well-greased 450g (1lb) loaf tins or, for rolls, into well-greased patty tins. Prove in the oven for 15 minutes, still at the lowest temperature possible. Raise the oven to 180°C, 350°F, gas mark 4 and bake for 20–30 minutes for the rolls and 50 minutes for the loaves. To test if a loaf is done, turn the tin on its side, slide out the loaf and tap it on the bottom. If it sounds hollow, it is cooked; if not, leave it out of the tin and bake for another 10 minutes or so. Cool on a wire rack.

Orange and Raisin Teabread

Traditionally tea cakes and teabreads were yeast-based but over the years, many teabread recipes also use bicarbonate of soda and/or baking powder, as this one does. The recipe makes one large, rich teabread, and the orange zest and juice make it particularly interesting.

350g (12oz) plain flour
1½ teaspoons baking powder
¾ teaspoon bicarbonate of soda
¼ teaspoon salt
175g (6oz) brown sugar
175g (6oz) seedless raisins
Grated zest of 1 orange
300ml (½ pint) orange juice
1 large egg, beaten
75g (3oz) melted butter

Makes 1 large teabread

Preheat oven to 180°C, 350°F, gas mark 4. Grease a 900g (2lb) loaf tin and line the base with baking paper. Sieve the flour, baking powder, bicarbonate of soda and salt into a bowl. Stir in the sugar, raisins and orange zest. Gradually beat in the orange juice with the egg and melted butter. Turn the mixture into the loaf tin and bake for 1 hour or until a knitting needle or skewer comes out clean. Cool in the tin.

Date and Walnut Loaf

Dried and semi-dried dates have been part of British cuisine since they first arrived in this country with the Romans, while walnuts arrived later from France. Britain is at the northern extreme for growing walnut trees, but so many old recipes exist – both ones that use the nut as an ingredient and ones that give instructions for pickling the whole fruit – that walnut trees must once have abounded in southern Britain. This big loaf keeps well and is best eaten buttered.

110g (4oz) butter
450g (1lb) chopped dates
110g (4oz) sugar
Pinch of salt
2 teaspoons bicarbonate of soda
300ml (½ pint) boiling water
110g (4oz) walnuts, cut in rough halves
2 eggs, beaten
450g (1lb) self-raising flour

Makes 1 large teabread

Preheat oven to 160°C, 325°F, gas mark 3. Grease a 900g (2lb) loaf tin and line the base with baking paper. Put the butter, dates, sugar, salt and bicarbonate of soda into a large mixing bowl. Pour over the boiling water and allow to cool. Add the walnuts, eggs and flour and mix until well combined. Spoon into the loaf tin and bake for 1–1¼ hours or until a skewer plunged into the middle of the loaf comes out clean.

Oatmeal Soda Bread

Oats grow best in cool climates; they were the principal cereal crop in Wales and Scotland. The Romans were rude about oats, thinking them only suitable for barbarians. Dr Johnson, in his famous dictionary, was even ruder, defining oats as 'a grain which in England is given to horses, but in Scotland supports the people'. However, it has the most protein (16%) of any grain and the undoubted success of Scots men and women throughout history is sometimes put down to the consumption of oats in the form of porridge. This oatmeal soda bread is easy to make and is delicious to eat straight from the oven or cold with a salad, pasta or nut roast. Soda bread does not keep well and should be eaten in one or two days.

450g (1lb) wholemeal flour
110g (4oz) fine oatmeal
1½ teaspoons cream of tartar
1 teaspoon bicarbonate of soda
25g (1oz) butter
425ml (¾ pint) milk and water mix (half and half)
1 teaspoon salt

Makes 1 large soda bread

Preheat oven to 350°F, 180°C, gas mark 4. Mix together the flour, oatmeal, cream of tartar and bicarbonate of soda. Using your fingers or a food processor, rub in the butter to resemble fine breadcrumbs. Add the milk and water and mix to a soft dough. Turn out the mixture onto a lightly floured surface and knead slightly into a loaf shape or slightly flattened round ball. If you wish, the surface can be deeply scored with a knife in portions. Place on a greased baking sheet and bake in the oven for 30–35 minutes.

Right: Oatmeal Soda Bread

Old Hannah's Cheshire Potato Cakes

North-west England grows superlative potatoes, so it is appropriate that this recipe comes from Styal in Cheshire. I don't know who Old Hannah was, but immortality through a recipe is the dream of every good cook.

225g (8oz) self-raising flour
¼ teaspoon salt
50g (2oz) butter or margarine
225g (8oz) left-over or fresh mashed potatoes
1 egg, beaten
A little milk if required

Makes approximately 12 cakes

Preheat oven to 375°F, 190°C, gas mark 5. Grease a baking tray. Put the flour and salt in a bowl with the fat. Rub the fat in the flour using your fingertips, then fork in the mashed potatoes. Make a well in the centre of the mixture and drop in the beaten egg. Fork it into the mixture using a little milk if necessary, to give a soft pliable dough. Finish by kneading the dough with your hands until smooth. Roll it out to approximately 1.25cm (½in) thick and cut into rounds with a pastry cutter. Space them out on the prepared baking sheet and bake for 30 minutes. Take out of the oven and wrap in a clean tea towel to keep them warm and soft. Split, butter and spread them with jam or syrup and serve while hot. Leftover cakes can be reheated, but they will have a crispy surface.

Left: Flapjacks

Wholemeal Bread

This is a standard handmade wholemeal bread recipe. In times gone by, many old country houses had their own bread oven, often built into a corner of the hearth. A fire was built in the oven, and when it reduced to ashes, these were raked out and the oven was ready for use. Bread was baked first, because it needed the hottest temperature, followed by pies and tarts.

250ml (9fl oz) tepid water
1 teaspoon sugar
2 teaspoons dried yeast or 10g (½oz) fresh yeast
450g (1lb) 100% wholemeal flour
  or 350g (12oz) wholemeal flour and 110g (4oz) strong plain flour
1½ teaspoons salt
15g (½oz) vegetarian lard

Makes 1 loaf

Preheat oven to 200°C, 400°F, gas mark 6. If using the dried yeast, place half the tepid water in a measuring jug and dissolve the sugar. Sprinkle the yeast over the top and leave in a warm place for 5–10 minutes until frothy (fresh yeast can be mixed in the water and used straight away). Put the flours and salt into a mixing bowl and rub in the lard. Add the frothed-up yeast and the balance of the water and mix with a wooden spoon to give a fairly soft dough (add more water if necessary). Turn out onto a clean work surface and knead for 10 minutes until the dough is smooth and supple. Place in a well-greased 450g (1lb) loaf tin, pushing the dough well down into the corners and sides of the tin to encourage it to form a dome-shaped loaf. Put the tin in a warm place covered with a damp tea towel or placed in a lightly greased polythene bag, tied loosely, and leave to rise for 30–40 minutes or until the loaf has doubled in size and within 6mm (¼in) of the top of the bread tin.

If you wish, the surface of the loaf can be sprinkled with poppy seeds, sesame seeds, rolled oats or cracked wheat. Brush the dough lightly with water or beaten egg to make the seeds stick.

Bake for about 40 minutes. Turn out the bread and, if cooked, the loaf will sound hollow when tapped underneath. Put it back for 10 minutes if it is not ready. Leave to cool on a wire tray.

Drop Scones

In Scotland, Wales and England, Drop Scones are small, thick pancakes, generally eaten with butter, jam or both, at tea or supper time. The Welsh name for these is froes. *Traditionally, the griddle on which the scones were cooked was greased with suet. Nowadays lard is best, but olive oil will do. Children (well supervised – the griddle is very hot) love to help make these and quickly become adept at flipping them over. If you haven't got a griddle, a heavy-based frying pan will do the job equally well. If it is non-stick it will need very little greasing indeed.*

225g (8oz) self-raising flour
½ teaspoon salt
1 tablespoon caster sugar
1 egg, beaten
175ml (6fl oz) milk
Lard or olive or sunflower oil

Makes 15–20 scones

Sieve the flour, salt and caster sugar together into a bowl. Make a well in the centre and add the egg and half the milk. Beat until the mixture is thick and smooth. Add the rest of the milk gradually, stirring all the time, until the mixture is the consistency of cream. Pour it into a jug. Leave to stand for 15–30 minutes.

Heat the griddle and rub a piece of lard over it, or grease a frying pan with sunflower oil. Pour tablespoons of the batter onto the griddle. Fry them until bubbles appear on the surface and the undersides are light brown. Flip them over with a palette knife and brown the other side. Add more lard to the griddle and start again. Keep the cooked scones in a folded napkin or tea towel. Serve warm with butter.

Cakes and Biscuits

Not that long ago, I walked into the dining room of a country house at around 3:30pm on a cold, wet, dark afternoon, feeling chilled and tired. The room was lit with warm lamps and the table, covered with a white damask cloth, was laid for tea, with plates piled high with succulent cucumber sandwiches, golden flapjacks and pale cream shortbread fingers. At one end of the table stood a plain sponge, dusted with icing sugar and filled with blackcurrant jam and cream – ready to be sliced. At the other end, a rich Dundee cake, packed with fruit and almonds. My spirits lifted immediately, even before I had taken my first sip of the steaming cup of tea that awaited me, or filled up my plate from all that abundance.

Cakes and biscuits, essential ingredients of such a sumptuous afternoon tea, share a long history with bread. The word *cake* comes from the Ancient Norse *Kaka*, originally a kind of fried dough. Every baked cake in this chapter evolved from bread, although cakes are now much sweeter and richer. Biscuits are also rich and sweet, but they have a crispness on the palate that makes them unique. While our traditional cakes are world-famous, and rightly so, biscuit-making is a field in which the British home baker can – and often does – excel.

The recipes in this chapter merely scratch the surface when it comes to the ingenuity and creativity of cake and biscuit makers over the centuries. Here are just a few of the traditional cakes and biscuits that are ideal to serve at afternoon or high tea. People have been drinking tea here since the middle of the 17th century, but the invention of afternoon tea, in the early 19th century, is attributed to Anna, Duchess of Bedford. Jane Pettigrew, in her book *Tea Time Recipes* (National Trust), writes that the marriage of Charles II to a Portuguese princess, Catherine of Braganza, in 1662, established the practice of drinking tea when, as part of her dowry, Catherine brought with her a large chest of it. In imitation of the court (and encouraged by merchants bringing tea back from the Far East), tea-drinking became a fashionable activity. By the 19th century, breakfast was taken at nine or ten in the morning, and dinner was not until seven or eight in the evening. Tea took on a new role for the Duchess of Bedford who, by four o'clock, was getting hungry. She began to ask for a light meal to be served in her room at this time, a practice enjoyed by her friends. This idea of 'afternoon tea' became popular, and by the end of the 19th century, when women were also starting to eat out, tea rooms had become an established part of the social scene. Today I live in Kew, near the famous botanical gardens, where we are lucky enough to have Newens, established in 1870, one of the last traditional tea rooms in London. Mr Newen once told me that his father described how in the 1920s, on weekends and bank holidays, people would walk six deep over Kew Bridge from the nearest train station to eat at the many tea rooms that lined Kew Green. Today, only Newens remains, serving speciality cakes and biscuits, all baked on the premises.

Many of the biscuit recipes here are particularly regional specialities, associated with a particular town. The towns themselves are often very proud of their recipe – the football team in Grantham is even called the 'Gingerbreads', after the local Grantham Gingerbreads. Some of these regional biscuits were sold at the fairs that were held regularly throughout the year. Cornish Fairings, a crisp, golden biscuit with a characteristically crackled surface, share their name with the small china souvenirs, or 'fairings', that used to be sold, or won, at fairs – presumably because a bag of biscuits was also a souvenir of a kind. Ashby Statutes, also known as Langley Wakes Cakes, were made to eat during 'Wakes Week', an annual week's holiday originating in Lancashire. Some recipes would be lost today if it wasn't for home bakers, perhaps because the locals tend to take them for granted. Laura Mason, collecting information about Shrewsbury Biscuits for her book *Traditional Foods of Britain: An Inventory*, found that 'little curiosity about them is expressed by the inhabitants themselves'. She comments 'it seems this once famous speciality has lost its identity and is ripe for a revival'. What better incentive to get baking?

In this chapter there are four recipes spiced with ginger, ranging from the aforementioned Grantham Gingerbreads to the sweet and sticky Yorkshire Parkin. These are a mere fraction of the many gingerbread recipes to be found in Britain, where ginger has been used as a spice since the Middle

Ages. Medieval gingerbreads were in fact made from spiced breadcrumbs, mixed with honey, and many towns had their own particular gingerbread, sold as treats at fairs. Another familiar tradition is the making of gingerbread men and gingerbread pigs – traditionally for November 5th, Bonfire Night.

Seed cakes were popular in the 18th century, when plain cakes were accompanied not by tea, but by a glass of fortified wine. They are represented here by a Caraway Cake and a superb Poppy-seed Cake. Lemon Madeira Cake tastes good, naturally, with a nice glass of Madeira. But if that's not to your taste, all these plain cakes are particularly good with a cup of coffee.

I was spoilt for choice when it came to apple cakes, eventually choosing two from the West Country which also use cider – one of our national drinks, it is much underrated in cooking but well represented in this book. Pear and Ginger Loaf couples two tasty ingredients in a marriage well made, while a more unusual fruit is the main ingredient in a delicious oddity, Quince Salami. If you are lucky enough to have quinces, this very old recipe with a modern name is quite delicious.

And, of course, I had to include a Victoria Sponge. The recipe I chose – in which you first weigh the eggs, then use the same weights of flour, butter and sugar – may sound odd, but gives very good results. A couple of tips: do make sure all the ingredients are at room temperature (eggs straight from the fridge do not give as good a result), and weigh your ingredients carefully. While I'm a great believer in doing without the measuring scales, particularly if you have cooked the recipe before, I do make an exception for baking.

Ashby Statutes

Ashby Statutes are also called Langley Wakes Cakes. Derbyshire villages marked their annual Wakes or Fairs week in July and August by baking their own versions.

125g (4oz) butter
75g (3oz) caster sugar
225g (8oz) plain flour
¼ teaspoon baking powder
1 egg, well beaten
110g (4oz) mixed dried fruit and/or nuts

Makes approximately 16 cakes

Preheat oven to 180°C, 350°F, gas mark 4. Either use mixed dried fruit or make your own mixture – I find finely chopped cherries, crystallised ginger and walnut pieces are a good combination. Either grease a baking sheet well or line it with baking paper. Cream the butter or margarine with the sugar until pale and fluffy. Sift flour and baking powder, mix with the fruit and nuts and add to the mixture alternately with the egg to form a stiff dough. Roll out on a floured surface approximately 1cm (⅓in) thick and cut into 7cm (3in) rounds. Bake for about 15–20 minutes, until nicely brown. Leave to cool on the baking sheet for a few minutes and sprinkle with caster sugar.

Centenary Celebration Fruit Cake

This plain fruit-cake recipe – the sort of cake that might be called a 'cut-and-come-again' cake – was developed to be served in all National Trust properties in East Anglia during their centenary year in 1995. It is a modern recipe but I chose it for this book partly because it is a National Trust book, but also because it illustrates my conviction that cooking is never static – plain fruit cakes (as opposed to rich fruit cakes) are traditional but new recipes are always being developed.

300g (10oz) plain flour
1 level teaspoon baking powder
3 level teaspoons mixed spice
175g (6oz) caster sugar
50g (2oz) ground almonds
175ml (6fl oz) sunflower oil
175ml (6fl oz) milk
3 eggs
50g (2oz) sultanas
75g (3oz) mixed peel
125g (4oz) glacé cherries, chopped finely

Makes 1 20cm (8in) cake

Preheat oven to 180°C, 350°F, gas mark 4. Either grease and flour or line with baking paper a 20cm (8in) cake tin. Sieve the flour, baking powder and spice into a large mixing bowl. Stir in the sugar and ground almonds. Beat together the oil, milk and eggs. Then pour the mixture into a well in the centre of the dry ingredients and blend together, mixing well. Fold in the fruit and pour into the prepared tin. Bake for approximately 1 hour, or until a skewer pushed into the centre of the cake comes out clean.

Remove the cake from the tin and allow to cool.

Dundee Cake

Dundee cake was first invented to use the spare citrus peel produced by the marmalade manufacturer Keillers, whose factory is situated in the city. According to Laura Mason, the city bakers had a gentlemen's agreement that only Keillers would make Dundee cake, which lasted until the firm was taken over in 1970. The main difference between a Dundee and other fruit cakes? No spice, more butter, the inclusion of ground almonds and, of course, the almond decoration on the top.

225g (8oz) plain flour
Pinch of salt
225g (8oz) butter
225g (8oz) caster sugar
4 large eggs
350g (12oz) sultanas
350g (12oz) currants
75g (6oz) chopped mixed peel
110 (4oz) glacé cherries
Grated zest of 1 lemon
25g (1oz) ground almonds
25g (1oz) whole almonds

Makes 1 20cm (8in) cake

Preheat oven to 150°C, 300°F, gas mark 2. Line a 20cm (8in) round cake tin with baking parchment, cutting the parchment so that the top is about 5cm (2in) above the top of the tin.

Sift together the flour and salt. Beat the butter until soft, add the sugar and cream the two until they are light and creamy. Beat in the eggs, a little at a time. Fold in the flour and the sultanas, currants, peel, cherries, lemon zest and ground almonds, taking care that all is well combined. Spoon the mixture into the tin and level the top. Split the whole almonds in two and arrange them in a pattern of concentric circles on the top of the cake. Bake the cake for about 2 hours, then test with a skewer to see if it is cooked (the skewer should come out clean from the centre of the cake). If the top is getting too brown too quickly, cover it with a dampened piece of greaseproof paper. Cool in the tin for 30 minutes, then turn out and cool on a wire rack. To store the cake, wrap it in its lining paper in foil. The cake will taste even better if you keep it for two weeks or so, before cutting.

Almond Cake

This is in the 18th-century tradition of plain cakes. The almonds keep it moist. It's the perfect cake for coffee, when nothing too rich or elaborate is required.

225g (8oz) butter
225g (8oz) caster sugar
4 eggs
1 teaspoon almond essence
225g (8oz) plain flour
1 teaspoon baking powder
50g (2oz) ground almonds
25g (1oz) flaked almonds

Makes 1 20cm (8in) cake

Preheat oven to 160°C, 325°F, gas mark 3. Grease and line a 20cm (8in) cake tin. Cream together the butter and sugar until pale and fluffy. Beat in the eggs one at a time. Add the almond essence. Sift together the flour and the baking powder and lightly fold into the cake mixture. Finally stir in the ground almonds. Spoon into the prepared cake tin and sprinkle the flaked almonds on top. Bake in the oven for approximately 1½ hours. Cool on a wire tray.

Lardy Cake

Although this is called a cake, it is really a fruity, spicy bread enriched with lard.

15g (½oz) fresh yeast or 1 teaspoon dried yeast
150ml (¼ pint) warm water
1 teaspoon sugar
225g (8oz) strong white bread flour
1 teaspoon salt

75g (3oz) lard
75g (3oz) currants or sultanas
75g (3oz) sugar
1 level teaspoon mixed spice
A little milk and sugar to glaze

Makes 1 20cm (8in) cake

To make the bread dough: mix the yeast in 2 or 3 teaspoons of lukewarm water and mix in the sugar. Leave until frothy (about 20 minutes) in a warm place. Sift the flour and salt into a large bowl, make a well in the centre, add the yeast mixture and the rest of the water and draw in the flour to form a dough ball. Knead the dough for about 10 minutes, then put it in a polythene bag which has a teaspoon of oil in it. Leave it in the bag to rise to double its size at room temperature. This should take approximately 2 hours. Knead again for about 10 minutes and put it back in the polythene bag for a further 30 minutes.

Preheat oven to 220°C, 425°F, gas mark 7. Chop the lard into small pieces and mix with the fruit, sugar and spice. Divide the mixture into three. Roll out the dough to a rough oblong shape, spread one-third of the fruit mixture onto two-thirds of the dough, fold in 3 by folding over the empty third, then fold again. Repeat the process twice more, rolling out, spreading the fruit mix and folding. The last time, form the dough into a 20cm (8in) square and place in a 20cm (8in) square tin. Brush with milk and sprinkle with a little sugar. Bake for 35–40 minutes. Leave in the tin for a few minutes so that the cake absorbs any extra lard. Then turn out and cool on a rack.

Lemon Madeira Cake

The 'madeira' in the title refers to the perfect accompaniment to this plain, old-fashioned cake – a glass of Madeira. I would add that a medium sherry tastes good, too. In the 18th century, cake was often eaten with a glass of fortified wine rather than tea, and was correspondingly plain. This recipe was given to me as the favourite of an old lady who always took her cake in this traditional 18th-century fashion.

100g (4oz) soft butter
125g (5oz) caster sugar
2 eggs
Zest and juice of 1 lemon
225g (8oz) self-raising flour

Makes 1 15cm (6in) cake

Preheat oven to 150°C, 300°F, gas mark 2. Grease and line a 15cm (6in) round deep cake tin. Cream together the butter and sugar until light and fluffy. Beat in the eggs a little at a time; then add the rind and juice of a lemon. Gently fold in the flour using a large metal spoon and spoon the mixture into the lined cake tin. Place in the centre of the oven and bake for approximately 1 hour. Cool on a wire rack.

Coconut Bakewell Tart

In 1820, Mrs Greaves, landlady of the White Horse Inn in Bakewell, Derbyshire, was entertaining. She told her cook to make a pudding out of an egg mixture cooked and spread with strawberry jam. The inexperienced cook put the jam at the bottom of the pudding. Mrs Greaves's guests commented favourably and Bakewell puddings, now called tarts, have been made in Bakewell – and elsewhere – ever since.

350g (12oz) shortcrust pastry
50g (2oz) butter
50g (2oz) sugar
1 large egg, beaten
25g (1oz) desiccated coconut
50g (2oz) ground rice
3–4 tablespoons jam or lemon curd

ICING
4–6oz (110–175g) sifted icing sugar
2–4 drops vanilla essence
1–2 tablespoons warm water

Serves 6

Preheat oven to 180°C, 350°F, gas mark 4. Grease a 25cm (10in) flan dish and line with the shortcrust pastry. Keep the pastry trimmings. Cream together the butter and sugar until light and fluffy and gradually add the beaten egg. Mix in the desiccated coconut and ground rice. Spread the uncooked pastry case with jam or lemon curd, spoon in the mixture and spread evenly. Roll out the leftover pastry and make lattice strips for the top. Bake in the oven for about 1 hour or until firm. While allowing the tart to cool, make the icing as follows.

Put the sifted icing sugar and (if you wish) a few drops of vanilla essence in a basin and gradually add the warm water. The icing should be thick enough to coat the back of a spoon. If necessary, add more water or sugar to adjust the consistency. Spread the icing on the cooled tart.

Grantham Gingerbreads

Grantham Gingerbreads were first created in 1740 when a local baker in Grantham, Lincolnshire, while making a flat, hard biscuit for travellers called Grantham Whetstones, added a raising agent to the mixture by mistake. Since then, Grantham has taken its gingerbreads to its heart. It is known as 'the gingerbread town' and its local football team are known as 'The Gingerbreads'.

100g (4oz) butter
350g (12oz) sugar
1 egg, beaten
2–3 teaspoons ground ginger
250g (9oz) self-raising flour

Makes approximately 30 gingerbreads

Preheat oven to 145°C, 280°F, gas mark 1. Grease a large baking tray. Beat the butter in a bowl with a wooden spoon to soften it, then work in the sugar followed by the beaten egg. Sift the ground ginger into the flour and add to the mixture, which will be quite dry and crumbly – a bit like shortbread. Using your hands, bring the mixture together into about thirty small balls the size of a walnut and place on the baking tray, leaving plenty of space between each one. Cook in the oven for 30 minutes. The gingerbreads should remain pale in colour and have a texture and appearance rather like a macaroon.

Caraway Cake or Seed Cake

Caraway cake was the original seed cake, and was very popular in the early 19th century, when the seeds would have been comfits *– seeds dipped in sugar. This is in the English tradition of plain cakes – perfect at coffee time when you want something that is not too rich.*

175g (6oz) butter

175g (6oz) caster sugar

3 eggs

3 teaspoons caraway seeds

225g (8oz) plain flour

Pinch of salt

1 teaspoon baking powder

1 tablespoon ground almonds

1 tablespoon milk

Makes 1 23cm (9in) cake

Preheat oven to 160°C, 325°F, gas mark 3. Grease and line a 23cm (9in) cake tin. Cream together the butter and sugar until fluffy and pale. Add the eggs one at a time, beating well after each addition; then mix in the caraway seeds. Sift the flour, salt and baking powder together and fold gently into the mixture. Then add the ground almonds and milk. Spoon into the prepared tin, level out, and bake for approximately 1 hour or until firm to touch.

Right: Caraway Cake or Seed Cake

Corfe Castle Rock Cakes

These are called rock cakes because they look like nobbly rocks, and they are my favourite 'I'd forgotten they were coming and there's no time to get to the shops' recipe, partly because they taste delicious just out of the oven. Experiment with the fruit; you could try dried cranberries or chopped ginger as an alternative to the currants and sultanas.

225g (8oz) self-raising flour
½ teaspoon nutmeg
110g (4oz) butter
110g (4oz) sugar
50g (2oz) currants
50g (2oz) sultanas
25g (1oz) mixed peel
2 eggs, beaten
Milk if needed

Makes approximately 8–9 cakes

Preheat oven to 190°C, 375°F, gas mark 5. Put the flour and nutmeg into a bowl and rub in the butter. Stir in the sugar; then mix in the fruit. Add the beaten eggs and mix to a stiffish dough, adding milk if necessary. Divide into 8 or 9 pieces and place on a greased baking sheet. Bake in the centre of the oven for about 25 minutes, until the cakes just start to brown at the edges. Cool on a wire rack.

Left: Caraway Cake or Seed Cake

Devon Cider and Apple Cake

I had trouble deciding which of the seven apple-cake recipes I have collected over the past years to include here. My final choice comes from Castle Drogo, the last castle built in England, designed by Sir Edwin Lutyens in the 1920s. It dominates the Teign Valley in Devon, high up on a spur of Dartmoor, one of the last wildernesses in the UK. However, Devon is not all wild country: its rich red soil produces superb apples and cider, both of which are used in this cake.

1 large cooking apple, peeled and chopped

50g (2oz) sultanas

Scant 150ml (¼ pint) dry cider

110g (4oz) butter

110g (4oz) soft brown sugar

2 eggs, lightly beaten

225g (8oz) wholemeal or plain flour

1 teaspoon baking powder

1 teaspoon allspice

1 teaspoon cinnamon

Zest of 1 lemon, grated

1 tablespoon demerara sugar

Makes 1 20cm (8in) cake

Preheat oven to 180°C, 350°F, gas mark 4. Grease or line with baking paper a 20cm (8in) cake tin. Soak the chopped apple and sultanas in the dry cider. In a separate bowl cream together the butter and sugar until light and fluffy. Gradually beat in, little by little, the eggs. Sift together all the dry ingredients and fold into the mixture together with the lemon rind. Add the soaked fruit and cider and gently mix until it is well incorporated. Spoon into the prepared tin, scatter the demerara sugar over the top and bake for 45–60 minutes.

Rich Fruit Cake with Guinness

This cake makes a perfect Christmas cake. The use of Guinness is an inspired touch. Rich but not too sweet, the cake stays wonderfully moist.

225g (8oz) butter
225g (8oz) soft brown sugar
4 eggs, lightly beaten
275g (10oz) plain flour
2 level teaspoons mixed spice
225g (8oz) seedless raisins
225g (8oz) sultanas
110g (4oz) mixed peel
110g (4oz) chopped walnuts (hazelnuts or dates could be substituted)
8–12 tablespoons Guinness

Makes 1 18cm (7in) cake

Preheat oven to 160°C, 325°F, gas mark 3. Prepare an 18cm (7in) cake tin with baking paper. Cream together the butter and sugar. Add the lightly beaten eggs, a little at a time, mixing well between each addition. Using a large spoon, carefully fold in the flour. Add the mixed spice, fruit, nuts and 4 tablespoons of Guinness. Turn into the prepared cake tin and smooth out evenly. Bake in the centre of the oven for 1 hour, then reduce the heat to 150°C, 300°F, gas mark 2 for a further 1½ hours. Remove from the tin when cooled and prick with a skewer. Spoon over the remaining Guinness. Keep for at least one week before using. This cake will keep well for months wrapped in foil.

Eccles Cakes

Eccles is a small town on the outskirts of Manchester. Eccles cakes seem to have caused nearly as much controversy as trifle. Two 19th-century bakers, James Birch and William Bradburn, both claimed to be selling the 'authentic' version from rival shops across the road from them in the early 19th century – who was right? Should they be round or square? Should they contain only currants, or other fruit as well? This recipe allows you to choose the fruit you put in. What is not in doubt is that they are rich in fruit and spices and very good served warm from the oven.

450g (1lb) puff pastry

FOR THE FILLING
225g (8oz) stale cake crumbs, or use crushed trifle sponges if not available
225g (8oz) jam of your choice
225g (8oz) dried mixed fruit
¼ teaspoon mixed spice
¼ teaspoon cinnamon
Caster sugar for decoration

Makes approximately 4 cakes

Preheat oven to 210°C, 425°F, gas mark 7. Grease a large baking sheet or line it with baking paper. Roll out the pastry and cut into circles approximately 10–13cm (4–5in) in diameter – this is probably easier to do if you use a saucer or something similar. Mix all the filling ingredients together until well combined and place a dessertspoon of filling onto each round. Brush the edge of each round with milk, bring up to the centre and pinch to seal well. Now turn your sealed pastry parcel over, so that the seam is underneath. Gently roll it flat to about 6mm (¼in) thick and pat it into a round shape. Place the cakes onto the greased baking sheet and cut three slits in the centre of each one. Brush them with milk, sprinkle with caster sugar and bake in the oven for about 15 minutes, or until the pastry is crisp and brown. Cool on a wire rack.

Cornish Cider Cake

Did you know that there is a Good Cider Guide *produced by CAMRA, the same organisation that promotes real ale? Cornish cider apples have wonderful names – Lord of the Isles, Tommy Knight and The Rattler are three varieties that are handpicked for using in Cornish cider. This cider cake recipe comes from Lanhydrock, a wonderful National Trust property set in a beautiful valley near Bodmin. It is a modern version of an old recipe associated with the house.*

110g (4oz) butter
110g (4oz) soft brown sugar
2 beaten eggs (room temperature)
225g (8oz) wholemeal flour
1 teaspoon bicarbonate of soda
¼ teaspoon nutmeg
240ml (8fl oz) dry cider

Serves 6–8

Preheat oven to 190°C, 375°F, gas mark 5. Grease an 18cm (7in) cake tin, and line the bottom with baking paper. Cream the butter and sugar together until light and fluffy. Sift all the dry ingredients and fold into the mixture. Add the cider slowly and beat to a soft dropping consistency. Put in the cake tin and bake for 1–1¼ hours. When cooked the cake should be springy to touch and leave the sides of the tin. When cold, store in an airtight tin for at least 24 hours before serving. It is delicious with butter and apple jelly or ginger preserve.

Fruity Gingerbread

This gingerbread recipe comes from Little Moreton Hall in Cheshire: a modern recipe for a medieval food from a medieval house. Early gingerbread recipes contained breadcrumbs and used honey as a sweetener. Black treacle or molasses has been popular since the trading ships started coming back from the West Indies in the 16th century.

110g (4oz) butter
110g (4oz) soft brown sugar
125ml (4fl oz) black treacle
1 egg, beaten
150ml (¼ pint) warm milk
110g (4oz) plain flour
110g (4oz) wholemeal flour
2 teaspoons ginger
2 teaspoons cinnamon
1 teaspoon bicarbonate of soda
50g (2oz) mixed dried fruit

Makes 1 20cm (8in) gingerbread

Preheat oven to 150°C, 300°F, gas mark 2. Grease and line a 20cm (8in) square cake tin. Melt the butter, sugar and treacle in a saucepan – cool and add the beaten egg and warm milk. Sift the flours, spices and bicarbonate of soda together in a mixing bowl and add the mixed dried fruit. Make a well in the centre of the dry ingredients, pour in the treacle mixture and beat very thoroughly. Pour into the tin and bake in the oven for approximately 1 hour. Cool for a couple of minutes in the tin, then on a rack.

Mrs Middlemiss's Rich Fruit Cake

This is the rich fruit cake for you if you prefer one without alcohol. Mrs Middlemiss baked cakes during the 1980s at Little Moreton Hall. She must have retired by now, but when she was baking the cakes, they were worth a detour as much as the house was!

110g (4oz) caster sugar

110g (4oz) soft dark brown sugar

225g (8oz) butter

50g (2oz) treacle

4 eggs

75g (3oz) self-raising flour

200g (7oz) plain flour

1 teaspoon mixed spice

700g (1½lb) mixed dried fruit: try candied peel, currants, sultanas, glacé
   cherries, crystallised ginger, chopped dates and chopped prunes

1 tablespoon milk

Makes 1 20cm (8in) cake

Preheat oven to 150°C, 300°F, gas mark 2. Grease and line a 20cm (8in) square cake tin. Cream together the sugars, butter and treacle and add the eggs one at a time, beating well between each addition until well combined. Sift the flours and mixed spice into a separate bowl, add the dried fruit and mix together. Gradually fold into the creamed mixture and finally add the milk. Spoon the mixture into the cake tin and bake in the centre of the oven for 2½–2¾ hours.

Yorkshire Parkin

Parkin is a gingerbread that contains oats. It was originally cooked on a griddle and eaten especially at Celtic and Christian festivals from 31 October to 11 November, including Bonfire Night. Parkin comes thick or thin, but in Yorkshire they prefer it thick, as in the recipe below.

225g (8oz) butter
225g (8oz) golden syrup
110g (4oz) self-raising flour
110g (4oz) wholemeal flour
110g (4oz) rolled oats
110g (4oz) oatmeal
225g (8oz) sugar
1 heaped teaspoon ground ginger
½ teaspoon baking powder
1 egg, beaten and made up to 180ml (6fl oz) with milk
½ teaspoon salt

Makes 1 20cm (8in) tin

Preheat oven to 160°C, 325°F, gas mark 3. Thoroughly grease a 20cm (8in) square cake tin. Melt the butter and golden syrup together in a saucepan. Mix all the dry ingredients together in a mixing bowl and stir in the melted ingredients. Add the egg and milk and thoroughly combine using a wooden spoon. Pour into the well-greased tin and bake for approximately 45 minutes. Remove from the tin whilst still slightly warm to avoid sticking. The parkin will keep very well in an airtight tin or will freeze. Parkin is traditionally kept in a tin with a sliced Cox's apple to keep it damp, and left to mature for at least a week.

Poppy-seed Cake

This delicious and unusual cake is in the British tradition of seed cakes (see page 256). It was given to me by a cook from Buckland Abbey in Devon, home of Sir Francis Drake, where it is a great favourite.

110g (4oz) blue poppy seeds
225ml (8fl oz) milk
225g (8oz) butter
225g (8oz) light raw cane sugar
3 eggs, separated
225g (8oz) self-raising wholemeal flour

Makes 1 20cm (8in) cake

Preheat oven to 350°F, 180°C, gas mark 4. Grease and line a 20cm (8in) cake tin. Bring the poppy seeds to the boil in the milk, turn off the heat and leave them to soak for 25 minutes in the covered pan.

Cream the butter and sugar together until light and fluffy. Add the egg yolks, one at a time, and beat thoroughly. Fold the flour gently into the creamed mixture and stir in the seeds and milk. Whisk the egg whites until stiff and carefully incorporate into the mixture. Spoon it into the prepared tin and bake for 1–1¼ hours or until the centre is firm and the cake has stopped 'singing'. Let it stand for 10 minutes, then turn out to cool.

Victoria Sponge Cake

Named after Queen Victoria, the Victoria Sponge is a creamed sponge cake (one in which the sugar and butter are creamed together before the eggs are beaten in), filled with whipped cream and raspberry jam. There are three important rules for making any sponge cake – firstly, all the ingredients must be at room temperature; secondly, the flour and sugar must be sifted very well; and finally, the longer you beat it, the lighter it is. I prefer to bake this cake in one tin and split the cake to fill it, but you can bake it in two sandwich tins – you may have to shorten the cooking time if you do.

4 large eggs
Equal weights to the eggs of butter, caster sugar and self-raising flour

FLAVOURINGS
Either a few drops of vanilla essence or zest of 1 lemon or zest of 1 orange.

FOR THE FILLING
3–4 tablespoons raspberry jam
150ml (¼ pint) double cream, whipped stiff

Makes 1 23cm (9in) cake

Preheat oven to 175°C, 350°F, gas mark 4. Line a 23cm (9in) springform tin with baking paper. Beat the butter with either an electric beater, a wooden spoon or a balloon whisk until pale in colour and creamy. Gradually beat in the sugar, and beat vigorously at least another 5 minutes once the sugar is in. The mixture should almost double in volume and be very pale in colour. Beat in the eggs, one at a time, beating vigorously between additions. If the mixture curdles, beat in a small spoonful of the measured flour with the egg. Stir in the chosen flavouring at this point. Finally fold in the flour, very gently.

Spoon the mixture into the prepared tin and bake for about 45 minutes in the preheated oven. The cake is cooked when a skewer inserted in the centre comes out clean.

Cool on a wire rack. When cold, cut the cake in half and spread the bottom half with raspberry jam and whipped cream. Put the top back on lightly and dust with icing sugar.

Pear and Ginger Loaf

Ginger has been used in British cookery for centuries. Medieval cooks in well-off households used dried ginger in every kind of dish, but from the 18th century it was in baking, specifically cakes and biscuits, that ginger was especially popular. The taste and texture of pear has a particular affinity with ginger.

225g (8oz) self-raising flour
¼ level teaspoon ground ginger
110g (4oz) soft brown sugar
110g (4oz) butter
1 ripe pear
1 egg, beaten
3 tablespoons milk

Makes 1 small loaf

Preheat oven to 180°C, 350°F, gas mark 4. Well grease or line with baking paper a small loaf tin. Sift the flour and ginger together and then stir in the soft brown sugar. Using your fingertips, rub in the butter. Peel, core and finely chop the pear and stir it into the flour mixture. Add the beaten egg and milk and mix to a stiff dough. Turn into the loaf tin and bake for approximately 55 minutes.

Macaroons

Macaroons were often served with wine in the 18th and 19th centuries, and macaroon recipes have appeared in cookery books since at least the late 17th century. The name comes from Italy – in the Neopolitan dialect, a maccarone *is a dumpling or small cake. I collected this recipe from a Cornish cook at Trelissick, a beautiful garden near Falmouth, Cornwall, in the 1980s.*

200g (7oz) caster sugar
25g (1oz) granulated sugar
110g (4oz) ground almonds
1 tablespoon rice flour
3 egg whites
2–3 drops of almond essence
Rice paper and split almonds

Makes approximately 9 macaroons

Preheat oven to 180°C, 350°F, gas mark 4. Mix the sugars, ground almonds and rice flour together in a bowl. Add the egg whites and essence and beat everything together with a wooden spoon for about 5 minutes. Scrape down the sides of the bowl and leave to stand for 5 minutes. Meanwhile, cut the rice paper into 7.5cm (3in) squares and place shiny side down on a baking sheet. Continue to beat the almond mixture for a further 5 minutes until thick and white. Using a bag and 12mm (½in) nozzle, pipe onto the rice paper – place a split almond in the centre of each macaroon and bake in the oven for 20–30 minutes.

Oat Biscuits

These oat biscuits are nutty and sustaining.

110g (4oz) margarine or butter
2 teaspoons golden syrup
¼ teaspoon bicarbonate of soda dissolved in 1 dessertspoon hot water
110g (4oz) granulated sugar
75g (3oz) plain flour
100g (4oz) rolled oats

Makes approximately 12–16 biscuits

Preheat oven to 200°C, 400°F, gas mark 6. Grease or line with paper a large baking tray. Gently melt the margarine and syrup in a saucepan. Add the bicarbonate of soda dissolved in the hot water and all the remaining ingredients. Stir with a wooden spoon until well mixed together. Place small drops on the greased baking tray, with plenty of space between each one for spreading. Bake for approximately 10 minutes.

Flapjacks

The name 'flapjack' was originally used for a griddle cake that had to be turned during cooking. 'Pancake, fritter or flapjacke' wrote John Taylor in 1634. Now it is a thick, sweet biscuit made with rolled oats.

50g (2oz) butter or margarine
110g (4oz) golden syrup
50g (2oz) demerara sugar
225g (8oz) rolled oats

Makes approximately 10 flapjacks

Preheat oven to 180°C, 350°F, gas mark 4. Grease a 20cm (8in) square cake tin. Melt the butter, syrup and sugar in a saucepan. Stir in the rolled oats, turn the mixture into the cake tin and spread evenly. Bake for 30–35 minutes. Take out of the oven and cut into pieces immediately. Leave in the tin until cold.

Shortbread

Shortbread is a biscuit with a long history. Tradition says Mary, Queen of Scots brought them to Scotland in 1550. The name harks back to the 'short cakes' baked in the 16th century. The classic proportions are always the same: 3 parts flour to 2 parts butter to 1 part sugar. I consulted the best shortbread cook I know for the perfect mix of flours; Kate has been cooking shortbread professionally for, among others, an acclaimed farm shop in the South West. She varies the flour by using one-third cornflour, and the variations I have suggested are hers.

110g (4oz) plain flour
50g (2oz) cornflour
110g (4oz) butter
50g (2oz) caster sugar
Caster sugar to decorate

Makes approximately 12 biscuits

Preheat oven to 160°C, 325°F, gas mark 3. Sieve the flour and cornflour together. Cream the butter until it is soft, then add the caster sugar and beat until the mixture is pale and creamy. Work the butter and sugar into the flour mixture a tablespoon at a time. Place the shortbread mixture onto a large baking tray and roll out to an 8in (20cm) circle. Pinch the edges and prick well with a fork. Cut through into 12 sections with the back of a knife, then sprinkle with a little caster sugar. Leave to chill in the fridge for 15 minutes, then bake in a moderate oven for 35 minutes or until pale and golden brown. Cool on the baking tray.

VARIATIONS
Orange shortbread: Add the zest of one orange to the mixture. The shortbread will be slightly softer than the plain version.
Walnut shortbread: Add 75g (3oz) chopped walnuts to the mixture.
Ginger shortbread: Add 50g (2oz) finely chopped crystallised ginger to the mixture. This shortbread will be slightly softer than the plain version.
Chocolate chip shortbread: Chop up a 75g (3oz) bar of fine milk or plain chocolate into chips and add to the mixture. This shortbread will be slightly softer than the plain version.

If you want fingers of shortbread, press the mixture into a shallow, oblong tin approximately 150 x 230cm (6 x 9in) instead of rolling it out. Cut into fingers as soon as the shortbread comes out of the oven, then leave it to cool in the tin.

Whittingham Buttons

Whittingham is a small village deep in the moors in Northumberland. This is a very local recipe, which was probably discovered by accident — who would have thought of putting custard powder in a biscuit? It works, though — they are crisp and sweet. In Northumberland you can buy them at the bakers, but anywhere else you will have to make them yourself.

175g (6oz) butter or margarine
75g (3oz) icing sugar
175g (6oz) plain flour
50g (2oz) custard powder

Makes 12–16 biscuits

Preheat oven to 180°C, 350°F, gas mark 4. Cream the butter and sugar together very thoroughly until light and flurry. Add the flour and custard powder and mix to form a firm dough. Break off small pieces, the size of a large walnut, and roll into a ball with your hands or place small spoonfuls on to a greased baking sheet and flatten slightly. Bake in a preheated oven for 10-15 minutes or until lightly golden. Cool on a wire rack.

Right: Whittingham Buttons

Quince Salami

This old and unusual recipe was once known as Quince Marmalade or Dried Suckets of Quince. Tudor marmalades were rather different from what we call marmalade today. Originally, they were made from quinces (imported from Portugal, where the name for quince is marmelo*). In those days, the marmalade was boiled for much longer than today, until it was solid. It was then eaten in chunks as part of the banqueting course, the last course of a feast. It also looks like salami!*

1 generous kilo (2–2¼lb) large quinces, thinly peeled
850g (1¾lb) caster sugar
Juice of 1 lemon
175g (6oz) mixed crystallised fruits, such as cherries, pineapple, pears, apricots
  and plums, chopped if large
225g (8oz) blanched almonds, roughly chopped

Serves 6–8

Put the quinces in a large saucepan, cover with water and bring to the boil. Boil, covered, until the quinces are soft (this may take quite a long time). Remove the saucepan from the heat and place the fruit in a colander to drain. Reserve the cooking liquid. While they are still hot, core the quinces and purée them in a food processor or blender.

Measure 225ml (8fl oz) of the cooking liquid into a saucepan. Reserve two tablespoons of sugar and dissolve the rest in the liquid over a very low heat. Stir continuously until the syrup is clear, then bring it to the boil without stirring and let it boil for a minute or two until it thickens. Add the quince purée and continue cooking and stirring until the mixture becomes very thick and leaves the side of the pan. Remove the saucepan from the heat, stir in the lemon juice, the crystallised fruits and almonds. Stir until they are well distributed throughout the quince paste.

Turn the mixture out on to a smooth surface, lined with clingfilm. Using the clingfilm as a container, work it into a sausage shape as soon as it is cool enough to handle. Then roll it in the remaining sugar and chill it well. Slice the salami thinly and serve with after-dinner coffee instead of petits fours or truffles.

Left: Quince Salami

Northumbrian Ginger and Cinnamon Biscuits

These are similar (except for the cinnamon) to the Cornish Fairings on page 277 — crisp biscuits are favourites everywhere. This recipe comes from the other end of England.

170g (6oz) butter
170g (6oz) sugar
1 tablespoon golden syrup
350g (12oz) plain flour sifted with
   2 teaspoons each of bicarbonate of soda, ginger and cinnamon

Makes approximately 30 biscuits

Preheat oven to 160°C, 325°F; gas mark 3. Line a baking sheet with baking parchment. Melt margarine, sugar and golden syrup in a saucepan. Add the flour, bicarbonate of soda, ginger and cinnamon and mix well. Roll small amounts of the mixture in your hands to form balls, approximately the size of a large walnut. Place these well apart on the baking sheet and flatten the top slightly of each one. Bake approximately 10–15 minutes until golden. Transfer to a wire tray to cool.

Shrewsbury Biscuits

This is a very old recipe. Shrewsbury Cakes, as they were then known, are mentioned in a document of 1561 but were probably made well before this date. The baker who made them famous is mentioned in the Ingoldsby Legends, *published in the 19th century: 'Palin, prince of cake pounders!/The mouth liquefies at the very name.' Palin the baker ran a confectionery shop on the corner of Castle Street and School Lane in Shrewsbury during the late 18th and early 19th centuries.*

50g (2oz) butter
50g (2oz) sugar
1 egg
50g (2oz) currants
175g (6oz) plain flour
¼ teaspoon mixed spice
Caster sugar to decorate

Makes approximately 20 biscuits

Preheat oven to 190°C, 375°F, gas mark 5. Either grease two large baking sheets or line them with baking paper. Cream the butter and sugar until pale and fluffy. Add the egg and beat in well. Fold in the currants, flour and mixed spice and knead lightly into a smooth ball. Roll out on a floured surface to about 5mm (¼in) thickness. Cut into rounds with a 6cm (2½in) fluted cutter and put on the baking trays. Bake in the oven for 15 minutes – after 5 minutes take out and sprinkle with caster sugar; then continue to cook until firm and very light brown in colour.

Honey Oatcakes

A cross between a flapjack and a biscuit, this recipe was given to me at Anglesey Abbey near Cambridge. There, the oatcakes are baked using flour which is stone ground using ancient millstones at the local water mill situated on the river Lode.

50g (2oz) butter
3 tablespoons clear honey
125g (5oz) light brown sugar
125g (5oz) coconut
50g (2oz) rolled oats
225g (8oz) wholemeal flour
1¼ teaspoons baking powder

Makes approximately 15–20 oatcakes

Preheat oven to 160°C, 325°F, gas mark 3. Grease a baking tin approximately 25 x 18cm (10 x 7in). Melt the butter and honey over a low heat. Mix all the dry ingredients together and add to the butter and honey. Spread in the tin and bake in the oven for 20 minutes. While still warm, cut into triangles and leave to cool in the tin.

Cornish Fairings

Fairings are thin, crisp, spicy biscuits, approximately 8–10cm (3–4in) in diameter with a characteristic cracked surface. They were sold at the Fairs that were held at certain times of year and each county or town had its particular type of biscuit (see also Ashby Statutes, page 248).

110g (4oz) butter or margarine
110g (4oz) caster sugar
100ml (3½fl oz) golden syrup
225g (8oz) plain flour
2 level teaspoons baking powder
2 level teaspoons bicarbonate of soda
2 level teaspoons ground ginger
1 level teaspoon mixed spice

Makes approximately 24 biscuits

Preheat oven to 150°C, 300°F, gas mark 2. Cream the butter, sugar and syrup together until well mixed, light and fluffy. Sift the flour, baking powder, bicarbonate of soda and spices together and add to the butter mixture until you have a soft dough. Make the dough into balls about the size of a walnut and put on a tray either well greased and floured or lined with baking paper. Flatten each ball slightly and keep them well apart; the biscuits spread as they cook. Bake for approximately 15 minutes. Cool on a wire tray.

Jams and Preserves

'The rule is, jam tomorrow and jam yesterday – but never jam today.' It seems unlikely that the White Queen in Lewis Carroll's *Alice Through the Looking Glass*, a hopelessly disorganised woman, ever made her own jam. Maybe if she had, there would have been 'jam today'.

Preserving food is a preoccupation we can all understand, although today it is more a pleasure than a necessity, when there are preserves aplenty to buy in the shops. Even so, the most expensive jams and pickles are often packaged to look as though they are home-made – because there is definitely something special about home-made pickles and preserves. Jams and preserves are not difficult to make, although they do take time. Generally they cost less than the shop-bought version, and if you grow your own fruit and vegetables, they can cost virtually nothing. If you don't grow your own fruit you can visit a 'Pick Your Own' farm, adding to the enjoyment.

Come January or February, when I was a child, our family kitchen was always full of steam and smelt of oranges – my mother was making her annual batch of marmalade. We had no freezer, so she watched the greengrocer's shelves like a hawk from Christmas onwards, awaiting the arrival of the Seville oranges. Much less beautiful than sweet oranges, knobbly, odd shapes and sizes, and sometimes still with their stalks and leaves attached, Seville oranges have an all-too-short season of just a few weeks. Today it is easy; you can buy the oranges and freeze them for later, if you haven't the time to make the marmalade now. But back then, once you had bought the oranges, you had to make your marmalade as soon as possible.

Good marmalade used to be expensive and in short supply. In my childhood, five of us ate mountains of toast and marmalade every morning, so it made good economic sense for my mother to make her own. When I got married, she bought me a preserving pan and gave me her recipe. I made it then because I loved the taste, but I make it now because, as well as the taste, I am hooked on the process. I love chopping the fruit, and the smell – I even like the time it takes. Because, although my Mum's recipe takes three days, making marmalade is a well-loved ritual, not a chore.

Preserves make wonderful presents, if you can bear to give them away. And you never have to worry about having made too much of anything because once made, (with the exception of Lemon Curd), preserves keep for a long time. Jams are probably best eaten within a year, but chutneys, like fine wines, improve with age.

There are, of course, recipes for jam for most fruits, across the world, and there is no shortage of recipes for strawberry and raspberry jam. But the recipes included in this chapter were chosen either for their particular ingredients or for a combination of ingredients that is particularly traditional to British cooking.

Marrow and Lemon Jam is an example of a good and tasty preserve, where ingenuity is part of the equation – marrow (or squash or courgettes) grows well in many parts of Britain, but the season is short and almost too bountiful. The recipe comes from Mrs Beddows, who was famous for her jams. Her Blackberry and Apple Jam solves the problem of blackberry pips by calling for both blackberry and apple purées, and then combining the two with sugar – the result is thick and aromatic. I love anything with quince as an ingredient, and the Quince Jam is a wonderful pale pink in colour, with a taste all of its own. Although cherries are available almost all year round, the season when the fruit is abundant and tastes best is short. Cherry Conserve extends the pleasure to be had from this gorgeous fruit, and can be used as a sauce with ice cream – or even one of the rice puddings.

Mincemeat and Mince Pies have a long history. With a filling of meat, preserved fruit, chopped nuts and apples, moistened with vinegar or lemon juice, they were called *chewettes* in the Middle Ages, but had become *mince* or *shred* pies by the 16th century. As Christmas pies, in the 17th century, they were banned by the Puritans, who tried to suppress the celebration of Christmas during Cromwell's time. No wonder Samuel Pepys comments – on Christmas Day, 1666 – that he left his wife in bed 'desirous to sleep, having sat up to 4 this morning seeing her maids make mince pies'. At that date the pies had only just come back on the menu, and would still have had meat in them. But in the 19th century the meat was replaced by suet (chopped fat of animal origin). Amy's Mincemeat, a 20th-century recipe, contains no fat at all. It just goes to show that traditional recipes are always changing.

Chutneys are Anglo-Indian. Malays, Indonesians and Indians traditionally serve *sambals* – uncooked relishes – and *chatnis* – cooked relishes – with meals. At the end of the 17th century the East India Company ships brought these strong, sweet pickles back to Britain, where they quickly became popular. A recipe for Piccalilli, a sweet mustard pickle of mixed vegetables, was recorded as early as 1694. I make Frances's Spicy Apple and Onion Chutney every year in September, using apples from a tree in our garden, species unknown. The apples don't keep well, and some years they don't even seem to ripen, but they make chutney that tastes good from the moment it is made. We like to eat it with cold meats and any kind of cheese.

Some relishes are traditional accompaniments to particular dishes. Irish Stew and Lancashire Hot Pot are generally accompanied by Red Cabbage Pickle. The recipe given here is milder and spicier than shop-bought pickle, and is simplicity itself to make. I pickle shallots and onion using Sara Paston-Williams's recipe for Sweet Pickled Onions, from her book *Jams, Preserves and Edible Gifts*, and also use her recipe for that old favourite, Lemon Curd.

A preserving pan is useful but not essential for these recipes. A sugar thermometer and a jam funnel for pouring mixtures into jars are also useful but, again, are not essential. You must wash the jars you are going to use for your preserves, then sterilise them by boiling in a large pan for 10 minutes, and drying them in an oven at 110°C (225°F) for 15 minutes, after which they will be ready for use. I store jams and marmalade in the fridge because I do not have a cool larder, but chutneys and pickles are fine on a shelf, or in a cupboard.

Amy's Mincemeat

Mincemeat originally contained meat and commercial mincemeat still contains suet, a meat product. With no suet, this home-made version, originally from West Devon, is suitable for vegetarians. Home-made Mincemeat rewards the effort of making it; both the taste and the texture are quite different from the commercial product. Don't worry about the quantity; it keeps for a long time.

**1.3kg (3lb) cooking and/or eating apples, peeled, cored and
finely chopped or grated
Juice and finely grated zest of 1 orange
Juice and finely grated zest of 1 lemon
600ml (1 pint) medium sweet cider
450g (1lb) brown sugar
1 teaspoon ground cinnamon
1 teaspoon grated nutmeg
1 teaspoon ground cloves
450g (1lb) raisins
450g (1lb) currants
225g (8oz) glacé cherries, halved
100ml (3½fl oz) rum**

Makes about 2.6kg (6lb)

Put the apples, juices and cider in a large pan or preserving pan. Bring to the boil, reduce the heat and simmer for 10 minutes. Stir in the sugar, cinnamon, nutmeg, cloves, raisins and currants. When the sugar has dissolved, simmer the mixture for a further 15 minutes. Remove the pan from the heat and stir in the glacé cherries. Allow the mixture to cool completely and stir in the rum. Pack into glass jam jars and cover.

Mince Pies

Use Amy's Mincemeat to create these delicious mince pies – a great British Christmas tradition.

225g (8oz) shortcrust pastry (see page 54)

FOR THE SWEET PASTRY
110g (4oz) plain flour
Pinch of salt
50g (2oz) butter
50g (2oz) icing sugar
1 egg yolk
2 teaspoons water

FOR THE FILLING
Approximately 225g (½lb) mincemeat
Sunflower oil

Milk, for brushing
Caster sugar, for sprinkling

Make up the sweet pastry as follows: combine the flour, salt, butter and sugar in a food processor and process until the mixture resembles coarse breadcrumbs. Add the egg yolk and water and process until the mixture forms a ball – stop the machine as soon as the ball has formed. Place the pastry in a plastic bag and chill for 30 minutes.

Preheat oven to 170°C, 350°F, gas mark 5. Roll out both types of pastry. Using fluted cutters, cut round bases 6cm (2½in) in diameter and lids 4cm (2in) in diameter. Brush a patty tin with 6cm (2½in) bowls with oil and line each bowl with shortcrust pastry. Prick the bases with a fork. Spoon a teaspoon of mincemeat into each one. Brush the edge of the pastry with milk and cover with sweet pastry. Prick the tops with a fork. Brush the tops with milk, dust with caster sugar and bake for approximately 15 minutes until golden brown. Cool on a wire rack. Serve warm with brandy butter. Mince Pies keep for a month in an airtight container.

Apple and Sage Jelly

Ellen Jefferies is famous at Erddig, North Wales for her spiced jelly preserves using fruits from the garden, orchard and hedgerow and either fresh herbs or spices from the store cupboard.

900g (2lb) apples, chopped but not cored or peeled
Large bunch of fresh sage
Pared zest and juice of 1 lemon
Sugar, granulated or preserving

Makes about 8 small jars

This recipe takes two days to make. Put the apples, sage, lemon zest and juice in a preserving pan. Add sufficient water to cover them. Cover the pan and simmer until the fruit is very soft. This should take around 30 minutes. Strain through a jelly bag overnight.

The next day, measure the juice into a clean preserving pan. Add 450g (1lb) sugar for each 600ml (1 pint) of juice. Heat gently until the sugar has dissolved, then boil rapidly until setting point is reached, stirring from time to time. Skim, pour the jelly into warm jars and cover. Seal when still hot.

Pear and Rosemary Jelly

This is another of Ellen Jefferies's wonderful jelly preserves recipes.

900g (2lb) pears
Pared zest and juice of 2 lemons
Large bunch of rosemary
Sugar, granulated or preserving
225ml (8fl oz) pectin, if necessary

Makes about 8 small jars

Proceed as for Apple and Sage Jelly, adding the pectin at the end if it is difficult to get the jelly to set.

Blackberry and Apple Jam

Supermarket blackberries can be used for the recipe, but in a perfect world this recipe is made with blackberries gathered from the hedgerow and windfall apples. You don't need perfect fruit for it. I like a mixture of cooking and eating apples because then the ultimate purée has more texture to it. It's also worth trying the PYO (pick your own) farms, if you can't find a suitable hedgerow.

900g (2lb) blackberries
300ml (½ pint) water
350g (12oz) cooking apples or eating apples (prepared weight)
1.3g (3lb) sugar

Makes approximately 8 jars

Pick over and wash the blackberries, put them in a pan with 150ml (¼ pint) of water and simmer slowly until soft – sieve to remove the pips. Peel, core and slice the apples and add the remaining 150ml (¼ pint) of water. Simmer slowly until soft and make into a pulp with a spoon or a potato masher. Add the blackberry purée and sugar, bring to the boil and boil rapidly, stirring frequently, until setting point is reached. Test for a set by cooling a little of the mixture on a cold plate (put the plate in the fridge first) – if a skin forms, it is ready. Pot into warm jars and cover.

Marrow and Lemon Jam

This was a popular jam during World War II when we could import no food and had to improvise with what we had. Fruit was too precious to be made into jam but marrows were plentiful. Fruit is not in short supply now but the jam is still pretty good and it's a great way to use up any excess marrows from the garden. In wartime, lemons were not available – but they do help to bring out the flavour.

900g (2lb) marrow (prepared weight)
900g (2lb) sugar
Thinly peeled zest and juice of 2 lemons

Makes approximately 6 jars

You need to start this recipe the day before it is cooked. Peel the marrow, remove the seeds and cut into pieces about 12mm (^{1}/$_2$in) square. Place in a basin, sprinkle with the sugar and allow to stand overnight. Tie up the lemon zest in a piece of muslin and place in a large, heavy pan with the marrow, sugar and lemon juice. Simmer until the sugar has dissolved, then boil until setting point is reached (see Blackberry and Apple Jam, page 285) and the marrow looks transparent. Remove the muslin bag, pot into warm jars and cover.

Cherry Conserve

'Take the best and fairest of cherries' begins the receipt from 1685, on which this recipe is based. Cherries will always be precious. Cherry conserve is very special, and the addition of alcohol (optional) turns it into a luxury. Cherries are low in pectin, so the availability of pectin sugar today takes the guesswork out of achieving a set. But even with pectin, don't expect a firm set. This is a runny treat.

900g (2lb) dark red cherries
Juice and zest of 2 lemons
800g (1¾lb) sugar with pectin
2–3 tablespoons cherry brandy or Kirsch

Makes 1.4–1.8kg (3–4lb)

Stone the cherries and place them with the zest and lemon juice in a large, heavy-based pan. Simmer very gently for about 15 minutes or until really soft, stirring from time to time to prevent them from sticking. Add the sugar and stir over a low heat until dissolved. Increase the heat and boil rapidly until setting point is reached (approximately another 5 minutes). Stir in the alcohol of your choice, if you wish, then ladle into the prepared jars and cover when cold with waxed discs and cellophane secured with rubber bands.

Trelissick Lemon Curd

This recipe, originally from Jams, Preserves and Edible Gifts *(National Trust), uses a slow cooker. I have also given instructions for those of you who don't have one. Lemon curd should be kept in the fridge and eaten within a month or so of making. If your curd curdles while you are making it, remove it quickly from the heat and stand it over a basin of cold water. Whisk hard until the curdling disappears, then continue as before.*

Finely grated zest and juice of 2 large lemons, preferably unwaxed and organic
4 large eggs, lightly beaten
175g (6oz) caster sugar
110g (4oz) unsalted butter, melted

Makes approximately 3 jars

Place the lemon zest and juice in a basin or dish that will fit in the slow cooker. Add the beaten eggs, sugar and melted butter and stir well. Cover with a piece of foil and place in the slow cooker. Pour enough boiling water into the slow cooker to come half-way up the basin or dish, then cover with the lid of the slow cooker. Cook for about 1½–2 hours until thick. Stir well with a wooden or plastic spoon (metal implements spoil the flavour), then pot in warm jars.

If you do not have a slow cooker, follow this method. Put the lemon zest and juice in a heatproof basin set over a pan of barely simmering water. Take care not to let the bottom of the bowl touch the water. Add the well-beaten eggs, sugar and melted butter. Stir the mixture frequently with a wooden or plastic spoon for about 20 minutes or until thick.

VARIATIONS
Lime Curd: Substitute 4 limes for the lemons.
Grapefruit Curd: Substitute 1¹/₂ grapefruit for the lemons.
Tangerine Curd: Use 2–3 tangerines (depending on size) instead of the lemons and reduce the amount of sugar to 110g (4oz).
Orange Curd: Use 1 large orange, preferably Seville or bitter orange when in season, instead of the lemons and reduce the amount of sugar to 110g (4oz).
St Clement's Curd: Use 1 medium orange and 1 large lemon instead of the 2 lemons and reduce the amount of sugar to 110g (4oz).

Right: Trelissick Lemon Curd

Marmalade

Seville oranges are the most popular fruit for marmalade because of their flavour and appearance. These oranges have a very short season, but they can be frozen for use later in the year. This is my mother's recipe, written by her into my blank recipe book when I got married. I use slightly less water than she did because I find it easier to get a good set, particularly if I have frozen the oranges. You need to begin this recipe two days before you pot the marmalade, but since all the real work is done on the first day, it is just a case of being patient.

About 1.6kg (3½lb) Seville oranges
2 lemons
Water
2.6kg (6lb) sugar
Butter

Makes between 9 and 12 jars

On the first day, cut all the fruits in half. Squeeze each half and retain the juice. Scrape out the shells, keeping the pips and pith. Put pips and pith into a piece of muslin lining a pudding basin. Slice the fruit shells into thin strips and put in a preserving pan. Measure the juice and make it up with water to 3.6 litres (6 pints). Tie up the muslin containing the pips and pith into a bag and hang it from the handle of the preserving pan so that it is covered by the water. Cover the pan with a clean cloth and leave the fruit to stand overnight.

On the second day, bring the fruit and water to the boil and simmer until the peel is tender. This should take about half an hour. Cover the pan and leave to stand overnight.

On the third day, preheat the oven to 100°C, 200°F, gas mark 1. Measure out sugar into a baking tin and warm it in the oven. Bring the fruit and water up to the boil. Put a saucer into the freezer compartment of the fridge at this point. When the fruit and water is boiling hard, tip in the warmed sugar and stir until it is dissolved. Replace the sugar in the oven with the pots you are intending to use for the marmalade. Boil rapidly, stirring to prevent burning until setting point is reached. Test for the setting point by dropping a teaspoon of liquid and peel onto the chilled saucer, putting it back into the fridge and waiting until it cools. If it forms a skin at this point, it will set. Once you have reached this point, put a knob of butter the size of a walnut into the marmalade. Leave it for 10 minutes to cool a little and put into the hot glass pots. Cover and label the pots when the marmalade is cold.

Left: Rhubarb Chutney

Quince Jam

A recipe to preserve a precious fruit. The quince was the original golden apple that Paris gave to the goddess Aphrodite in the garden of the Hesperides. If you find the earthly version on sale, buy them immediately. Better still, if you have a garden, plant a quince tree. Quinces ripen in October, when the leaves start to fall, and are even better if used after a frost.

900g (2lb) quinces, peeled, chopped and cored
Water
1.4 kg (3lb) sugar
Juice of 1 lemon

Makes approximately 3–4 jars

Put the prepared quinces in a pan with enough water to cover and cook slowly until the fruit is really soft – this takes at least 30 minutes. Then add the sugar and lemon juice and stir until dissolved. Boil rapidly until setting point is reached. Pot and cover in the usual way. Makes about 2.2kg (5lb).

Frances's Spicy Apple and Onion Chutney

This recipe from Northumberland is simplicity itself. It tastes good with all cold meats and is superlative with cheese. Don't worry about what apples to use, as it's a very easy-going recipe. I prefer to use a mixture of eating and cooking apples, which I feel gives the best texture, but use what is best value and available to you. By the way, it will probably get eaten, but it does keep – even improve – for at least a year.

1.3g (3lb) apples, peeled, cored and chopped
900g (2lb) onion, sliced finely
225g (8oz) raisins
50g (2oz) yellow mustard seeds
1.2 litres (2 pints) wine or cider vinegar
225g (8oz) fresh tomatoes, chopped
4 teaspoons salt
225g (8oz) caster sugar
2 teaspoons cayenne pepper or 1 teaspoon of minced chilli

Makes approximately 10 jars

Put all the ingredients in a preserving pan and bring to the boil, stirring while the sugar dissolves. Boil all together for an hour. Pot and cover when cold.

Red Cabbage Pickle

This is a traditional – and delicious – accompaniment to Irish Stew (see page 88) and Lancashire Hot Pot (see page 100).

1.3kg (3lb) red cabbage
1 onion
About 1 tablespoon salt
4 teaspoons soft brown sugar
700ml (1¼ pints) cider or wine vinegar
225g (8oz) caster sugar
¼ teaspoon mixed spice
6 peppercorns
1 teaspoon whole cloves
1 cinnamon stick

Makes approximately 4 jars

Slice the cabbage and the onion finely and mix with salt in a large bowl. Put all the rest of the ingredients in a pan and bring to the boil, stirring while the sugar dissolves. Transfer to a china or plastic container and leave both to stand overnight. Next day, put the cabbage and onion into jars, packing it as tightly as you can. Pour over the vinegar mixture and leave it at least three days before using as a relish. It will keep for several months.

Piccalilli

'Take vinegar one gallon, garlic one pound, ginger one pound, turmeric, mustard seed, long pepper and salt of each 4 ounces'. These are some of the ingredients for an Indian pickle written down in 1765. By this time the East India Company had familiarised the well-off with chatnis *from the East. In Piccalilli the mustard acts as a preservative as well as the vinegar. This recipe comes from Oxburgh Hall in Norfolk, where they pickle seasonal vegetables from their kitchen garden.*

2.75kg (6lb) prepared vegetables (a mixture of diced cucumber, marrow, courgette, beans, cauliflower florets and small onions)
450g (1lb) cooking salt
25–40g (1–1½oz) mustard powder
25–40g (1–1½oz) ground ginger
175g (6oz) white sugar
1 litre (2 pints) distilled malt vinegar
20g (¾oz) cornflour
15g (½oz) ground turmeric

Makes approximately 6 jars

Layer the prepared vegetables on a large plate with the salt and leave overnight covered with a cloth. Next day, drain and rinse the vegetables under cold running water, then dry well. Stir the mustard, ginger and sugar into most of the vinegar, retaining just enough to make a thin paste with the cornflour and turmeric. Add the vegetables and simmer until you have a texture you like; crisp or less crisp, your choice. Add the cornflour and turmeric paste to the pan. Bring to the boil, stirring carefully, and boil for 2–3 minutes. Pour into warm jars and cover with a cloth. Leave until completely cold, then seal. Store for 2–3 months before using.

Rhubarb Chutney

Rhubarb reached Europe in the 16th century and was originally grown in physic borders for medical use. It wasn't until the 19th century that it began to be appreciated as a fruit, an ingredient of pies, pastries and for eating as chutney.

900g (2lb) rhubarb
225g (8oz) onions
700g (1½lb) brown sugar
225g (8oz) raisins
1 teaspoon mustard seeds
1 teaspoon mixed spice
½ teaspoon ground pepper
1 teaspoon ground ginger
1 teaspoon salt
600ml (1 pint) wine or cider vinegar

Makes approximately 6–8 jars

Cut the rhubarb into 2.5cm (1in) lengths. Peel and chop the onions finely. Put all the ingredients into a large heavy pan and simmer gently, stirring frequently until the mixture is of a thick consistency (like jam) with no excess liquid. This should take less than 45 minutes. Put into warm pots and cover tightly.

Sweet Pickled Onions

This is the best recipe I have ever used for pickling onions. The resulting onions are sweet and crisp. Do be careful not to cut away too much when you trim the tops and roots of the onions or they will disintegrate and become soggy. Do not worry if any small yellow spots appear on your pickled onions, they are perfectly harmless. This recipe originally appeared in Jams, Pickles and Edible Gifts. *Please note that this recipe takes two days to make.*

1.35kg (3lb) small pickling onions, trimmed
50g (2oz) cooking salt
2–3 fresh tarragon sprigs
1–2 green or red fresh chillies, halved
1–1.5 litres (1¾–2½ pints) white wine vinegar
350g–450g (12–16oz) sugar

Makes approximately 4 jars

Put the onions into a large bowl and cover with boiling water. Leave for about 20 seconds and then pour off the water. Cover with cold water, then peel the onions, keeping them under the water when peeling. Put them into a bowl, sprinkling each layer with salt. Cover with a clean cloth and leave overnight.

Rinse well and shake off as much water as possible. Pack into clean, dry jars, adding a washed tarragon sprig and half a chilli to each jar. Boil the vinegar and sugar together for 1 minute, adding 225g (8oz) sugar to each 850ml (1½ pints) vinegar. Pour the hot vinegar over the onions. Cover tightly and store for 2–3 weeks before eating. Use within 6 months.

Drinks

'A delicate combination of ingredients, all of which contribute their share in building up a unique beverage, possessing an individualism of its own.' This general definition of a good mixed drink is from a small book of drinks recipes, published in 1958 by 'Bernard' – evidently so well-known as a barman that he didn't need a surname. I think his definition applies equally well to this chapter's select list of recipes for traditional alcoholic tipples, and some non-alcoholic coolers.

In the Middle Ages, everybody drank ale – from the moment they were weaned. Water wasn't safe and most milk was made into butter or cheese, with the whey and any spare milk generally given to the old and the sick. Broadly speaking, any drink brewed from malted grain and water was considered ale. The best ale came from the south of England, and was made from malted barley. But elsewhere oats – and even beans – were added to the mash. The drink wasn't as strong as today's version, and it didn't keep as well. Beer – made from hops – kept better than traditional ale, but it needed more specialist equipment and if possible, a brew house. Hops for beer were brought to Britain by merchants from Flanders and Holland, in the 1400s, but it was only in the 16th century that a hop-based ale – or beer – became popular. Just as today, beers were brewed to different tastes and strengths. The malt would be used several times when brewing: its first use produced the strong beer, used again it would be weaker, and the third or subsequent brew would be weak or 'small' beer. Beer was often heated in winter – Lamb's Wool is so-called because of the froth on the top of this warmed drink. Spiced and sweetened, they are celebration drinks for any time of the year when it's cold.

Cider was only drunk in regions where there were cider orchards, and was generally for special occasions. In 1587, speaking of cider and perry (the latter made from pears, rather than apples), William Harrison remarked that 'Certes these two are very common in Sussex, Kent, Worcester and other steads where these sort of fruit do about, howbeit, they are not their only drink at all times'. My recipe for a cooling Cider Punch comes from a book of cider recipes produced for H P Bulmer, a family-run cider company in Herefordshire, a county famous for its cider apples.

Cider-drinking was bounded by place, but wine-drinking was restricted to those who could afford it. Although there had been vineyards in England, custom – and probably bad weather, too – dictated that wine was imported, from the 16th century onwards. All imported goods were expensive but wine had an additional import duty, and sweet wine – very popular, and stronger than ordinary claret – was subject to yet another, separate tax. Because of its cost, the drink became a status symbol for Elizabethans, and it was considered the mark of a gentleman to offer your guests some wine. Like beer and cider, wine was sugared and spiced, and heated up as a winter drink. The old Christmas tradition of 'wassailing' – drinking a toast to your fruit trees from a wassail cup of heated beer, cider or wine, ostensibly to encourage a good crop next year – was a much-loved seasonal pastime, enjoyed by gentry and commoners alike. The Mulled Wine recipe here is from Buckland Abbey, home of that Tudor buccaneer, Sir Francis Drake – it makes a good modern wassail cup.

Distilled wine, or *aqua vitae*, was introduced here in the 16th century. Originally consumed for reasons of health, it quickly became drunk for pleasure. By the 18th century, rum or brandy-based hot punches, ladled from a steaming bowl into glasses called 'rummers', were all the rage – and you can try out a Georgian recipe for Milk Punch. In Scotland, Usquebaugh, or Whisky – fermented barley and water – remains the country's national drink. Since toddies are supposed to originate from Scotland, the Hot Toddy recipe has a whisky base. Last but not least, there are three delicious recipes for non-alcoholic coolers. Orange Cordial and Lemonade are recipes served daily to thirsty visitors at Sissinghurst, the beautiful National Trust garden in Kent, while Barley Water is a modern reworking of a 17th-century recipe.

Mulled Wine

This particular mull is rather like a hot sangria – rather appropriate as the recipe comes from Buckland Abbey, the home of Sir Francis Drake, commander of the English fleet that defeated the Spanish Armada in 1688.

1 orange
12–14 whole cloves
1 litre (1¾ pints) red wine
1 litre (1¾ pints) lemonade
50g (2oz) brown sugar
150ml (¼ pint) orange juice
1 cinnamon stick 15cm (6in) long

Makes 6–8 glasses

Stud the orange with the cloves and cut in half. Place all the ingredients in a large pan and bring very slowly almost to a simmer. Serve hot but do not allow to boil.

Hot Milk Punch

This lethally delicious concoction is based on a Georgian recipe. It makes an unusual drink and guarantees any party will go with a swing. Note you must start this recipe the day before you want to serve it.

4 large lemons
600ml (1 pint) brandy
350g (12 oz) sugar
600ml (1 pint) still mineral water
600ml (1 pint) milk

Serves 6–8

Grate the zest from the lemons into a large bowl. Squeeze the juice from the lemons and reserve. Pour the brandy over the lemon zest and leave for 2–3 hours. Then strain the mixture and add the lemon juice, sugar and mineral water. Stir well. Bring the milk to the boil and pour into the mixture which will immediately curdle. Cover and leave the bowl overnight. The next morning strain the mixture through a jelly bag. The liquid will run clear. Reheat to just below boiling and, if possible, serve from a punch bowl, ladling the mixture into small glasses.

Cider Punch

'Good cider 'tis a drink divine
Better by far than all your wine
Good in grief, good in joy,
Good for maid, man and boy'
　　　　　Anon, 19th century

Recipes for alcoholic punches abound. Everyone loves a celebration, and something fruity, alcoholic and fizzy adds to the occasion. I thought this recipe of Mary Berry's tasted particularly delicious. After all, cider is the wine of the West Country. You will need to start preparing this punch the day before you need it.

175g (6oz) strawberries
Zest and juice of 1 orange
3 tablespoons orange liqueur (I used Cointreau)
600ml (1 pint) medium cider
600ml (1 pint) sparkling water

TO SERVE
Ice cubes
Mint leaves

Makes 6–10 glasses

Wash and hull the strawberries, then place in a small bowl. Shave the zest from the orange carefully so that the strips are really thin. Put them in the bowl with the strawberries and add the orange liqueur and squeezed orange juice. Cover the bowl and leave to stand overnight.

Next day, just before you are going to serve the punch, add the cider, sparkling water and ice cubes. A fresh mint leaf in each glass is the finishing touch.

Hot Toddy

Hot Toddy is the name used in the English-speaking world for a mixed drink with a spirit base that is served hot. (It doesn't refer to a particular recipe.) For me, it conjures up thoughts of steaming mugs of something slightly sweet and definitely alcoholic, and a hazy picture of people in oilskins or heavy outdoor clothes sitting round a roaring fire. They have just been out in very inclement weather and their fingers are clasped around the mugs; their faces are still very cold, but inside they are glowing.

Scotland is thought to be the original home of the Hot Toddy, so I am giving a whisky-based recipe for this deeply comforting drink. Other spirits, such as brandy or rum, can be used. Oh, another thing – Hot Toddy won't cure the flu or a bad cold, but it will help to make the symptoms bearable.

1 tablespoon honey
Juice of ½ lemon
200ml (7fl oz) very hot (but not boiling) water
50ml (2fl oz) blended whisky

Makes 1 mug

Mix the honey and lemon juice together with a little of the hot water until blended. Add the measure of whisky, then fill the mug with hot water. Drink while the mixture is still very hot.

Lamb's Wool

This comforting drink was originally devised for warming cold Oxfordshire herdsmen coming in from the fields. Oxfordshire has always been famous for its wool, so the name is particularly appropriate. Lamb's Wool got its name from the white, woolly-looking froth on the surface of this steaming drink.

600ml (1 pint) brown ale
1 glass white wine
A pinch of grated nutmeg
A pinch of ground ginger
1 tablespoon soft brown sugar
600ml (1 pint) milk

Serves 4

Place the ale and wine in a pan and heat gently until just below boiling. Stir in the spices and sugar. Heat the milk in another pan and beat it into the ale so that it froths. Serve hot.

Mulled Ale

Who better than Mrs Beeton to provide a recipe for Mulled Ale? She considers the amount below 'sufficient for 4 persons', and the cost – in my edition of 1881 – is given as one shilling.

1.25 litres (2 pints) good ale
1 tablespoon caster sugar
½ teaspoon whole cloves
½ standard wine glass rum or brandy
Freshly grated nutmeg, to taste

Serves 4

Heat the ale with the sugar and cloves. Don't allow it to boil. At the same time, warm a jug by rinsing it out with boiling water. Pour the hot ale into the jug, adding the brandy or rum and grated nutmeg to taste.

Right: Mulled Ale

Lemonade

Sissinghurst Castle Garden in Kent on a very hot day – not only were the flowers wilting, but so was I. I was rescued with a glass of home-made lemonade, so I rang up Mark Britcher, head chef at Sissinghurst Restaurant, for the recipe. It is simple, but carefully thought out – and he should know what works best: on some hot days they make over 114 litres (25 gallons) of lemonade for their thirsty customers. Lemonade is best made the day before you intend to serve it.

3 unwaxed lemons
75g (3oz) granulated or lump sugar
750ml (1¼ pints) water

TO SERVE
Ice cubes
Mint leaves or borage flowers and leaves

Makes 6 glasses

Chop the lemons and put them in a food processor with the granulated or lump sugar. Process until you have a fairly fine pulp: the processing 'pulls' the natural oils from the lemons. Put the mixture in a glass jug and stir in the water. Chill overnight before use. Serve with ice cubes and a sprig of mint or borage. This lemonade will keep for two to three days in the fridge.

Left: Lemonade

Barley Water

The recipe is based on a drink from 1685 called 'A Dainty Cooling Drink for a Hot Fever: 'Take French barley one ounce, boil it first in a quart of fair water a good while, then shift it and boil it in another quarter of water. Shift it again and boil it in a bottle of fair spring water to a quart, then take 2 ounces of sweet almonds, lay them to soak all night then stamp and strain them in the last barley water. Put to it 4 spoonsful of damask rose water, the juice of one lemon and with sugar sweeten it to your taste. Drink of this often when you are dry or hot.'

Barley water was thought to be medicinal but there is no proof of this. But it is agreed that it is a great thirst quencher.

50g (2oz) pearl barley
1.25 litres (2 pints) water
2 lemons
sugar to taste

TO SERVE
Ice cubes
Mint leaves

Serves 4

Wash the barley and put it to boil with the water and the thinly peeled zests of the lemons. Boil very gently for 2 hours, then strain. Add sugar to taste, stir to dissolve it and leave to cool. Just before serving, add the juice from the 2 lemons. Serve poured over ice with a mint leaf to decorate.

Home-made Orange Cordial

Keep this cordial in the fridge. Serve poured over ice cubes with slices of fresh orange or lemon in the glass and use still or sparkling water to top up. It will keep for two to three weeks.

1 lemon
3 oranges
675g (1½lb) granulated or caster sugar
25g (1oz) citric acid
300ml (2 pints) boiling water

Makes approximately 1.5 litres (2½ pints)

Rub the zest from the lemon and oranges, cut the fruit in half and squeeze out the juice. Chop the shells into chunks. Put sugar, citric acid, lemon and orange zest, juice and chunks of shell in a large bowl. Add the boiling water, stir to help the sugar dissolve and leave to cool and stand, preferably overnight. Strain to remove lemon and orange pieces. Pour cordial into a jug or clean bottles and store in a refrigerator. Use diluted as required. The cordial can be kept for two or three weeks.

Confectionery

Making sweets is hobby cooking – totally unnecessary but enjoyable. I have only included in this section recipes for sweets that can be achieved reasonably easily in a domestic kitchen, with nothing too technical or too dangerous, although you do need to take care making fudge. The fudge recipe is borrowed from an expert. Laura Mason has written a scholarly and fascinating history of sweets, delving into the ancestry of sherbet lemons, liquorice allsorts, toffee and love hearts.

Chocolate Fudge

Fudge, apparently, reached this country from the United States but since that was over a hundred years ago, I think a recipe can now be considered traditional. Laura Mason has developed this recipe from one written down just after the World War I.

500g (18oz) sugar
250g (9oz) butter
250g (9oz) dark chocolate (60% cocoa solids – check the label)
600 ml (1 pint) milk
Vanilla essence to taste
110g (4oz) walnuts (optional)

Line a 20cm (9in) square tin with baking paper. Put all the ingredients into a large pan over a low heat. Allow the butter and chocolate to melt and bring to a gentle boil, stirring constantly. Cook over a moderate flame, still stirring constantly, and boil gently until a little of the mixture forms a soft ball when it is dropped into cold water. Add the vanilla and the walnuts if used. Leave to cool in the pan for about 20 minutes, then stir until it stiffens. Pour or press into the lined tin and leave to set before cutting into squares.

Note: Laura says this is not the easiest recipe to handle: the mixture tends to separate while you are heating it, but keep beating – the end result is delicious.

Chocolate Truffles

Chocolate truffles probably acquired their name in the 1920s, according to Alan Davidson, because they look like the savoury truffle, which is a fungus, a highly rated delicacy which emerges from under the ground usually as a smallish lump, covered in earth, having been tracked down by either a pig or a dog trained for the purpose. These, however, are easy to make and wickedly indulgent: home-made chocolate truffles really are special.

75g (3oz) plain chocolate
2 tablespoons brandy or rum (optional)
50g (2oz) unsalted butter
50g (2oz) icing sugar
75g (3oz) ground almonds
Cocoa powder or vermicelli for decoration

Melt the chocolate in a basin over hot water. Stir in the brandy or rum and add the icing sugar and ground almonds. Cover the bowl and chill until firm. Divide into small balls, roll in vermicelli or cocoa and store covered in the fridge. They keep well for several days. Grated orange rind or coffee essence can be substituted for the brandy or rum, if preferred.

Coconut Ice

This recipe comes from Sara Paston-Williams's Jams, Preserves and Edible Gifts. *Easy to make, good to eat and very pretty, coconut ice makes an excellent edible gift.*

Tasteless vegetable oil, for preparing tin
450g (1lb) caster sugar
150 ml (¼ pint) milk or single cream
150g (5oz) desiccated coconut
Cochineal or pink food colouring

Lightly oil a shallow 20 x 15cm (8 x 6in) tin with the vegetable oil and set aside. Place the sugar and milk in a heavy pan over a low heat and stir until the sugar dissolves. Increase the heat and bring to the boil, then allow the mixture to boil gently for about 10 minutes or until a little dropped into cold water forms a soft ball between finger and thumb (112–116°C or 235–240°F on a sugar thermometer).

Remove from the heat and beat in the coconut. Quickly pour half the mixture into the oiled tin and spread it evenly, using a wet knife. Stir a few drops of colouring into the remaining mixture so that it turns pale pink. Spread this evenly over the white coconut mixture and leave to cool. As soon as it begins to set, mark the mixture out into neat squares.

Leave until completely cold and set firm. Cut or break the coconut ice into pieces and eat it within a few days.

Peppermint Creams

Another perfect edible gift, these pretty-looking sweets have a delicate mint flavour.

450g (1lb) icing sugar
1 teaspoon lemon juice
1 egg white, lightly whisked
A few drops of oil of peppermint or peppermint essence

Sift the icing sugar into a bowl and mix with the lemon juice and enough egg white to make a pliable mixture. Flavour with the peppermint oil. Knead on a work surface lightly dusted with icing sugar, then roll out to a 6mm (¼in) thickness. Cut into small rounds with a 2.5cm (1in) pastry cutter. Leave in a cool place for 24 hours to set and dry.

Appendices

Roasting

'The English men understand almost better than any other people, the art of roasting a joint.'
Per Kalm, 18th-century Swedish visitor

Britain's climate and topography produces superb beef, lamb, pork and turkey. Here is some advice on the best cuts to buy, storage and preparation, cooking times and accompaniments. Finally there is a recipe for gravy, which can be made either thin or thick.

I shall concentrate on cuts that are available, by and large, at both the butcher and the supermarket. But if you and those you cook for really enjoy meat, then a good relationship with a butcher is essential. Bear in mind that you are talking to a real professional whose expertise is much greater than yours or mine, and whose advice is invaluable. A butcher knows the best time of the year for the best cuts and how long you can store the joint, and will have cast an expert eye over what is available. Take your butcher's advice on the quantity needed to feed the number of people you are cooking for: if the meat has the bone in, he will know what proportion of the joint is bone and allow accordingly.

One more point: the larger the joint, the easier it is to cook well. Rest the joint for 15 minutes after cooking and before carving. This relaxes the meat and makes it more tender – and it also gives you time to make the gravy.

A large joint of meat may seem an expensive investment, but bear in mind that all these meats taste good cold. There are recipes elsewhere in this book that use cooked meat (for example, see Devilled Fowl on page 76 and Shepherds Pie on page 91). When you count up the number of meals your joint of meat has provided, you may find that your expensive big joint has worked out to be more economical than several smaller cuts.

Storing meat

Raw meat and poultry should be stored in the fridge. It should be put on a plate and covered, or placed in a clean, air-tight container. Put raw meat on the bottom shelf of the fridge, so that there is no danger of any meat juices contaminating other food. And remember to wash your hands after handling raw meat, and before handling any other food.

Beef
What to buy
Forerib on the bone, rolled back rib, aitchbone cut, sirloin, topside, top rump or fillet.

Preparation
All the joint needs before cooking is a brush of olive or sunflower oil and a dusting of salt and pepper. Roast the joint on a rack, or you can put it on the bottom of the roasting pan, with a quartered onion and a sliced carrot underneath – these will prevent burning, and add flavour to the gravy.

Roasting

Beef is generally roasted 'rare', 'medium', or 'well done'. Preheat the oven to 230°C, 450°F, gas mark 8, and roast the joint for 10 minutes at this temperature, before reducing the heat to 175°C, 350°F, gas mark 4, for the rest of the time required. Rare roasting times are 12–15 minutes per 450g (1lb). Medium roasting times are 15–18 minutes per 450g (1lb). Well-done roasting times are 18–20 minutes per 450g (1lb). Let the joint rest for 15 minutes before carving it.

Accompaniments

Horseradish Sauce (see page 120), mustard and Yorkshire Pudding (see page 154).

Lamb

What to buy

Leg or half leg, shoulder or half shoulder, best end of neck or saddle. Also available are the very showy joints prepared from rack of lamb, sometimes known as Crown of Lamb or Guard of Honour.

Preparation

As for beef. If you like the flavours, lamb responds very well to the insertion of slivers of rosemary and garlic into the meat before cooking. Make incisions with a sharp knife on all sides of the joint. Let the joint rest for 15 minutes before carving it.

Roasting

The same timings and instructions as for beef.

Accompaniments

Mint Sauce (see page 121), or redcurrant jelly.

Pork

What to buy

A whole or half leg, sparerib, shoulder, belly, rolled hand, neck end or tenderloin.

Preparation

Crackling (the skin of the joint, which should crisp up during cooking) is an important part of a pork joint. Choose a joint that has a good layer of fat under the skin, and see that the butcher has cut the crackling into thin strips for you. Rub oil and salt into the skin before roasting.

Roasting

Pork is best served well done. Roast for 20–25 minutes per 450g (1lb), then place the joint on a rack to cook. Start roasting the joint upside down and turn it halfway through cooking so the crackling can crisp. Let the joint rest for 15 minutes before carving it.

Accompaniments

Apple Sauce (see page 123).

Turkey

What to buy

Free range and/or organic is best. A turkey is only on most people's menu once or twice a year, so buy the best you can afford.

Preparation

I stuff the carcass with a mixture of chopped apple (either eating or cooking apples), chopped onion and garlic, and cook the stuffing that we eat with the bird separately (see recipe for Roast Duck on page 74). I stuff the breast of the bird with 450g (1lb) sausagemeat mixed with 4 chopped shallots and 225g (½lb) chopped chestnuts (you can buy them vacuum-packed). Either brush the skin of the bird with melted butter or, my preference, mix together 110g (4oz) full-fat cream cheese or butter with 1 tablespoon finely chopped parsley, 2 crushed garlic cloves, pepper and salt. Put your hand under the skin of the bird and spread this mixture over the breast and, if you can, the top of the legs of the bird. It is a messy business but very rewarding. The cream cheese and butter bastes the meat as it cooks, giving you a succulent bird.

Roasting

For a turkey weighing less than 6½kg (14lb): 18 minutes per 450g (1lb).
For a turkey weighing more than 6½kg (14lb): 15 minutes per 450g (1lb).
Cover with foil until the last 45 minutes of cooking. Let the bird rest 15 minutes before carving it.

Accompaniments

Bread Sauce (see page 121), cranberry jelly or Parsley and Lemon Stuffing (see page 152). Tiny sausages and bacon rolls: roast these during the last 45 minutes of the cooking time – either alongside the bird or, if there is no room in the pan, in a separate tin.

Gravy

This is a recipe for a classic gravy, the perfect accompaniment for roast meat.

2 tablespoons pan dripping
2 tablespoons tawny port or sherry
300ml (½ pint) vegetable stock. For turkey, make a stock from the giblets of the bird.

Make a thin gravy as follows: either make up the vegetable stock or strain off the stock from the turkey giblets. Pour off the excess fat from the roasting pan, also discarding the onion and carrot, if used, and leaving about two tablespoons of fat behind. Give the bottom of the pan a good scrape, heat up the pan juices, adding the stock from the giblets and 2 tablespoons of port or sherry. Boil vigorously for a minute or two, adjust the seasoning and serve.

If you prefer a thicker gravy, work 1 tablespoon flour in with the pan juices and cook it for 2–3 minutes. Gradually add the stock and the 2 tablespoons of port or sherry, stirring vigorously. Bring the mixture to the boil, taste and adjust the seasoning, simmer for a couple of minutes and serve.

What does the National Trust believe about food?

The National Trust wants to help 'reconnect' the food chain between producers and consumers. We want consumers both to understand the benefits and to enjoy preparing and eating food that comes from a known source and is healthy and enjoyable. At the same time we want to see farmers rewarded for producing quality food while protecting and enhancing the countryside.

We want both producers and customers to share our passion in sourcing and selling food that has integrity based on animal welfare, food safety and environmental principles. So, we buy and sell quality food and drink that is good value. We aim to source local seasonal produce that has been produced and prepared to high standards.

We have a responsibility to ensure that minimum standards are met by our suppliers and that we are confident food is produced in a safe way and that unnecessary pollution or environmental damage does not occur.

While we aim to source food produced in close proximity to where it is processed and eaten, we realise this is not always possible or appropriate. Local food does not necessarily mean it is high quality and produced to high standards. For this reason we are focusing not just on where food came from but also the standards it has been produced to, so we are confident we are sourcing food that is as sustainable as possible.

In helping build a local food culture we have set ourselves some very demanding tasks and ambitions. This cannot be achieved overnight, so a pragmatic approach is in order.

So what does the National Trust food policy mean?

All fresh eggs used in our restaurants should be sourced to the Free Range Freedom Food Standard or be certified organic. Our current minimum standard demands that all fresh meat products used should be of UK origin. Work is in progress to raise this minimum standard to Freedom Food or certified organic standards. Where possible, eggs and fresh meat should be sourced from a local producer who complies with this standard; otherwise food is sourced from national suppliers who comply with the standards of the Ethical Trade Initiative.

Our aim is that all fish and seafood used in our catering outlets should come from sustainable sources. We take our lead from the guidelines produced by the Marine Conservation Society and we have worked with our suppliers to produce a product list that reflects these guidelines.

All our tea and coffee is sourced from nationally appointed suppliers who are members of and therefore comply with the standards of the Ethical Trade Initiative.

We try to use English fruit and vegetables in season, but do use foreign products where there is no substitute. Where possible, properties seek to link garden production with catering to produce best examples of the shortest possible supply chain providing the freshest possible ingredients. When ordering fruit and vegetable from local suppliers, catering managers first seek to purchase British produce, but acknowledge that this is not always possible.

Virtually every property will be able to feature a locally produced beer and (in certain areas) cider. It is important that local ingredients are used. In the South East, Scotney Ale should be featured because it uses hops produced on our own estate. Some properties will be in the fortunate position to have local wine producers, and these should be supported.

Understanding why we all should support local food is key as local food can only ever be successful if consumers demand local, seasonal and quality food products.

Farm foods

Food is at the heart of everything we do. The Trust's commitment to food stretches from using high-quality produce in our restaurants to supporting our tenant farmers in selling direct to the public via farmers' markets at Trust properties. With hundreds of tenant farms, more than 25 working kitchen gardens and farms that we manage, the Trust has an important stake in every part of the food journey.

Farm foods for sale

Some of the most visited National Trust properties are now holding regular farmers' and food markets, including Stourhead and Lacock Abbey in Wiltshire, Waddesdon Manor in Buckinghamshire, Sissinghurst in Kent and Dunster Castle in Somerset.

Yew Tree Farm

Food lovers are in for a real treat when they order the top quality mature Herdwick seasonal lamb or belted Galloway beef, now available nationwide from the National Trust's tenants at Yew Tree Farm in the Lake District, formerly owned by Beatrix Potter. Jon and Caroline Watson took over in 2002 and have not looked back since. They have set up a business selling their meat, but what is their secret?

Herdwick sheep are unique to Cumbria and have grazed the local hills for centuries. They are very distinctive with their grey coats and white faces. Unusually hardy, they can live on the fells all year round, on a mixed diet including berries and leaves. This lifestyle means that they grow slowly and produce a particularly sweet-tasting meat.

Belted Galloway, otherwise known as 'Belties', graze differently to sheep and are the ultimate conservation tool to manage certain habitats. The Belties take longer to mature than commercial breeds, so that the meat is not only beautifully marbled for the very best rich flavour and texture, but is also high in beneficial Omega 3 fats.

With our support, and local funding, the Watsons have built a white room at Yew Tree Farm. Here their home-grown lamb and beef can be stored and packed before being sent by carrier directly to customers. Jon and Caroline have both been on a butchering course to equip themselves with the skills necessary to provide that extra-special service for their customers. The hampers maximise the income potential from the livestock produced on the farm. With every phase of production, from breeding to the despatch of the boxed meat under the control of the farmer, a high-quality product is guaranteed. As Caroline sums it up: 'We want the people who buy our meat to learn more about the environment where the food comes from and the whole food story.'

Stourhead Farm Shop

The Stourhead Farm Shop is a mouth-watering new fixture at one of the most popular National Trust properties. It has been open since May 2005. Managed by two farm tenants from the Stourhead Estate, the shop provides visitors with the opportunity to buy high quality local and seasonal food. One of its aims is to reconnect people with real food. Visitors to Stourhead and local people will have the chance to buy a wide range of local food that tastes good. It could be

high-quality beef that's been hung for three weeks, freshly picked seasonal vegetables or herbs without the food miles, or local cheese and eggs, as well as mineral water bottled on the Stourhead Western Estate. The Stourhead farm shop is open seven days a week from 10am-6pm.

Little Scotney Pale Ale
This beer with 'body' is brewed from hops grown by tenant farmer Ian Strang at the National Trust's Little Scotney Farm, on the Scotney Castle Estate in Kent.

Scotney Castle has our only remaining working hop farm and is one of the few surviving in Kent, a county which was at the centre of the hop industry. The delicate, papery blooms of hops have been grown and picked in this area for centuries. This enterprise began life both from Ian's need to stay afloat and our desire for hop growing and production to continue at Scotney as a vital part of Kentish and British tradition. While only a fraction of Ian's hop crop is used to flavour Little Scotney Pale Ale (the rest continues to be sold wholesale), the hope is for sales to eventually underwrite losses on the entire crop. Ian will be able to re-invest both in the hop enterprise and the rest of the farm.

The four 'roundel' oasts at Little Scotney Farm are still used only for the process of handling and drying hops. Working with Ian is Robert Wicks. Robert took up the tenancy on a farm building at our Crockham Grange Farm near Westerham, converting a redundant dairy building into Westerham Brewery. In turn, this has provided additional rent for our farm tenant and a new source of employment in a rural area. The brewery began brewing its first beer in May 2004 and currently brews eight beers, all of which are available in the local area. Robert's ambition is to make Ian's crop sustainable.

Little Scotney Pale Ale is available at National Trust shops, licensed tea-rooms and restaurants across the south-east. You can order also Little Scotney Pale Ale direct from Westerham Brewery: 0870 9315628.

National Trust tenant farm shops and produce
The National Trust has many tenant farmers who run their own farm shops and box schemes. To help support our tenants, the National Trust compiles a directory of farm foods and crafts on an annual basis.

All our tenants are, of course, independent. As a result, the standards of their individual products or services are entirely the responsibility of each tenant and not the National Trust.

Left: Lemon Curd
Previous page: Fruit Crumble

US conversion chart

Dry measures

1 US cup	50g	2oz of breadcrumbs
1 US cup	75g	3½oz of rolled oats
1 US cup	90g	3½oz of desiccated coconut
1 US cup	100g	3½oz of walnut pieces, icing sugar
1 US cup	120g	4oz of white flour
1 US cup	150g	5½oz of wholemeal flour
1 US cup	175g	6oz of mixed peel, sultanas
1 US cup	200g	7oz Demerara sugar, rice
1 US cup	225g	½lb of cream cheese
1 US cup	300g	11oz mincemeat
1 US cup	350g	12oz of treacle, jam

Liquid measures

¼ US cup	60ml	2fl oz
1 US cup	240ml	8fl oz
1 US cups (1 US pint)	480ml	16fl oz

Butter and lard measures

¼ stick	25g	2 level tablespoons
1 stick (1 US cup)	100g	8 level tablespoons

Acknowledgements

First of all I would like to thank all the cooks at restaurants at National Trust properties whose recipes feature in this book.

Special thanks to Laura Mason whose advice and recipes I much appreciate; also Sara Paston-Williams, particularly for her historic recipes and her wonderful puddings; Kate Steggles, the shortbread supremo; and Mark Britcher at Sissinghurst for the Lemonade and Orange Cordial recipes.

Alan Davidson's *The Oxford Companion to Food* has been my constant companion, as has Jane Grigson's *English Food* and Michael Smith's *Fine English Food*. Thank you to Tina Persaud for commissioning the book and Nicola Birtwisle for encouraging and helping me all along the way.

Friends and family helped to test the recipes but a final thank you to the ever-supportive John, Fiona, Jules, Lucy, Dan and Rich.

All recipes are © Sarah Edington except the following:

Cornish Pasties (p108), Faggots (p109), Game Pie (p114), Jugged Peas (p132), Maids of Honour (p206), Pork Pie (p110), Welsh Rarebit (p153) all © Laura Mason 2005.

An 18th-Century Trifle (p207), Apple Fritters in Ale Batter (p173), Apple Hat (p171), Baked Apples (p181), Boodles Orange Fool (p215), Brown Bread Ice Cream (p211), Casseroled Pigeon with Herbs and Spices (p77), Chicken or Rabbit Fricassee (p105), Claret Jelly (p209), College Pudding (p187), Custard Tart or Sweet Egg Pie (p163), Damson Snow (p218), Elderflower and Gooseberry Fool (p200), Fine Almond Blancmange (p205), Florence Nightingale's Kedgeree (p49), Lamb Casseroled in Ale with Prunes and Raisins (p97), Pears in Red Wine Syrup (p177), Pickled Herring and Fruit Pie (p52), Scotch Collops with Forcemeat Balls (p106), Spiced Bean Pottage (p135), Spicy Ground Rice Pudding (p180), Sussex Pond Pudding (p185), Sweet Pickled Onions (p295), Trelissick Lemon Curd (p288) all © National Trust, various dates.

Bibliography

Beeton, Isabella, *The Book of Household Management,* Ward Lock & Co, London, 1888

Campbell, Susan and Conran, Caroline, *Poor Cook*, Sphere Books, London, 1972

Dallas, E S, *Kettner's Book of the Table*, Centaur Press, London 1968

David, Elizabeth, *An Omelette and a Glass of Wine*, Penguin Books, Harmondsworth, Middlesex, 1986

Davidson, Alan, *The Oxford Companion to Food*, Oxford University Press, Oxford, 1999

Edington, Sarah, *National Trust Recipes*, National Trust, London, 1996

Edington, Sarah, *The Captain's Table*, National Maritime Museum Publishing, London, 2005

Edington, Sarah, *The National Trust Book of Healthy Eating*, National Trust, London, 1990

Edington, Sarah, *The National Trust Book of Recipes*, National Trust, London, 1988

Edington, Sarah, *Vegetarian Recipes*, National Trust, London 2002

'Farmhouse Fare', *The Farmers Weekly*, London, 1950

Fitzgibbon, Theodora, *A Taste of Scotland*, Jarrold & Sons, Norwich, 1970

Grigson, Jane, *English Food*, Ebury Press, London, 2002

Grigson, Jane, *Jane Grigson's Fruit Book*, Michael Joseph, London, 1982

Grigson, Jane, *Jane Grigson's Fish Book*, Penguin Books, London, 1994

Hammond, Peter, *Food and Feast in Medieval England*, Sutton Publishing, Stroud, 1998

Humble, Nicola, *Culinary Pleasures*, Faber and Faber, London, 2005

Maher, Barbara, *Cakes*, Penguin Books, Harmondsworth, Middlesex, 1982

Making a Meal of It, English Heritage, Swindon, 2005

Mason, Laura, *Farmhouse Cookery*, National Trust, London, 2005

Mason, Laura, *Sugar-Plums and Sherbet*, Prospect Books, Totnes, Devon, 1998

Mason, Laura with Brown, Caroline, *Traditional Foods of Britain*, Prospect Books, Totnes, Devon, 2004

Paston-Williams, Sara, *Traditional Puddings*, National Trust, London, 2002

Paston-Williams, Sara, *A Book of Historical Recipes*, National Trust, London, 1995

Paston-Williams, Sara, *Jams, Preserves & Edible Gifts*, National Trust, London, 1999

Paston-Williams, Sara, *The Art of Dining*, National Trust London, 1993

Pepys, Samuel, *The Shorter Pepys*, Penguin, London, 1993

Pettigrew, Jane, *Tea-time Recipes*, National Trust, London, 2001

Sabieri, Helen and Davidson, Alan, *Trifle*, Prospect Books, Totnes, Devon, 2001

Sim, Alison, *Food and Feast in Tudor England*, Sutton Publishing, Stroud, Gloucestershire, 1997

Smith, Michael, *Fine English Cookery*, Faber Paperbacks, Whitstable, Kent, 1983

Spry, Constance, *The Constance Spry Cookbook*, Pan Books, London, 1972

Stein, Rick, *Rick Stein's Seafood Odyssey*, BBC Worldwide, London, 1999

The Cookery Year, Readers Digest, London, 1974

Thompson, Flora, *Lark Rise to Candleford*, Penguin, Harmondsworth, Middlesex, 1977

Weir, Robin and Liddell, Caroline, *Recipes From The Dairy*, National Trust, London, 1998

WI, The and Smith, Michael, *A Cook's Tour of Britain*, WI Books, London, 1984

Willan, Anne, *Reader's Digest Complete Guide to Cookery*, Dorling Kindersley, London, 1989

Wright, Carol, *The Cotswolds*, Cassell, London, 1975

Index

Figures in *italics* refer to captions.

334

National Trust Membership

Whether you're interested in gardens, castles, wildlife, places linked to famous events and people, looking for a new coastal path to walk or just somewhere peaceful to relax and enjoy a nice cup of tea, National Trust membership gives you a wide variety of things to do, as often as you like, for free.

Join today and you can start to explore some of Britain's most beautiful places, while helping to protect them for future generations.

As a member you'll receive a comprehensive membership pack featuring places cared for by the National Trust.

What's more, National Trust membership gives you free entry to more than 300 historic houses and gardens and information about 700 miles of coastline and almost 250,000 hectares of stunning countryside, so visiting couldn't be easier.

Visit www.nationaltrust.org.uk or phone 0870 458 4000
for more details.